Big Steel

Big Steel

Black Politics
and Corporate Power
in Gary, Indiana

by Edward Greer

Monthly Review Press
New York and London

Library of Congress Cataloging in Publication Data

Greer, Edward.
    Big Steel.

    1. Gary, Ind.—Economic conditions.
2. Gary, Ind.—Politics and government.
3. Afro-Americans—Indiana—Gary—Politics and
suffrage. 4. Community power. I. Title.
HC108.G3G73   309.1'772'99   79-13178
ISBN 0-85345-490-6

Monthly Review Press
62 West 14th Street, New York, N.Y. 10011
47 Red Lion Street, London WC1R 4PF

Manufactured in the United States of America

10 9 8 7 6 5 4 3 2 1

Dedicated to the memory of my editor,
Harry Braverman

Contents

Acknowledgments

Foremost among those helping this study reach fruition was my late editor, Harry Braverman, whose confidence and warm support was decisive. Jules Geller and Karen Judd at Monthly Review Press, along with John Ehrenreich, undertook the many tasks associated with converting a rough manuscript into a book.

Numerous colleagues and friends, of varied politics and unvaried kindness, helped out in offering critical observations on sections of the draft. Special mention must be made of Professor Bob Ross, who meticulously critiqued the entire draft manuscript and encouraged me to rewrite it in its entirety.

All relevant contemporaneous notes, tapes, memoranda, and letters cited in the text are in my possession and available upon request by qualified scholars.

Introduction

The main aim of this book is to show how political power actually works in the city of Gary, Indiana.[1] Because of the nature of the city and its political battles, it is a tale of high drama.

A second theme, which is explicitly discussed here and in comments interspersed throughout the text, and which implicitly defines the focus of the work, is a theoretical one. It represents a view quite different from the one I held in 1968, when I went to work as a special assistant to Mayor Richard Hatcher of Gary. This view emerged gradually, as a response to the reality of social relations I experienced in attempting to carry out a series of reforms in local government, and has required a revision of my own political beliefs.

Briefly, the position I have come to hold is that liberal or pluralist theory of American society is incorrect; that "power elite" theory, along with many versions of Marxism which approximate it, is similarly inadequate; and that Marxist theory in the tradition of Italian communist Antonio Gramsci comes closest to providing an explanation of political power in this country.

Thus, this second theme is a critique of the fundamental political beliefs of most Americans, including most scholars, about how political power works in the United States. As a theory of political power, pluralism asserts that our country is a fundamentally democratic society, in which the people are sovereign over the state. From this perspective, the government is

11

seen as legitimate and owed alliegiance; hence, needed reforms can and ought to be achieved within the limits of the existing system.[2] This is the hegemonic ideology of our society. It is proclaimed by virtually all of our leaders and largely followed in practice by most of the citizenry. But if one carefully examines the character of political power in Gary, Indiana traced in this book, an alternative concept proves more fruitful, an alternative embedded in the Marxist tradition, and congruent with the conditions and prospects of the working people in that city and throughout our nation.

A Story of Local Reform

No one doubts that our nation's cities are in severe difficulties. The political and economic priorities of our society make it likely that these difficulties will continue. Moreover, there is currently no political coalition with any prospect of changing these priorities to the extent necessary to compel a sharp alteration of the existing urban plight. This book illuminates the fact that the problems most urban places experience are due to basic structural characteristics of our contemporary political economy. The absence of genuine full employment, for example, results in a permanently degraded mass of unemployed and marginally employed youth, largely minority, concentrated in the central cities—with appalling social effects. Equally basic is a politics which does not seriously consider, let alone adopt, mandatory controls on the free flow of capital between regions and even beyond the borders of the nation. This free market in capital and private decisions to maximize profits has in the period since World War II resulted in a gradual draining of the economic vitality of most American cities.

The fundamental importance of these structural features means that there is no realistic prospect of overcoming the urban crisis without the implementation of governmental policies to achieve full employment and to compel the investment of private capital in ways that are contrary to free market forces. As long as such dramatic national reforms are not on the political agenda, it is meaningless to discuss whether or not a particular city or its government is "successful." The best that can be said for either is the degree to which the inexorable slide downward of urban conditions is retarded. Even by this minimal criterion, as we shall see, the possibilities of maneuver open to a city administration are marginal. The difference in the daily life of the average city dweller made by a change in the occupant of the mayor's office is too small to be noticeable.

Therefore, this book does not attempt to determine the answer to the main question it asks: namely, whether the election of a black mayor in Gary resulted in the city becoming a better place to live. The answer is simply that by most measures, life in Gary is significantly worse than it was a decade ago. (Of course, more likely than not, it would be even a tiny bit worse than it is today had the previous administration in City Hall been able to maintain itself in power.) Instead, the book attempts to assess the limits of political reform in the existing system. It tries both to discover what these limits are and to figure out ways to go beyond these limits, that is to say, to open up political pathways for changing the system itself. In this inquiry the central question raised is that of *class power*, and the exploration is one of the relationship between class, race, and political power.

No examination of any single city can hope to fully resolve these large questions because no city encompasses the heterogeneity of American society. But within that intrinsic limit, Gary is a representative case, as a microcosm of heartland industrial America. Gary is an industrial suburb of Chicago and a middle-sized manufacturing city of 180,000 inhabitants, of whom a majority are black. At its core is the mammoth Gary Works of the United States Steel Corporation. For half a century this complex of steel mills, stretching for ten miles along the south shore of Lake Michigan, was the nation's largest. When fully operational, it employs 25,000 workers. And the surrounding community illustrates the circumstances of the industrial proletariat in the United States today.

Gary was built beginning in 1906 to provide housing for the employees of U.S. Steel's new mill. Until the New Deal period,

City Hall, like those of numerous other industrial communities, was dominated by a Republican Party machine that in turn was a direct creature of the dominant local economic power. Successive administrations closely followed the public policy preferences of the corporation.[3] A second phase in Gary's political history began with the ascendency of the New Deal coalition to local political power. This ascendency was part of the larger historical process which saw the organization of industrial workers into stable mass unions and the initiation of a series of major social reforms by the national government.

The third phase in Gary's political evolution began in 1967 with the election of black insurgent Richard Gordon Hatcher as mayor, as a black majority coalition wrested power from the entrenched Democratic Party machine. His victory was part of the national civil rights movement, which has also led to major social reforms throughout the nation.

Both the New Deal and the current "blackening" of municipal politics have resulted in genuine changes for the mass of urban people. While there is no doubt as to the positive significance of the New Deal in ameliorating the daily lives of working people, the extent of urban black power is problematic. As the city with the longest uninterrupted regime of "black power," Gary is probably the leading example of this phenomenon. The most useful insights on the character of black power and its impact on our national destiny may therefore emerge from a close study of its limits in that city.[4]

Pluralist Theory

As a microcosm of urban American society, Gary is also representative of the nature of community power. The examination of black mayoral politics in this city will demonstrate that neither pluralist nor "power elite" theories, the ways in which American political power is generally conceptualized, adequately explain how municipal government works.

Fundamentally, pluralism fails as a description of community political power in Gary because it has no concept to incorporate the reality of monopoly economic power. Yet the local economy of the city is overwhelmingly dominated by the U.S. Steel Corporation. And as we shall see throughout the book, this massive economic presence inexorably dictates narrow limits for governmental reform. Pluralist notions of political power, which deny that the capitalist class controls the state, therefore also deny that any single group can or does hold a preponderant position across the entire range of political issues. Thus, pluralist studies of community power in Gary portray U.S. Steel as simply one among numerous significant actors.[5] In part this is a result of conceptual and ideological biases which tend to ignore evidence of subtle or covert exercise of monopoly capital control over political processes and outcomes.[6] The pluralists acknowledge that there are limits to reform regardless of who governs, but view these limits as intrinsic to the nature of the world or consequential to what the population wants, instead of seeing that democratic control is sharply constrained by the capitalist political economy.

In reply to the evidence of U.S. Steel's power over local government in Gary, pluralists assert that the city is atypical. It is true that Gary is in a small minority of American cities in having a majority black population and depending upon a single employer, and its historical evolution also has some unique features. But every city is distinctive to some degree, and the main structural features of Gary's economy and governing bodies fall well within our national urban norms.[7] Every problem or aspect of community life here addressed is essentially replicated in numerous other cities.

More to the point, not a single one of the case studies in this book is about a policy area with features distinctive to Gary. Quite the reverse. The problems discussed, along with the range of practical policy options for responding to them, are broadly true for almost all American cities. Badly skewed property tax patterns, corruption and incompetence in local government, racially biased police departments, inadequate pollution controls, declining housing stock, and racial tensions are ubiquitous. We will see that the constraints which Mayor Hatcher faced in dealing with these problems substantially derive from aspects of the national political economy which are common to all urban places.

A fallback objection to this evidence could be that the choice of issues discussed in detail—police, housing, taxes, and pollution—are not representative of the city's politics. But they have been chosen precisely because of their salience to Gary's political life: they are the problems with which I was most deeply engaged as a special assistant to Mayor Hatcher because they were major problems confronting City Hall. Furthermore, since some are mainly local and others largely dictated by national government, some are more directly subject to mayoral control than others, and so on, taken as an ensemble they fairly represent the nature of local politics.[8]

Power Elite Theory

If mainstream pluralist theory is inadequate as explanation, power elite notions are even less satisfactory. These kinds of ideas have a long populist tradition in the United States. The attraction of this posture is that it directly addresses the hegemony of monopoly capital over the political economy. Thus although as a theoretical approach it is alien to Marxism,[9] many Marxists are influenced by it. When I went to work for Mayor Hatcher, I viewed a power elite framework as roughly adequate.

The difficulty with the power elite perspective is that it is reductionist. Political power is not an epiphenomenon of economic power. Thus, the immense economic resources of U.S. Steel in Gary do not translate into equivalent political influence. This study reveals that political power in that city is broadly shared between monopoly and competitive capital.

In many ways the direct political self-interest of the corporation is effectively countervailed by a wide variety of other community actors. For instance, we will see in detail that despite the fact that Gary was a deliberate creation of U.S. Steel, from the very outset the corporation found important preferences checked.

After the first couple of years it was unable to control the physical environment of the city; free market competition played more than an equivalent role. Thus, the corporation was not able to get the local transit system built along its preferred route, nor could it prevent the ubiquitous saloons, despite Judge Gary's notions about proper worker deportment. More significantly, its careful efforts to maintain a permanent division between its skilled native and unskilled foreign-born employees were undermined by forces beyond its control: war and depression and political and social evolution within the American working class resulted in industrial unionism. In turn, working-class organization entailed a substantial and permanent reduction in the power of capital over labor at the point of production. Nor was U.S. Steel able indefinitely to perpetuate its direct hegemony over City Hall. The significance of this defeat is exemplified by its loss during the 1930s of the use of the local police department as a strikebreaking force. At the national level, this shift was part of the changed balance of class power under the New Deal, with capital compelled to make major concessions to the working people.

Some radicals attempt to uphold power elite notions in the face of this kind of evidence by asserting that the monopoly capitalists, exercising a form of corporate liberalism, deliberately made such concessions to preclude the growth of mass socialist sentiment. They aver that the absence of a popular revolutionary movement in the United States and the continued viability of the existing political system demonstrate that all reforms which occurred are really in the self-interest of the ruling class.

However, this defense fails on both theoretical and empirical grounds. Since in principle everything short of a socialist revolution is necessarily compatible with the continuation of the capitalist system, no actual event could refute the power elite hypothesis. While this may be satisfying to its proponents, it destroys the viability of the theory and reduces it to mere expostulation. Furthermore, notwithstanding the claims of the corporate liberal historians, almost without exception the major democratic and social gains of the mass of the people over the course of our national history were won against intransigent capitalist resistance.[10] Without any doubt, this was the case in Gary. Whether we look to the growth of trade unions, struggles against Jim Crow laws, weakening of corporate hegemony over City Hall, or efforts to control pollution, U.S. Steel was compelled to accept outcomes it bitterly opposed.[11]

More recently, in the period discussed in detail in this book, U.S. Steel was unable to preserve its comfortable working relationship with the local Democratic Party machine. It was not able to seriously intervene to prevent the assumption of local political power by insurgent blacks who were a potential threat to many of its vital interests. Controversies with the Hatcher administration over employment patterns at the mills, pollution control measures, and local property taxes each represented a significant danger, even though they were substantially contained. And the struggle is not over: a more coherent mass civil rights movement or militant Steelworkers' Union would have the current and future potential to inflict major defeats on the corporation. Any power elite theory which views the economically dominant class of monopoly capitalists as a political ruling class with equivalent power over the state apparatus is thus clearly inadequate.

Marxist Theory

As community power is not explicable in either pluralist or power elite paradigms, an understanding of political power in advanced capitalism has to proceed along other conceptual paths. From the standpoint of Marxism, the starting point for an investigation is the question of how the capitalist class sustains a civilization based on the exploitation of the large majority of the people.

Traditionally, of course, Marxists have drawn attention to the coercive power of the state in answering this riddle. American history, after all, provides ample evidence of capitalists resorting to antidemocratic violence to protect their class privileges, both internationally and domestically. And such episodes have occurred in Gary. But while no sober observer doubts the capacity of American elites to resort to force, this alone is not an adequate explanation of the way that power works in the United States. Indeed, with the class struggle at an ebb, as it has been since World War II, the amount of violence has been relatively desultory.

Generally, the stable maintenance of consent by the oppressed to the existing system is the mechanism by which power is sustained in the United States. One school of thought has it that this consent is ideologically manipulated, and while there is some merit to this view, it is only a partial truth. In the modern world, the consent of the masses to the existing social order must and does entail substantial concessions by monopoly capital to the real interests of other social classes. As the Italian Marxist theoretician Antonio Gramsci put it:

> The dominant group is coordinated concretely with the general interests of the subordinate groups, and the life of the state is conceived of as a continuous process of formation and superceding of unstable equilibria (on the juridical plane) between the interests of the fundamental group [i.e., the monopoly capitalists] and those of the subordinate groups—equilibria in which the interests of the dominant group prevail, but only up to a certain point, i.e., stopping short of narrowly corporate economic interests.[12]

Gary exemplifies this understanding of political power. On the one hand, the interests of U.S. Steel do prevail in a general and overall sense. Its ownership over the means of production is unchallenged; government taxes and regulation are constricted so as not to undermine this ownership. Regardless of formal popular sovereignty, in practical terms the government does not have available policy options which would involve superseding the private economy, and political reforms which would have such an effect remain outside of the political agenda. Juridically, this is expressed by the constitutional protections provided to private property. In schematic Marxist terms, this relationship can be expressed by pointing to the role of the state as guarantor of the fundamental conditions for the accumulation of capital: namely, the preservation of the right to extract surplus value from wage labor.

On the other hand, as Gramsci's observation makes clear, ownership of the Gary Works represents the limits of state-guaranteed rights. The corporation may have to pay taxes which substantially reduce its profits; it may have to concede a variety of workers' rights at the point of production (such as the protections afforded by trade union organization and "welfare state" regulations); it may be subjected to controls over its production processes through pollution controls. In each of these matters, and innumerable others as well, a shifting balance of power between various class actors determines the actual outcomes.

What I learned in Gary is that in local government it is the petty bourgeoisie which is the decisive political actor.[13] Let us now turn to Gary itself.

I
Evolution of a Steel City

1
The Beginnings of Reform

For Gary's civil rights activists the early 1960s were an exciting time. After decades of arduous struggle, major victories seemed possible. A black physical education teacher at a local high school, Jesse Bell, Jr., filed suit against the local school board to try to redress the de facto racial segregation in the local schools. (In 1962, black students made up 50 percent of those enrolled in the schools, but 70 percent of them went to all-black schools; and expenditures per pupil were about 20 percent less for blacks than for whites.) This case, which ultimately was lost, became a pivotal one of the period and was handled by the nation's leading civil rights attorneys. Their local counsel was a young black attorney, Richard G. Hatcher. In the course of the litigation Bell and Hatcher became close friends, and a few years later Bell served as manager in Hatcher's campaign for mayor.[1]

Like most of the new black mayors, Hatcher is a self-made man. Born in 1933 in the nearby industrial town of Michigan City, where his father worked as a laborer for the Pullman Company, he was one of thirteen children. Six died, and during the Depression his father eked out a meager living as a junk peddler. Hatcher suffers from blindness in one eye as a result of his family's inability to afford medical treatment for a childhood accident. After great personal effort, Hatcher obtained both a college degree and a law school education. Upon graduation in 1959 he not only entered private law practice, but also found a job in the Lake County, Indiana prosecutor's office. Employment in the public prosecutor's office is the traditional first step for a political career in Indiana—and Hatcher from the outset determined upon such a path.

Immediately upon becoming an attorney, Hatcher involved himself in local civil rights activity. He participated in direct action campaigns against a local hospital's Jim Crow patient assignment policy, organized a Gary delegation to the 1963 Civil Rights March on Washington, took on local cases alleging police brutality, and participated in the coalitions fighting to obtain a municipal ordinance for open housing. In 1960 Hatcher also co-founded an independent black political group called Muiguithania. Muiguithania started as a small clique of young black professionals interested in affecting Gary's political life, but it rapidly developed into the core of a reform Democratic club seeking political office for its members. While its participants initially were ignorant of the art of electoral politics, they systematically taught themselves how to run effective campaigns.[2]

In 1963 Muiguithania successfully sponsored Hatcher for one of the three at-large seats on Gary's nine-member city council. The role played by the local Democratic Party machine in this election remains somewhat obscure. But in any event, upon his election Hatcher demonstrated himself to be a formidable and independent force on the council.

In Gary, as with other cities dominated by entrenched political machines, the general posture of council members is to follow the machine's bidding in legislative matters in return for various pecuniary rewards. The tradition in Gary was that the machine channeled certain jobs, such as those with the police and fire departments, as personal patronage to council members. In return for a substantial payment by the job seeker, the council member provided the position, regardless of formal civil service rules. For example, to become a fire fighter in Gary in the early 1960s, one had to pay one's councilman $1,700. To obtain a general contractor's license—which was prerequisite to engaging in construction work—the formal requirement was a fee of $150 and passing a written examination. In reality, one passed the exam if and only if a payment of $1,200 (or $1,500 if the applicant were black) was tendered to the relevant member of the city council. Hatcher refused to participate in these arrangements.

Once Hatcher became mayor, he ended these traditional sources of revenue to the city council, earning in return the bitter enmity of a group of petty bourgeois deprived of their livelihood. Both black and white council members responded with a generalized opposition to his legislative program, and it was not until the election of new city council members in his second term of office that Hatcher was able to obtain favorable results from the local legislature.[3]

Soon after Hatcher was elected to the city council, his incorruptibility, independence from the machine, and militancy on civil rights questions became common knowledge in Gary's black community. The skepticism resulting from disappointments in previous insurgents was replaced by a growing enthusiasm as Hatcher's personal capability and his willingness to fight the machine became manifest. A habit even developed among local civil rights activists of attending city council meetings to watch Hatcher champion their causes. And the two two-year terms that Hatcher served saw many exciting political battles in which Hatcher acted as a militant leader of the oppressed black community of the city. The most important of these was his leadership in the struggle for an omnibus civil rights ordinance. After much complex parliamentary maneuvering, the ordinance, which included an open occupancy housing provision, was passed, and Hatcher became the most popular political figure in Gary's black community. From that time on, Hatcher was a symbolic figure to the local civil rights movement and the beneficiary of an emerging mood among many blacks that the time had come to achieve a new relationship with local government.[4]

Hatcher's primacy among Gary's black politicians made him the natural candidate in the event of a black insurgent political effort to obtain the Democratic mayoral nomination in 1967. And it was evident that Hatcher's entire career was organized around that quest. He wanted to challenge the machine, and many black people in Gary would have liked him to be mayor. But even among his closest supporters there was grave doubt about the prospects for such an insurgency. The local machine had deeply entrenched itself in power since the New Deal period, both in the city and in Lake County. In addition to its own substantial resources of political power, patronage, and followers it had powerful allies in the business community and the Calumet region trade union bureaucracies. Moreover, its candidate would be white. Political tradition in both the society and community reserved major executive roles for whites: there were no black mayors in the United States.

Moreover, Hatcher had troubles raising funds for a serious campaign. The black businessmen, professionals, and ministers were either economically and politically obligated to the local machine, or ideologically uneasy about Hatcher's political militancy. With the exception of a group of school teachers organized by Jesse Bell, Jr., Hatcher's appeals for campaign funds from the black middle-income strata were largely fruitless. The machine, of course, had access to substantial funds through its ties to Gary's white business community. The result was that Hatcher's 1967 primary effort was run on a minimal budget of $37,000, while his machine-backed opponent spent perhaps ten times that amount.[5]

However, Hatcher won the backing of a small but active force in Gary politics, known as the "Miller mafia." At the time Henry Wallace ran for president in 1948 an informal group of small business and professional people, largely Jewish and radical, who lived in the section of town known as Miller, actively participated in the campaign. Over the years which followed, the group supported a large variety of reform and civil rights struggles in Gary. When Hatcher ran for the city council in 1963, the Miller mafia began to play an important support role in his effort, providing him with substantial technical skills, at least limited entry into parts of the white community independent of the machine, poll watchers for white neighborhoods, and the bulk of his financial backing.

In contrast with Hatcher's inability to raise significant sums from Gary's black middle-income strata, the generosity of the Miller group was particularly striking. In addition, this group developed the basic strategic document around which the campaign was organized. On December 6, 1966, this document was presented to Hatcher. It made three points. First, that popular white racism would make it impossible for Hatcher to obtain more than 10 percent of the white vote in the Democratic Party primary. Second, that the main strategic objective of the campaign would have to be obtaining the most black votes.

> It should not be diluted by fear of white reaction. The pertinent question must always be: "What will elicit the greatest black response?" The purpose is to induce Negroes to perform three vital acts: register, go to the polls, and cast a vote for a black mayoral candidate.

Third, to accomplish this end, it would be necessary to disengage the black vote from the machine control which characterized it.

The document also provided a detailed numerical breakdown of Gary's voting patterns, showing that demographic changes in the city's population had resulted in a potential black electoral majority. Soon the main points of the document were summarized in a popular brochure, *Tell It Like It Is: Hatcher Can Win*, which was distributed in thousands of copies as the key piece of campaign literature.[6] With it, a speculative venture took on reality. It was evident that a united black population had the ability to elect its own candidate regardless of the preferences of the machine and the voting pattern among whites. Thus Hatcher became a credible candidate.

The Machine

This analysis did not alter the fact that in order to become the mayor of Gary Hatcher had to win against the opposition of the local Democratic Party machine. Over the years, the radical movement in America has taken the position that the urban machines are an opponent of the interests of the urban working class,[7] a view confirmed by the legacy of machine politics in Gary. When Hatcher ousted the long-entrenched Democratic Party machine from City Hall in 1967, his new administration was confronted with the outcome of decades of machine politics. Virtually no governmental regulation on behalf of the public welfare was taking place.

For example, the health department did not enforce any of the local and state ordinances requiring sanitary conditions. When Hatcher's new health commissioner personally inspected local restaurants to determine if their dishwashers were being run at temperatures hot enough to sterilize, it was simply assumed he was coming around for bribes.[8]

Road maintenance provided another example. A loss of front-end alignment from driving an automobile on Gary's pot-holed streets was common. For many years the practice had been to put only one-third of the contracted road paving material on the streets. The difference in value was jointly pocketed by the municipal bodies responsible for granting the contract and the recipient.

School construction costs ran perhaps double those attainable by genuine competitive bidding. In Gary's newest school, the sewer line was installed directly above that of the fresh water line.[9] The building department enforced neither the building nor the housing codes; fire department response time was slow, as fire fighters on the payroll worked full time in the steel mills and paid a portion of their salary to their supervisors to mark them on duty; and in the jail, supervised by the police department, there was only gruel, as the food consumption funds for the prisoners were siphoned off. In short, within the constraints of the existing municipal budget, the local population received only a fraction of the services for which they were paying. A similar phenomenon existed on the appropriation side. Chapter 7 examines the way in which those with substantial vested interests paid far less than their legally mandated share of the local property tax. Moreover, the machine in Gary had adopted fiscal policies which favored "small city budgets, especially for departments oriented toward services."[10]

Curiously, this kind of highly negative assessment of the city machine is not shared generally by mainstream American social scientists. Instead, one commonly encounters what amounts to a defense of the political machine as a functionally beneficent part of the American political system.[11] Early in the Cold War, social theorist Robert K. Merton argued that the indignation against machine politics reflected a "naive moral judgment . . . that political machines violate moral codes." While Merton agreed that the machines were corrupt and granted that they provided unwarranted profits to both the small and large business interests associated with them, he also asserted that they performed a socially useful function, benefiting the mass of city dwellers.

Although he did not introduce any empirical evidence in support of his contentions, Merton claimed that the machine benefited the urban poor in two ways. First, for ethnic manual workers otherwise lacking opportunity for occupational advancement, municipal employment provided by the machine offered a route for upward social mobility. Second, the machine—in contrast to impersonal rationalized bureaucracies—was ready to help the poor regardless of formal eligibility requirements, and this aid was dispensed in a humane and personalized fashion. In return, the urban immigrant masses naturally followed the electoral preferences of their ward committee.[12]

These speculations rapidly became embedded in mainstream American social science as descriptive of the underlying reality.[13] And by the early 1960s proponents of liberal pluralism generally accepted this benevolent perspective. The concensus view rested on three propositions. First, the machine stood above ideology: the machine boss simply brokered disparate sectoral interests in the community. This balancing led to a general interest which made the community governable and moderated potential class conflicts. Second, the machine served the interests of working people by integrating them into the larger society and by helping them achieve upward social mobility. In contrast to discrimination in the private employment sector, machine patronage provided ethnic groups with a major route for occupational advance. Third, these very successes led to the machine's natural decline, as the end of mass immigration, New Deal reforms, mass upward social mobility, and the assimilation of the ethnic immigrants into the larger political culture combined to make it obsolete. The vestiges of the machines which endure do so because new black central city dwellers live in conditions similar to those lived in by the immigrant groups who preceded them.[14]

The apparent plausibility of this presentation has persuaded some "new left" academics. One has recently asserted: "The big-city political machine is, whether we like it or not, a working-class institution."[15] Once one has reached this conclusion, it is only a short step to argue, as some radicals now do, that it makes sense for socialists to work inside the Democratic Party just as it does to work inside trade unions. But while in general trade unions do defend the immediate interests of working people, the urban machines do nothing of the sort.

The problem with the elaborate justification of machine politics is that it is not sustained by empirical evidence. The urban machine simply has not been an instrument of class mobility for working people. Historically, municipal jobs have constituted only a small fraction of the urban labor market, and the large majority of patronage jobs (such as garbage collector) are relatively low paid and provide little chance for advancement. Instead, the main benefits of the patronage contracts have been skimmed off by a relative handful of entrepreneurs. And the personal fortunes made by the machine bosses and their business cronies, whatever their individual ethnicity, have not provided a basis for a general amelioration of the immigrants' lot.[16]

Case studies show that the capture of City Hall by a previously oppressed ethnic group has not advanced the economic welfare of the group as a whole. If anything, by diverting popular energies from efforts to penetrate into the more decisive private sector of the economy, the overall effect may have been to actually retard the ethnic group's rate of economic advance.[17] Furthermore, the machines were actually far less responsive to the successive ethnic groups than their defenders allege. Just as markets in reality do not follow the perfect fluidity of liberal economic theory, so too, despite academic notions, the machines did not move quickly to incorporate the newcomers so as to maximize their voting strength. In few cities was there intense competition between the two major parties for the voting allegiance of immigrant masses. Nor did the ethnic immigrants assume positions of power in the machine proportional to their voting contribution. Generally, a lag of decades preceded new ethnic takeovers, especially for executive positions which involved the power to distribute significant amounts of patronage. This time lag in incorporating the ethnic groups makes it most unlikely that the machines could have served as a major element in immigrant upward social mobility.[18]

Despite the sophistication of their exponents, in reality the urban machines have neither served the working class nor stood above class interests. Rather, the urban ethnic machines have been a political instrument of the petty bourgeoisie.[19] Both the ideology and the policy of the machine reflect this class character.[20] It is true that the machine leaders, who run the machine like a business, prefer not to antagonize their constituents by taking avoidable political stands. But beneath this apolitical facade lies a petty-bourgeois orientation. As with small businesses generally, the ideology of the machine bosses "rests upon their identification with business as such." Thus, machines prefer to buy off their opponents individually rather than make substantive policy concessions to them. Their general political orientation has been centrist and moderate.[21]

The political machines have always been hostile to efforts to forge mass socialist or labor parties, and traditionally they have opposed trade union organization. (The relatively recent convergence of urban machines and the industrial unions has been accomplished mainly by accommodation on the part of the unions and their diminished role in conveying working-class demands into political life.) More recently, the machines have attempted to prevent the development of autonomous community organizations directed at urban structural reforms.[22]

The petty-bourgeois character of the machines is also evident in their operation. One crude manifestation is the plundering of the city treasury, legally or otherwise, by the bosses and the local businesses providing the municipality with goods and services. It is in this sense that "the rewards of machine politics are essentially issue-free in that they will flow regardless of what politics are followed" by the City Hall incumbents.[23] For the machine, the politics of business and the business of politics fuse. Thus, the local business community has generally served as a firm base of financial and political support.

Even more significant than the endless "deals" which characterize the economic activities of machine-dominated city halls is the machine's policy pattern, which consistently favors the well-to-do. Thus, ordinary workers and black people make up the difference when machine assessors favor major property owners; central city dwellers pay with their health when local machines fail to enforce environmental regulations; and slum dwellers are the losers when landlords bribe municipal building departments. Similarly, the general fiscal conservatism of the machines serves the local business community, who, in direct contradiction to the mass of working people, both prefer and benefit from lower taxes as opposed to higher social welfare expenditures.[24]

The local political alliance between business and property interests explains why machine politics continue to predominate among the manufacturing cities of America's heartland, and machine politics remain the normal way of life in urban working-class America.[25] Yet machine politics in industrial communities serve above all to deflect political activity from taking on an explicitly class form. The ability of urban machines to co-opt potential leaders from working-class and minority communities results in its functioning to incorporate embryonic working-class movements and to prevent them from reaching the stage of autonomous politics.[26]

Thus, the fact that Hatcher had to contest against an urban machine for office was not particularly unusual; for representatives of working-class or black struggles this will prove to be the typical pattern. For a black candidate to defeat such a machine meant that a powerful obstacle to the black liberation movement would be removed.

The Black Sub-Machine

Just as the machine institutionalizes the subordination of the working class to the hegemonic political forces of the society,[27] the black sub-machine institutionalizes the subordination of the black community to the dominant political power.

Since World War II, central cities have experienced a sharp increase in their black populations, obliging political machines to rely more heavily on the black vote to obtain electoral majorities. Their chief mechanism for turning out these votes is the black sub-machine, doubtless the single most powerful and coherent community organization in the northern ghettos.

Prior to the New Deal period, the northern black sub-machines were affiliated mainly with the Republican Party, and both were loyally supported by the mass of black voters. During the New Deal period these sub-machines were largely broken up and reconstituted as part of the Democratic Party coalition, a shift that brought some gains to the black community.[28] But the relationship of the black sub-machine to the overall Democratic Party apparatus was a distinctly subordinate one. For instance, blacks remained underrepresented in patronage jobs and other benefits both quantitatively and qualitatively.[29]

As Hatcher and his associates realized, the advance of Gary's black community in the political arena required the formation of a popular base of support independent of the local black sub-machine. In that sense there is a distinct parallel between the multiethnic New Deal coalition which won Gary's mayorality contest in 1934 and Hatcher's black coalition which won in 1967: in both cases the victories turned on drawing into political life a mass of previously nonparticipating potential voters from the lowest economic strata of the city.

The difference of course is that in the 1930s blacks constituted only a fifth of Gary's electorate, while Hatcher's coalition was overwhelmingly black. To appreciate this difference, a brief review of Indiana's long racist history is useful. Slavery in Indiana lingered on for years after its formal abolition in 1816, and the state constitution of 1851 forbad blacks from living in Indiana. Prior to the Civil War one of Indiana's senators was a slaveholder (domiciling his slaves in Kentucky), and the majority of the state's congressional delegation voted for the Fugitive Slave Act. Nor did the small number of blacks in the state prevent the continuation of a racist tradition over the following decades. The southern part of the state maintained segregated schools under local option ordinances until 1949, and from the 1920s until after World War II, Jim Crow laws kept public facilities segregated throughout the state.[30]

Racial segregation in Gary increased sharply during the 1920s. While the elementary schools were segregated from the outset, it was not until 1927 that blacks were required to attend an all-black high school. During this period the Gary park system was also put on a Jim Crow footing, and the Ku Klux Klan virtually came to control the state's political life. The United States Steel Corporation played the key role in the institutionalization of racism, particularly in the employment arena. As Mohl and Betten conclude in a study of the development of racial discrimination in Gary:

> Racism was imposed on the community by those who controlled the city. U.S. Steel was primarily responsible through its promotion and hiring policies, its control of the Gary Land Company, and its influence on the school board and park commission. Local politicians, through municipal policy and realty codes, reinforced trends established by the steel corporation.[31]

One particularly striking case of U.S. Steel's leading and initiating role in this process is the behavior of William Gleason, superintendent of the Gary Works, who also served as head of the Gary Park Commission from 1915 until 1935. When some black parents in 1930 attempted to racially integrate a small park in their neighborhood which had previously barred them, Gleason personally appeared on the scene and threatened to fire any black Gary Works employee who did not leave.[32]

The subordinate position of Gary's blacks also manifested itself in their relationship to the local Republican Party. With appropriate symbolism, the Gary black Republican club was founded in 1908 in the basement of the Gary Land Company— U.S. Steel's subsidiary real estate company. Despite increasing feelings of Republican Party neglect, black voters in Gary, as elsewhere, continued to be loyal to "the party of Lincoln" throughout the 1920s and early 1930s. As late as 1932 Republicans continued to command large black voting majorities in the city.[33]

This sub-machine-generated support for the Republicans was

buttressed by small favors, such as the allocation of three black city council seats. These captive councilors had their analogue in Gary's black middle class as a whole, which often had "profitable connections" with the U.S. Steel Corporation. As one black minister at the time put it:

> Because the company controls this city, there are few of us who are not afraid to go against the wishes of Mr. [H.S. Norton], who runs this town. To work here you must work for some part of the mill directly or indirectly. . . . There is no way the colored have to say anything against this. . . . What has happened is that the churches have become subsidiaries of the steel corporation and that the ministers dare not get up and say anything against the company.[34]

This power was exercised both to control the black vote and to block trade union activity in the black community.

The maintenance of Republican machine hegemony over the black vote became increasingly vital during the 1920s, as a growing number of children of immigrants were beginning to vote in the cities, and their allegiance was going to the Democrats. Beginning in 1928 large numbers of skilled and semiskilled white workers joined the most oppressed white workers in voting Democratic, leaving the Republican machine utterly dependent upon its bloc of black voters for its electoral majorities.[35]

As late as 1934, when this emerging Democratic coalition captured Gary's City Hall, a majority of the black voters were still in the Republican camp. But when they did shift allegiance, blacks did so in a manner more complete and decisive than any other group. By 1936 most blacks in Gary, and throughout the nation, had lined up behind Roosevelt and the New Deal.[36]

This black voting shift was highly pragmatic. In 1930 (when the Gary Republican machine relied heavily on their votes), blacks held only two-thirds of their proportional share of municipal jobs. The transfer of black support to the New Deal coalition resulted in a rise in this share to virtual parity by 1944.[37]

Since the New Deal blacks have played an ever greater numerical role in the voting strength of the Democratic Party, both nationally and in particular urban centers. As late as 1944 (due to massive disenfranchisement in the South, where most blacks still resided) blacks provided only 5 percent of Roosevelt's vote. But by 1968 they accounted for a full 19 percent of the national Democratic vote.[38] The sheer size of this black vote helps to explain the support Hatcher received from the Democratic Party national leadership after he won the nomination for mayor.

But in Gary itself, the rising black vote did not automatically translate into important benefits for the black people of that city. The more entrenched the machine became, the *less* it returned to blacks. One key indicator of responsiveness to ethnic demands is municipal jobs; by the mid-1960s blacks were reduced to about half of their proportional share of municipal employment (see Table 1.1).

Apparently, as a result of the exhaustion of the reform impulse of the New Deal and the disappearance of the local Republican Party as a serious electoral threat, the Gary Democratic machine felt little need to make substantive concessions to the black community. Indeed, by the time Hatcher ran for mayor the racial

Table 1.1
Representation of Blacks in Gary Municipal Jobs

Year	Percent of population	Percent in municipal employment
1930	17	12
1944	18	16
1955	29	20
1966	50	28

Sources: for 1930, Richard Julius Meister, "A History of Gary, Indiana: 1930-1940" (Ph.D., University of Notre Dame, 1967); for 1944, J. Harvey Kerns, *A Study of the Social and Economic Conditions of the Negro Population of Gary, Indiana* (New York: National Urban League, 1944), p. 14; for 1955, Warren M. Banner, *A Study of the Social and Economic Conditions in Three Minority Groups: Gary, Indiana* (New York: National Urban League, 1955), pp. 10-12; for 1966, Alex Poinsett, *Black Power Gary Style: The Making of Richard Gordon Hatcher* (Chicago: Johnson, 1970), p. 77.

biases in City Hall's hiring practices had become a major campaign issue in the black community.

The Democratic machine continued the practice developed by the Republican Party of effectively purchasing the support of the bulk of the black middle-income strata. Together with its allies in the local business community it provided "many of the lines of advancement in work as well as prestige" for this group.[39] The majority of black ministers, for example, publicly urged their parishioners to vote and to cast their ballots for the machine candidates. (It was reliably reported to me that the machine regularly dispensed substantial sums of cash to many of these ministers, both for their own use and to dispense to particularly needy members of their congregations.) Similarly, a variety of small favors were extended to black professionals and petty bourgeois whose marginal economic position rendered them easily influenced.

The black precinct committeemen, who constituted the core of the black sub-machine, were essentially paid machine employees; almost three-fifths of them personally held patronage jobs with City Hall. They in turn dispensed various favors to a huge proportion of the black people living in their precincts. Such favors might include paying an overdue electric bill, aiding a constituent in applying for relief benefits, or getting some minor criminal charge dropped. In any given year a full quarter of Gary's black population received some direct assistance from their precinct committeemen.[40]

Moreover, the committeemen regularly paid poll watchers on election day and, if necessary, individual black voters. The machine also added its campaign workers (both black and white) to the public payroll for the duration. For instance, when the township assessor ran (unsuccessfully) for mayor in 1963 he simply hired more than 1,000 temporary employees, and in his reelection campaign in 1966 he hired 750, at a cost to the public of $37,500. On the primary day in 1967 when Hatcher ran for mayor, an armored truck cruised from precinct to precinct in the black community, dispensing to the black committeemen sufficient cash to pay every black voter in the city $10.[41]

From the standpoint of the machine, these payments were

a necessary cost of business. In one sense, such behavior is "ideologically neutral," but it served to block popular reform candidates who lacked comparable resources. An entrenched machine thus serves to set a "cost of entry" into the electoral marketplace, which tends to exclude autonomous working-class political forces. The control by the Gary machine over City Hall gave it the basis for running a profitable venture even after paying out the sums needed to obtain the vote.[42]

By the time Richard Hatcher decided to challenge the Gary machine in 1967 it was even more dependent upon the black vote than the Republican Party machine had been in the 1920s. As one leader of the Gary Democratic Party organization explained it:

> You depend on your solid vote, where you know the people are for you. It's very foolish to waste all your time and effort in an area where you know you're not going to get the vote no matter what you do. . . . [In the 1960s] you had to rely upon the heavy Democratic Negro precincts to carry the lead. It made sense. If you were going to break even in the white areas, you had to concentrate in Negro areas to get your majority.[43]

Thus for Hatcher's candidacy to succeed, it had to break the electoral power of the Gary ghetto sub-machine.

Hatcher's Primary Campaign

When Hatcher announced his candidacy in 1967, the median age of white central city dwellers was 32 years, and the black median was 22 years, a difference which remains today. While most of the younger members of the white population have moved to suburbs, the more vigorous part of the black population has concentrated in the cities. This means that urban black candidates face an aging leadership and constituency among the entrenched machines throughout the country.[44]

Hatcher's machine opponents were viturally all in their late fifties, having achieved local political power as young insurgents during the New Deal. For instance, in 1934 the campaign manager of the first Democrat to win the mayoralty in Gary against the then-entrenched Republican machine was Ray Madden. He was rewarded with the post of city chairman of the party and made city controller. In 1942 Madden went on to become Lake County's representative to Congress, a post he still held in 1967 at the age of 72.[45]

By this time the machine had also solidified its ties to the conservative trade union bureaucracies of the Calumet region. For instance, the Steelworkers' Union district leadership "tended to support some of the regions's most reactionary and corrupt public officials. . . . especially . . . in Lake County."[46] In 1967, Joseph Germano, then regional director (though now retired), was one of the key machine supporters.

However, Gary's machine was in serious disarray at the time, its boss, former mayor George Chacharis, having been imprisoned for income tax evasion. (One part of the evidence adduced during his trial was that he and his associates had set up a dummy corporation to which a construction company building the Indiana Toll Road through Gary had been obliged to pay $100,000.) In 1960 Chacharis had delivered 70 percent of Gary's vote for John F. Kennedy. He was an honored White House guest and apparently was considered seriously for appointment as ambassador to Greece. But an organized crime campaign under the supervision of Attorney General Robert Kennedy inadvertently caught Chacharis in its net, and after much waffling he was indicted. This resulted in internecine warfare within the machine, as different factions fought to obtain control.

Chacharis, a poor immigrant boy from Greece, had made his way in Democratic Party politics simultaneously with advancing himself in the employ of U.S. Steel. He had started at the Gary Works as an unskilled laborer, and left in 1950 as chief project engineer in charge of all new construction at the mills. While at U.S. Steel he acquired a controlling interest in a fuel company, the General Coal and Oil Company.[47] Thus he was at the interface of U.S. Steel and local petty bourgeoisie interests seeking construction contracts. While mayor, Chacharis held occasional meetings with the mill superintendent "to hammer out decisions in face-to-face conferences."[48] The mutual cordiality was buttressed by the favorable local property tax treatment provided to the Gary Works by Chacharis' protégé, Township Assessor Tom Fadell, a subject which will be discussed in more detail in a later chapter.[49]

When Chacharis was sent off to prison, Gary's business community discreetly severed their ties with him.[50] Moreover, the orderly succession in office was disrupted. The machine tradition was to rotate the mayoralty each term to a member of a different ethnic group, each of whom retired from office a millionaire. But in 1963 no fewer than five candidates fought for the Democratic Party designation. The winner, A. Martin Katz, was reputed to have spent the largest sums to gain the support of the precinct committeemen.

The machine's internal difficulties affected white and black voters differently, however. Although Katz's close ties with the machine resulted in his getting only a quarter of the white vote, he still obtained a majority of the black vote; at least two-thirds of his total primary vote came from the black community.[51]

A parallel development occurred in Chicago. In 1963 Mayor Daley received only 44 percent of the general election vote in the all-white, nonreform wards, but 84 percent in the black wards.[52] Despite his appeal to a white "blacklash" vote, Daley's machine remained coherent enough throughout this period to continue to roll up majorities among Chicago's black voters. Katz, by contrast, would not be able to sustain such a pattern into the 1967 election in Gary.

Katz's ability to obtain large numbers of white votes was not aided by the general perception that he was favorable to civil rights legislation. Katz was sympathetic to such legislation, and as a shrewd politician he believed that substantial concessions had to be made to Gary's black community to ensure its continued electoral loyalty. He thus both supported local civil rights legislation and provided blacks with better municipal jobs than they had previously been able to obtain.

For the first time under his administration, blacks were hired as inspectors in the building department, and every city commission and board was integrated. Thirty-two blacks were added to the fire department—doubling the number previously hired in Gary's entire history. Blacks even were given a few leading administrative positions, such as corporation council member and superintendent of general services, but by the time Katz ran for reelection in 1967, many blacks felt that these concessions were too few and too late (see Table 1.1).[53]

Thus, while Katz believed that he was very far advanced on the race question, particularly in view of Gary's traditions in this matter, and that black voting loyalty therefore would be assured, a good part of the black community felt differently. On the other hand, Katz correctly feared that he would have trouble in obtaining sufficient white votes in the 1967 primary, especially if confronted with a "law and order" candidate to his right. Given a serious insurgency from the black community of the sort that Hatcher presented, Katz was unable to achieve the kind of support from both blacks and whites that Mayor Daley put together in nearby Chicago.

The first major story about the forthcoming Democratic Party primary contest for mayor appeared in the Gary *Post-Tribune*—the only local newspaper—on February 8, 1967. The discussion of Hatcher's candidacy read as follows: "Hatcher, a lawyer, is a Negro. He's been told the city is not ready for a Negro mayor."

Over the next few weeks, Katz, Hatcher, and Bernard Konrady (a local white businessman running a populist-style "law and order" campaign) each announced his candidacy. The Gary *Post-Tribune* carried the story of Hatcher's formal declaration on February 28:

> Richard G. Hatcher launched his Gary mayoral candidacy Monday night with a plea that the campaign not be branded a "black-white" conflict. Speaking before 800 to 1,000 persons at a testimonial dinner . . . Hatcher emphasized that his primary concern is to meet the needs of all people, black and white together.

The article went on to discuss Hatcher's platform, in which he blamed U.S. Steel for the community's pollution and inadequate local property tax, and pointed out the gross underrepresentation of blacks in municipal jobs, especially among the police and fire departments.[54]

These two stories essentially constituted the press coverage. With the exception of a brief item on the campaign's main election rally—a gala meeting of 4,000 people with singer Harry Belafonte and boxer Muhammad Ali—and a few obscure references to problems of voter registration, the *Post-Tribune* essentially blacked out Hatcher's efforts. Their posture reflected that of the white business establishment: Hatcher was persona non grata. A few years later Hatcher commented that in Gary "there is only one major newspaper, and by far the overwhelming bulk of its news has to do with the lives of the white people either in Gary or in its surrounding, nearly all white, suburbs."[55]

At the same time that the wealthy white owners of the *Post-Tribune* were exercising their freedom of the press by ignoring Hatcher, they provided his opponents with ample coverage. The endorsements by George Chacharis and the Lake County Central Labor Council for Katz were prominently reported, as was Katz's opening campaign speech, which implicitly accused the Hatcher forces of advocating racial violence:

> Any violence occuring in the next few weeks must be laid at the feet of those preaching the doctrine of division, using their outside agitators and advisors, and manipulated by interests foreign to democratic principles. . . . Gary has no room for people who wish to be catapulted into public office on the rocket ship of violence, using the fuel of race hatred.[56]

The *Post-Tribune* was created in 1921 through the merger of two newspapers, which were both voices for the United States Steel Corporation in civic affairs. It was run by the prominent local Republican Synder brothers, one of whom had served on the Board of Public Works during the Republican epoch. During the New Deal, the newspaper bitterly opposed both Roosevelt and the efforts of the CIO to organize the steel industry. It was also virulently racist. During the 1930s, for example, a black criminal defendant was described as having an expression of "childlike irresponsibility characteristic of his race."

In recent years the *Post-Tribune* has been bought by a national chain, but it continues under the same editorial leadership and continues to support the local machine, under whose aegis it remains grossly underassessed for property tax purposes. The paper has been a lucrative business: when Henry B. Synder died his estate was valued at over $1 million. The staff continues to be virtually all white; and the reporters assigned to City Hall continue to evidence hostility to Hatcher and black people generally. The newspaper consistently has been the voice of the larger business community in Gary.[57]

With little exposure in the mass media, public perceptions of Hatcher's candidacy in the white community were shaped to a large degree by the Democratic Party campaign committee. The machine, in addition to its public hints that Hatcher was a dangerous person, systematically began to spread rumors and literature in white neighborhoods, primarily ridiculous charges about his personal life, along with outlandish claims that his election would lead to Gary's rule by personal agents of Premier Fidel Castro of Cuba. The traditions of popular racism in the society made this type of political manipulation feasible; the respectable business community of Gary permitted it, and the machine needed it.

Attempts by Hatcher's white supporters to distribute their campaign literature in white neighborhoods were met by so many individual acts of violence that it was necessary to suspend the effort. It even became necessary to provide armed guards to protect the homes of his most publicly prominent white supporters.

In the black neighborhoods, violence by machine supporters was countered successfully by comparable methods on the part of the insurgents. After several months of sporadic encounters, it was the Hatcher organization which was able to distribute its materials freely and the incumbent who found himself in difficulty. This victory was not primarily the result of having more toughs, but an indicator of the truly popular character Hatcher's campaign took on in the black community. At its height, twenty-five hundred volunteer workers (of whom 90 percent were black) participated. The black community was organized on a block-by-block basis to carry out mass voter registration and to assure a massive vote on primary day.[58]

Although 48 percent of the registered Democrats at the outset of the campaign were black, Hatcher faced the problem that traditionally a larger proportion of white than black registrants actually voted. (In the 1956 Democratic Party primary, for example, 56 percent of the registered whites but only 46 percent of the registered blacks voted.) So one part of the campaign effort involved the registration of 3,700 additional, mostly black, voters, despite substantial impediments placed in the way by the Lake County Democratic Party machine. This effort was remarkably successful: the excitement generated by Hatcher's campaign was enough to reverse the traditional racial voting pattern. Evidently a mass of blacks who ordinarily felt that voting was a wasted effort believed differently this time, because in the 1967 primary, while 50 percent of registered whites cast ballots, 61 percent of registered blacks did so.[59]

As the primary campaign moved toward a close it became obvious that Hatcher was going to win a majority in the black community. One indicator was that Hatcher stickers began to be displayed prominently on the windows of black homes, evidence of the excellence of Hatcher's organizing. The shift took place notwithstanding the original hegemonic position of the black sub-machine in which

> grass-roots campaign workers found that many blacks were reluctant to cast their votes for Hatcher not because he was black, or they did not think he could win, or because they did not trust him, but because they had become accustomed to receiving cash rewards, gifts, groceries, and other benefits from their precinct committeemen for voting for machine candidates, and they feared these would be cut off if they voted for anyone else. Apparently, many black voters genuinely believed that machine politicians had accurate information about how each person voted and would use this information to punish those who did not vote as they were told.[60]

When this became clear, Katz's campaign took a new turn. He began to give up on the black vote and concentrate on winning a majority of the white vote. In the last week of the campaign throughout the white community the argument was made that a vote for the "law and order" candidate was—by splitting the white vote—in effect a vote for Hatcher and black domination of Gary. This argument clearly influenced a large number of voters, but the lateness of this tactic (and the reluctance of a large bloc of white voters to endorse a candidate whom they perceived as pro-black) was such that the white vote remained split between the two white candidates, each obtaining about half. Katz obtained a quarter and Hatcher three-quarters of the black vote. Thus Hatcher won the primary with a plurality of 38 percent.

The General Election

Since victory in Gary's Democratic Party primary had been tantamount to election ever since the New Deal period, there was dancing in the streets of the black community when the primary results were announced. Participants called it a "festival of the oppressed." Hatcher's campaign organization prepared to essentially dissolve itself. His volunteer workers had prevailed with only a fraction of the funds, electoral experience, and institutional advantages possessed by the incumbent. The general election was foreseen as a mere formality, especially after the chairman of the Lake County Democratic Party, John Krupa, announced his "full support" for Hatcher.[61]

There was the ominous fact that only 5 percent of the white voters in the primary had cast their ballots for Hatcher. But it was reasonable to assume that the Republican Party opposition would again mount only a nominal effort, and that in the general election whites would manifest their traditional Democratic Party loyalties. The intensity of popular white racism in Gary, however, made another pattern possible.

One measure of the extent of white racism in Gary was the remarkably high support for George Wallace. In 1964 when Wallace ran for president in the Indiana Democratic primary he obtained 67 percent and 77 percent of the vote in the two main white sections of the city. The core of Wallace's support came from former white southerners who had moved to Gary to work in the steel mills. The foreign-born workers, very poor workers, and workers with strong ties to their ethnic communities were the least likely to vote for Wallace. But younger skilled white workers, particularly those who felt dissatisfied with their situation in society, generally supported Wallace.[62]

A white working-class racist backlash seems also to require proximity to a large black urban population which is actively seeking political or social advances. In this circumstance, the immediate fear of racial integration, viewed "as threatening to the stability and respectability" of white neighborhoods, can trigger popular white backlash. The large Wallace vote of 1964 followed by one month the 10,000-strong open housing demonstration in Gary led by City Councilman Richard Hatcher.[63]

In a situation of crisis when the machine found itself in a critical situation, it considered the reserve option to save itself by appeal to a mass racist sentiment. At first, the machine seemed inclined to support Hatcher in the general election; Krupa, at a party rally attended by 1,500 announced "full support" of Hatcher's bid for mayor. Yet within a few weeks it had reversed itself, deciding to evoke a white backlash. It took extraordinary measures to block Hatcher from office: urging Democratic Party voters to vote for the Republican candidate, openly branding Hatcher a "Kremlin agent," and engaging in massive illegal vote stealing.[64]

The decision to take these measures had little to do with the personal racism of the Democratic machine leadership. Hatcher himself insists that their posture was not based on racial intolerance: "In me they knew they were getting not just a black man but one they couldn't control."[65] To the machine, Hatcher's problem was not his color but his politics.

Hatcher's biographer colorfully described Lake County boss Krupa as a "middle class extoller of the virtues of hard work and self-reliance, super-American patriot, passionate anti-Communist." Krupa first demanded that Hatcher purge his campaign organization of both its white and black "radical elements." This was, of course, the means to a more profound end. As Hatcher recalls, after his victory in the May primary:

> Krupa met with me and said he wanted to name the police chief and controller and several key officers. And I told him, "Look, too many people have worked too hard on this and I'm not going to abdicate my responsibilities or sell them out. I'm going to name my own police chief and controller."[66]

Once it was clear to the machine that Hatcher was not prepared to permit it to choose the officials who would make the key
decisions which involved economic control over the city government, they then resorted to opposition and backlash. In the
secret negotiations between Hatcher and the machine, it was
made clear that the price of support in the general election
was to permit the machine continued control over the police
department and a majority on the Board of Public Works, which
controlled all municipal contracts. In return, not only would
Hatcher be supported in the election, but his personal economic
position, and that of his key advisors, would be greatly amelio-
rated. A refusal to cooperate would be not only politically but
personally dangerous.

Thus, in a crisis, the "neutrality" of local machine politics
transformed itself into organized political reaction. Once their
pecuniary interests were seriously threatened, the machine
petty bourgeoisie demonstrated a class interest for which they
were prepared to carry on a coherent battle, one in which they
did not feel restricted by the limits of political liberalism, or
"law and order."

After Hatcher's refusal of this corrupt bargain, the machine
began to publicly support the Republican candidate, a colorless
local businessman named Joseph Radigan. It did so on the
grounds that Hatcher was a dangerous radical. For instance,
John Krupa was quoted in the *Post-Tribune* as saying:

> It would be the greatest thing for the city of Gary to elect a Negro
> mayor. But it must be a man who denounces Black Power advo-
> cates. And it must not be someone who is going to force housing
> integration on people. The people of Gary had better wake up. If
> these people are able to capture city hall, they also gain control of
> the police and fire departments, leaving the steel mill and indus-
> trial complex at their mercy. The leaders in Moscow and Havana
> must be rubbing their hands in glee over this situation.[67]

To Gary's black community, such charges were patently
ridiculous. Regardless of whether they had voted for Hatcher in
the primary, the consensus among blacks was that just as all
other candidates in the past, once nominated, Hatcher should
automatically be supported by the Democratic Party in the gen-

eral election. To suddenly introduce additional criteria made it obvious that the machine was appealing to racial bigotry and serving to maintain an undemocratic tradition of blocking blacks from higher positions. Gary's black community was outraged, and the entire black population of the city united behind his candidacy.

But the unanticipated behavior of the machine demoralized Hatcher's campaign organization. The strategic planning for his insurgency had extended only as far as the primary. Morale visibly dropped among the campaign workers, and a bitter fratricidal dispute took place between Hatcher's key advisors. This was based largely on an underlying opposition to the new role Hatcher assigned to the black district committeemen.

Hatcher believed that to win in the general election it would be necessary to further increase the number of black voters. And since Krupa—secretary of the Lake County Election Board, among other posts—controlled voter registration, only official committeemen could register new voters in the period prior to the general election. Thus, Hatcher approached the black committeemen for support and insisted that they be given prominent positions in the campaign. While the large majority of the committeemen simply sat out the general election (not daring to publicly oppose Hatcher in the black community), a small minority did support Hatcher and registered the new voters. Many in Hatcher's campaign believed that these men were actually spies and saboteurs for the machine; and a substantial number of volunteers resigned in disgust over what they considered an unprincipled decision. But the strategy did yield an additional 5,000 black registrants.[68]

Meanwhile, the machine stance was a source of increasing concern to the Democratic state and national leadership. State party leaders and national figures such as Vice President Hubert Humphrey and Senator Robert Kennedy went out of their way to indicate their support for Hatcher, even aiding his fundraising efforts. These leaders were not direct beneficiaries of the existing nexus of local machine politics, but were concerned to maintain black support for the Democratic Party during a period of mass activism among blacks.[69] But the Lake County machine ignored their entreaties.

As election day approached, ominous rumors began to circulate that the machine was going to utilize its control over balloting to falsify returns and steal the election, common practice in communities dominated by machines. For instance, the machine-dominated local Board of Health, as the source of death certificates, had the only complete and accurate list of those who had died since the previous election. With this list, it was simple for "ghost" voters to appear at the polls claiming to be a deceased person and cast a vote with virtually no chance of challenge. Also, since the board was responsible both for certifying the licenses of nursing homes and for supervising the votes of the aged who were not physically able to go to the polls, it was able to falsify many of these votes. Control over the Board of Health was translatable into over 2,000 extra votes.

Moreover, the machine was able to see to it—and did—that on election day numerous voting machines in the black precincts were "out of order." Hatcher's organization prepared for this eventuality by hiring on its own over a dozen voting machine mechanics from nearby Chicago to be on hand on election day to fix broken machines. Coordinating this effort, along with providing sufficient poll watchers to prevent flagrant miscounting of ballots, was another organizational triumph of the Hatcher insurgency. And Gary police officers, who stood in front of polling booths in black neighborhoods to prevent their opening, were driven away by armed gangsters from outside the city hired by unknown persons prepared for this machine tactic.

In addition to these traditional machine tricks, a few weeks before the election the Lake County Board of Elections challenged 5,286 black voters and (despite grave questions as to the legality of this act) struck them from the voting rolls. Hatcher and his legal advisors felt that it would be futile to try to challenge this action in the state court system. Moreover, the machine prepared to falsely register 15,000 nonexistent white voters!

Fortunately for Hatcher, one of the white registrars was unwilling to participate in this fraud, and went to him with an affidavit detailing the scheme. With this evidence in hand Hatcher requested that the Justice Department intervene on his behalf and filed suit in federal district court. Initially, the Justice

Department refused to intervene, but at the last moment reversed itself in the first federal engagement in a northern civil rights election controversy. The decision is still shrouded in some mystery; it may be that during the period of black ghetto uprisings, the possibility of an armed conflict between machine incumbents and enraged Hatcher supporters if the election were so palpably stolen played a role. In any event, sending numerous federal agents to Gary, the Justice Department provided detailed testimony in federal court as to 1,100 new false registrants in white sections of the city. The three-member federal court issued a strong order, and the machine desisted at this point. With virtually the entire Indiana State Police Force in the city, and thousands of National Guardsmen on alert right outside, a relatively quiet election was held.

Both whites and blacks voted in massive turnouts, 72 percent of registered whites and 76 percent of registered blacks. With the exception of the Spanish-speaking voters, the majority of whom cast their traditional Democratic Party ballots, almost all of the white people of Gary voted for Radigan. But 96 percent of the black voters chose Hatcher. Hatcher won the election, by a vote of 40,000 to 38,000.[70]

On January 1, 1968, Hatcher took office and proceeded to try to make Gary a better community in which to live. But this was not so easy, for formal authority and real political efficacy do not always coincide. As this book will try to demonstrate, in the case of a crusading black mayor the gap was a chasm.

2

The Origins of an Industrial Center

When Richard Hatcher entered Gary's City Hall on January 1, 1968, he assumed the mayoralty of a city with a particular historical evolution and economy. In large measure, this historical legacy set the limits within which he was able to function. No realistic assessment of his achivements and failures, therefore, is possible without some comprehension of the historical development of the city. Simply to know that Gary is an industrial city with a black majority hardly suffices.

The existence of Gary, Indiana resulted from the need for the United States Steel Corporation to expand its productive facilities during the heroic period of American capitalism at the turn of the century, when massive industrialization was the order of the day. When in 1906 U.S. Steel began construction of the world's largest and most modern steel complex, it was initiating a project whose scale was truly grand.

U.S. Steel was the world's first and, at the time, only billion-dollar corporation. At the time of its initial capitalization in 1901, the true value of the corporation's plant and equipment was only about half of its nominal book value. But so successful was the new venture that this discrepancy was rapidly overcome. U.S. Steel had an annual budget which exceeded that of the federal government. And, because of its position of monopoly, its rate of profit was so high that it was able to construct the Gary Works with internally generated funds.[1]

U.S. Steel was created in 1901 by combining 213 manufacturing plants and transportation companies. Among its initial resources were the bulk of the Mesabi Range's iron ore—the basis of its monopoly power, a third of the shipping tonnage on the Great Lakes, and 770 miles of railroad track. It produced three-fifths of all American steel and a far larger share of many finished steel products. (For instance, it produced 80 percent of the steel plate, 85 percent of the wire, 90 percent of the street and interurban rails, and virtually all of the steel sheets, tubes, and tinplated steel.)

From the Civil War to the turn of the century there had been no two years in which the price of the main steel product of the period, railroad rails, had been the same. But within two months of the formation of U.S. Steel, the price of steel rails was stabilized at $28 per ton and maintained there until the onset of World War I. This not only illustrated the corporation's monopoly position, but also provided the capital necessary for building the Gary Works.[2]

A Burgeoning Industry

The expanding railroad system of the late nineteenth century was the decisive stimulus to the American steel industry. In turn, the steel industry led the general growth of manufacturing through World War I. While total production of manufactured goods almost doubled during the first decade of the century, steel grew even more rapidly. In 1900 steel mills constituted 7 percent of the nation's total manufacturing capital, but by 1919 the industry's share had increased to 11.4 percent. In 1890 the United States surpassed England to become the world's leading steel producer. By 1900 it produced two-fifths of world steel production; and by the end of World War I, three-fifths of the world total. Between 1900 (when American production was 11 million tons) and 1920, production more than quadrupled. The Gary Works was a central component of this spectacular burst of industrial expansion.[3]

Commercial steel production in the United States began after the Civil War; and for the remainder of the century the railroad industry was the main steel consumer. Between 1880 and 1900, 260,000 miles of new track were laid, and steel rails were substituted for the older iron ones. Rail equipment, too, used increasing quantities of steel. Thus, not only were 50 percent more locomotives built in 1900 than in 1880, but whereas in the earlier year each one required fifty tons of steel, in 1900 each locomotive required twice as much.

New York's Pennsylvania Station, built between 1903 and 1910 for $112 million, also used vast amounts of steel, not only for the terminal, but also for the tunnels under the Hudson and East rivers and the connecting links between the Pennsylvania and Long Island railroad systems. In fact, Pennsylvania Station was the only engineering project of the period to exceed the Gary Works in cost.[4]

While the bulk of the track was being laid west of the Mississippi River for such transcontinental lines as the Santa Fe, Rock Island, and Northern Pacific, the center of gravity of the steel industry remained in western Pennsylvania. In 1902 Allegheny County alone produced 38 percent of the nation's steel. But Chicago, which was closer to these rapidly expanding markets (as well as to iron ore supplies), also experienced rapid growth of its steel facilities. Despite this expansion, rail production in the Chicago area at the turn of the century ran about .5 million tons per year short of the demand.

During this period other major uses for steel developed. For instance, the use of structural steel in the building of skyscrapers—a revolutionary innovation when first used in the 1880s for the Statue of Liberty—became commonplace. Other kinds of construction projects such as the interurban transit lines and factories came to utilize large quantities of steel. The use of structural steel quadrupled between 1900 and 1920 to reach almost 4 million tons annually. At the same time, the development of steel-reinforced concrete made possible such giant new dams as the 246-foot high Roosevelt Dam. The Roosevelt Dam, constructed between 1906 and 1911, was the first to produce substantial amounts of electricity. And the burgeoning electrical power industry of the early twentieth century itself became a substantial user of steel in power stations and electrical equipment.

Large quantities of steel also came to be utilized in the machine tool industry, the electrical equipment industry, and for agricultural implements, including the new giant combines and caterpillar tractors. Steel wire rods began to be produced in quantity in the 1890s for nails, cans, and barbed wire. And the expanding petroleum industry also needed substantial amounts of steel for drilling rigs, wells, and pipeline, as well as for the refineries themselves.[5] Another major user of steel was the steel industry itself. The period between 1880 and 1900 saw a transition to steel in the construction of ships, and over half of American tonnage was in Great Lakes' iron ore ships. By 1920 almost 90 percent of the industry's ore was shipped from the Mesabi Range via the Great Lakes.[6]

As the steel industry expanded, so too did manufacturing and urbanization in general. Urbanization was based upon large-scale manufacturing: over the period from 1870 to 1920 the country went from one-fourth urban to over one-half urban. By 1910, three-quarters of all the cities with populations over 50,000 were located in the industrial belt. Chicago exemplified this trend. Its population of over 2 million people had multiplied eighteen times from the end of the Civil War until 1910, as it was the combined beneficiary of manufacturing growth and its strategic location as the national railroad center. At the base of its manufacturing enterprises were its steel mills, which directly employed 17,000 workers, and its foundries and machine producing factories, which employed an additional 40,000.[7]

Chicago's explosive growth rapidly led to the elimination of the central city as a location for new or rapidly expanding industries. As early as 1890 an acre of land in the heart of the downtown cost $3.5 million, and so by the close of the century the city's industry was expanding southward and eastward into the Calumet region.[8] The dense network of railroads, and the growing new interurban lines, assured adequate transportation. An early example of this trend was the decision of the Pullman Company in 1880 to build a new "company town" south of

Chicago. (Steel for its cars could be obtained readily from the nearby South Works of the Illinois Steel Company, soon to be merged into U.S. Steel). Other firms, such as Western Electric, with its Hawthorne Works in Cicero, followed suit, some, such as Standard Oil's Whiting Refinery, going eastward across the Indiana border.

The eastward expansion was facilitated by the Elgin, Joliet, and Eastern Railroad which paralleled Lake Michigan in Indiana. Constructed in 1887, it essentially formed an outer belt around Chicago and provided virtually limitless sites for industrial expansion. The 192-mile Elgin, Joliet, and Eastern Railroad became part of the United States Steel Corporation upon its founding in 1901.[9]

The Need for a New Mill

Early in the twentieth century the processes of monopolization and technological progress combined to increase the scale of plants in heavy industry. Steel production came to be more concentrated in those cities, such as Chicago, which already had large, efficient plants. However, U.S. Steel's Chicago South Works already had been expanded to the limits of its 330-acre site, leaving two options for substantially expanding steel production in the Chicago area: engage in massive landfill into Lake Michigan, radically expanding the South Works site, or construct a new facility. Since it was doubtful whether it would be economically feasible to cram vast new facilities into the congested South Works site even with landfill, and since Illinois political conditions created substantial obstacles to landfill, a new site in the Calumet region thus seemed appropriate.[10]

But the location decision was not unchallenged. Despite the rapidly rising demand for steel in the Midwest and West, U.S. Steel, as a monopoly, was not obliged to follow the dictates of the market. In fact, all prices for steel products under the "Pittsburgh plus" system were held constant regardless of where they were produced.[11] Charles Schwab, the first president of U.S.

Steel, proposed that the new facilities be built in Pennsylvania. But Board Director Marshall Field of Chicago favored a midwest location. He argued that in steel in particular, total transport costs are lowest by locating at the market rather than at the raw materials point. This economic advantage would be increased if it were possible to eliminate a "break of bulk" point, where raw materials have to be transferred between different modes of transportation. Placing a new steel mill on the shore of Lake Michigan, where ore boats could be unloaded directly into the mill, would give both advantages. Field's position carried the day. As Board Chairman Elbert H. Gary explained:

> We selected [Gary] because it was the best point in our judgment. Why? Because in looking all over the United States and Canada we found by actual figures we could assemble the raw materials and we could manufacture at less cost than at other points; because more than anything else it had a very large market for its products, the market having grown to such an extent that the mills of [the South Works] were not sufficient to supply these markets.[12]

Moreover, the native Americans to whom the land had once belonged had long since been expelled, and the northern part of Lake County, Indiana was relatively underdeveloped. "There was no reason for people to settle among the dunes," a grade school text commented, "and no one thought that a big city would ever be built at the south end of Lake Michigan."[13] However, by the turn of the century, the Calumet was clearly marked for industrialization and urbanization, a trend foreshadowed by the growth of Lake County's population, from 15,000 in 1880 to 38,000 in 1900. (Population was to double again in each of the next two decades, reaching a total of 160,000 in 1920.) The seven railroads passing through northern Lake County guaranteed its development; there had already been numerous efforts by speculative promoters to stimulate urban industrial development along rail routes.[14]

An initial speculative land boom had been set off in 1890 over rumors that the large Chicago meatpacking firms were going to move to the Calumet area. The firms actually did purchase over 4,000 acres of land, at an average price of $175 an acre, including a parcel from the Calumet Gun Club, later sold to the corporation.

Amidst the speculation, real development was occurring, as the cities of East Chicago, Whiting, and Hammond grew along with the industrialization of the Calumet region. East Chicago began with the introduction of manufacturing plants that built railroad car wheels and agricultural implements. Soon a chemical plant moved in to take advantage of the nearby Whiting Refinery. Between 1895 and 1901 the Inland Steel Company purchased a large tract and constructed the Indiana Harbor Works (which by 1903 employed 1,200 men). Youngstown Sheet & Tube also began to carry on steel operations in East Chicago. The area, in short, was an ideal industrial location.[15]

U.S. Steel decided to expand its facilities into the Calumet area. As H. S. Norton, Judge Gary's personal representative in Gary, summarized it:

> Gary is really a part of the Chicago development and represents the expansion of Chicago south and east in accordance with the dictates of economic necessity and advantage. . . . It is difficult to tell where Chicago ends and Gary begins.[16]

The corporation chose a large, moderately priced tract of land on Lake Michigan and adjacent to the Elgin Railroad for expansion. As the historian of the Calumet region, Powell A. Moore, describes the site:

> Sand ridges, low dunes and lakelike sloughs characterized the area, which was covered by a heavy growth of scrub oak, marsh grass, and tangled vines. The sluggish Grand Calumet, more like a bayou than a river, lay half a mile from the lake across the proposed plant site.[17]

Elbert Gary himself directly supervised the site choice, with the assistance of Eugene G. Buffington, president of the subsidiary Illinois Steel Company. (Buffington was ultimately rewarded for his managerial role with a place on U.S. Steel's board of directors.) Having made the decision in July 1905, U.S. Steel engaged the former mayor of Hammond, Armanis F. Knotts, to purchase the tract secretly. As the agent, Knotts paid out over $7 million for 9,000 acres: stretching out over ten miles of lake shorefront, and reaching a width of over two miles. As a bonus, the corporation's own Elgin Railroad ran through the site, providing a direct link to the South Works in Chicago.[18]

The Construction of the Gary Works

With its baronial site (once the exclusive hunting preserve of Chicago magnates) safely purchased, the corporation announced publicly its intention to build the world's largest and most modern steel works. As its Annual Report boldly stated: "The total cost will be large. The conclusion to build this plant has been made after a very careful consideration by the Finance Committee and the Board of Directors of this Corporation."[19] Every care was lavished on the Gary Works. The initial plan was to construct a mill of 1.75 million tons annual capacity, or one-twelfth of American production when operational. But ultimately it achieved a full one-eighth of the nation's steel ingot capacity. Its capacious site and advanced design enabled it to reach the "optimum efficiency" for steel production.

As a strictly secondary aspect of the project, the decision entailed the construction of a new city as well.[20] When Graham Taylor interviewed top corporation executives, he was informed that

> the building of the town was incidental, that their main concern was to construct a steel plant, and that citymaking was a side issue into which necessity alone drove them. They must have a place for their employees to live. This could not be expected to develop at all proportionately to the sudden need, unless the company assumed much of the responsibility.[21]

The rail links to Chicago—which would suffice to bring commuting construction workers to the site—were inadequate for a large permanent workforce, and a mill on the scale of the proposed Gary Works necessitated an entire city. But the city was merely a means to staff the mills; it was the Gary Works which was to be the source of profit.

The location on the shore of Lake Michigan was necessary not only to obtain iron ore at minimum transport cost, but also for the hundreds of millions of gallons of water needed daily in the manufacturing process itself. When fully developed, the Gary Works would consume almost as much as the entire population of Chicago. Moreover, the lakeside location made massive land-fill possible, a process which had the dual virtue of providing a repository for slag waste and adding additional land at minimal cost. Initially, a tract a half mile in length and extending 700 feet into the lake was thus created; by now a total of 1,370 acres has been created in this fashion.[22]

Political obstacles by the state of Illinois to landfill were a factor in the decision to locate in Indiana. Before the site was definitely chosen, high Indiana government officials privately promised Gary that they would pass a special statute to make such landfill legal. And at the next session of the Indiana legislature this promise was fulfilled. Legislation was quickly passed, without public debate, providing that for a payment of $25 per acre Lake Michigan could be filled in up to the federal harbor line depth of 22 feet.[23]

Another external factor facilitated the use of the newly chosen site: the development of the electric interurban railroads. While there were several railroads passing through the Gary area besides the Elgin, none of them were providing adequate passenger service from the Calumet region to Chicago. The interurbans—electrically powered and designed specifically for passenger service—filled this gap, and in the first decade of the century, thousands of miles of track were laid. In 1901 regional entrepreneurs planned an interurban between Chicago and South Bend, Indiana, and construction of this $4 million South Shore line took place between 1906 and 1908. Regular service commenced late in 1908, and by 1910 there were trains leaving Gary every half hour for the forty-five minute commute to Chicago's Loop. The existence of the interurban made it both easy to tap the Chicago labor market to build the mill and also to tie the Gary Works tightly to Chicago's burgeoning economy.[24]

Thus facilitated, site preparation began. Over a five-year period commencing in 1906, U.S. Steel invested $78 million in the Gary project. Purchasing the land, developing the new city, and creating additional facilities for the Elgin, Joliet, and Eastern Railroad took $16 million; site preparation and construction of the mills cost $60 million. During this period an average of 3,000 construction workers were on the job, though at times the number reached 6,000.[25]

The railroad tracks of three lines were moved southward from the mill area and elevated so that streets could cross into the mill without interference; in all 55 miles of new track were needed. Similarly, the Grand Calumet River was shifted a quarter of a mile southward and confined to a specially prepared channel. (It had previously been a meandering and marshy stream whose width reached 1,000 feet during storms.) The bulk of the site, north of the newly rechanneled Grand Calumet and encompassing the entire lake frontage, was reserved for the mill; only the southernmost section was left for the city. Observers quickly noted that the rechanneled Grand Calumet served as "a veritable moat in times of stress. . . . Perhaps no great industrial plant . . . occupies a position so impregnable to mob attack and so calculated to withstand a prolonged industrial siege."[26] Finally, a new harbor was specially constructed to allow even the largest Lake Michigan ore vessels to dock readily. Two parallel piers, 250 feet apart, were run out 2,000 feet from the shore; and a 3,600-foot channel was dug from the shore into the site, culminating in a large turning basin. Iron ore thus could be directly unloaded into blast furnaces.

And the largest electric unloaders in the world (with 35,000-ton daily capacities) were built at the dockside. Indeed, the Gary Works was the first major plant designed around the concept of electrification. An electric powerhouse of 46,000 horsepower—including the "largest installation in one unit of gas engines that has ever been made"—was installed to power both the Gary Works and the new city. Through a subsidiary, the Gary Heat, Light, and Water Company, U.S. Steel provided the city with gas and electricity from the mill.[27] To obtain water a three-mile intake tunnel was passed under the Gary Works at a depth of 80 feet and extended 8,000 feet into the lake. Designed for a city of 200,000, it sufficed for all Gary's wants until the late 1960s.[28]

The extensive site preparation and infrastructure served the world's most modern mills. Initially, the main plant consisted of eight blast furnaces, fifty-six open-hearth furnaces, a billet mill, plate mills, merchant bar mills, and all the auxiliary shops necessary to service them. This was joined by the world's largest rail mill, with an annual capacity of 1.5 million tons, and the coke plant, exclusively the more modern byproduct type, with an initial annual capacity of 2.5 million tons. By the end of World War I the coke ovens were further expanded to 4.5 million tons, which provided for all the corporation's installations in the Midwest.[29]

By January 1909, the first steel rails were shipped out of the Gary Works. That year, even as construction was proceeding, .5 million tons of rails were produced. In 1909 construction also began on two giant finishing plants, the American Bridge Company Works, and the American Sheet & Tin Plate Company Works. Situated on the site so as to most conveniently process the Gary Works' raw steel, they became an integral part of the entire complex. In 1910, the Gary Works produced 1 million tons of steel. The cost of steel production was a full fifth below that of U.S. Steel's Pennsylvania facilities, rendering the Gary Works a successful technical and economic undertaking, and giving the corporation dominance over the Midwest steel market. When World War I began, the Gary Works had a steel producing capacity of 2.2 million tons annually, making it by far the world's largest steel complex.[30] Its success demonstrated that a careful choice of location and a spacious site, combined with the modern engineering techniques, were decisive in modern heavy industry.

Choice of a City

As mentioned, once U.S. Steel decided to build the Gary Works out in the Calumet marsh, it was necessary to build a city to house the workers. But while the mill could be constructed according to engineering specifications, a city was somewhat more elusive: the people who would inhabit it were not subject to the same kind of control as were machines. Both the character of the decision to build the city, named after the chairman of the board of directors, and the immense gap between what was decided and what actually developed illustrate the limits of monopoly capital's power. At the extremes, two routes of urban development were possible: company town or tract development. While various commentators have considered Gary to be one or the other, in reality the city possesses elements of both these extremes, and falls in between. A characteristic American manufacturing city, in which some of the vital contours of urban life have been set by the priorities and necessities of U.S. Steel while others have been determined by free enterprise market forces, Gary is the combined result of both monopoly and competitive capital. And it is that combined class bloc, interacting with the working people who live there, that has determined the kind of community Gary is today.

Today, most housing takes the form of tract developments. Private builders use a large amount of suburban land to put up housing and proceed to sell it off to individual buyers. Once the last lot is sold off, the interest of the developer in the community ceases. On the other hand, a company town is one in which the workforce is employed largely by one corporation, which also owns the bulk of the land and houses the community. There are two types: one is a satellite city of some larger industrial center (e.g., Homestead, built in 1872 as an extension of Pittsburgh); the other is a remote and isolated community built to tap some mineral resource. Since the constant discovery and development of new raw material sources leads to the ongoing creation of new company towns, the latter are a direct result of advanced capitalism. A larger part of their workforce is engaged in employment for a national, rather than local, market than is the case with most cities. The parochial character of these towns is the result not of their marginal relation to modern capitalism, but of their extreme subordination to it. They are a part of the distorted, uneven development between regions that the private economy engenders.[31]

In addition to these structural elements, American company towns have been notorious historically for the harsh economic exploitation and direct, tyrannical company control over the community. While company towns originated with the rise of modern industry, American company towns never played more than a minor part in the urban life of the United States. In 1938 only 2 percent of the population lived in such communities.[32]

In the early twentieth century, company towns were a prominent part of the bituminous coal and southern textile industries, and fairly common among industrial belt steel communities. The housing was generally cheap and of low quality, often without utilities and running water, and commonly located near the fumes of industrial processes, without any regard for the consequences. Although there was substantial variation in individual cases, the overall planning of the company towns generally was inferior to the standards of the time.[33] Among the exceptions, two are relevant to Gary: Vandergrift, Pennsylvania and Pullman, Illinois.

Beginning in the 1890s, the American steel industry, as part of its overall policy of paternalism toward its skilled workers, began to encourage its crafts workers to become private homeowners. A key example was Vandergrift, near Pittsburgh, designed by the firm of Frederick Law Olmstead and built in 1895 by the Apollo Iron and Steel Company. (Apollo Iron was later merged into American Sheet & Tin Plate Company, which in turn was merged into U.S. Steel.) Apollo Iron formed a land company, which sold individual lots with utilities already installed to the skilled workers at modest prices. Aside from banning alcoholic beverages, there were no controls on the individual lots, and the company provided mortgage money to facilitate purchases. Workers who bought homes in Vandergrift found themselves effectively locked into their jobs. As one inhabitant put it: "When you can't get work here you must leave, and if your property is not paid for you can lose it."[34] The steel companies liked this situation and encouraged it.

The top executives of U.S. Steel were also close to events in Pullman, Illinois. The Pullman Company, as a manufacturer of railroad equipment, was a major steel consumer, and Andrew Carnegie was a personal friend of George Pullman. After the Pullman strike of 1893, J. P. Morgan joined Pullman's board of directors to help overcome the strike's aftereffects.

Pullman had decided to build a "model city" for his employees along with his new factory, so as to develop a workforce which would be immune from labor unrest. As he put it: "With such surroundings and such human regard for the needs of the body as well as the soul . . . the disturbing conditions of strikes and other troubles that periodically convulse the world of labor would not need to be feared here."[35] Instead of simply having a company engineer plan the town, as was the norm, Pullman hired two professional architects, who were given substantial autonomy in elaborating a town design. The most modern planning methods were utilized, such as mixing types of housing, breaking up the grid pattern of streets for public squares, separating residential from industrial uses, and providing areas for a large park, a library, and a theater. Every effort was made to give a pleasing aesthetic form to the factory buildings. There was only one bar and no brothels. By 1885, the Pullman Company had invested over $8 million in 1,400 dwellings: sturdy, multi-family brick row houses, provided with utilities and set on wide, tree-lined streets.

Moreover, Pullman had a well-defined public square, surrounded by a major hotel, an arcade with shops as well as the theater and library, and residences. In short, the physical plan implied an active civic life on the part of the inhabitants. Yet through his control over the housing and employment, Pullman was in authoritarian control. This contradiction was a factor in the labor explosion which led the 5,500 employees (mostly skilled "old immigrants") to engage in a bitter strike in 1894, with the support of Eugene Victor Debs' American Railwaymen's Union. Until the strike was broken with the use of federal troops, Pullman did not dare to evict the strikers, although they had ceased to pay rent.[36]

A New Steel City

To U.S. Steel's top executives, the Pullman experience was a searing lesson of what to avoid. As Eugene J. Buffington, chosen to direct construction of both the city and the mill,[37] stated at the time, it was Vandergrift, Pennsylvania to which the corporation looked as a model. This was in accord with U.S. Steel's labor policies of concessions to its skilled workers and oppression of its unskilled laborers. Buffington was determined to avoid a repetition of the open class strife at Pullman:

> The most successful efforts at industrial social betterment in our country are those farthest removed from the suspicion of domination or control by the employer. Fresh in the minds of all of us is the failure of the Pullman Company to maintain its authority over the village affairs of Pullman, Illinois. . . . American ideas and atmosphere are inherently antagonistic to such plans of community life.[38]

But the corporation never contemplated permitting Gary to develop completely on its own, regardless of how its own interests would be effected. It wanted to exercise a kind of hegemony over the community without resorting to overt control.

Later historians have missed this distinction, concluding that Gary was simply a tract development, rather than a city modeled on Vandergrift. This confusion has arisen largely because of a 1931 newspaper article by A. F. Knotts, the land agent responsible for purchasing the Gary site, in which he asserted that he was responsible for the character of the community. His self-enhancing tale ultimately passed into the scholarly literature. For instance, Harold M. Mayer and Richard C. Wade assert:

> A. F. Knotts, attorney for U.S. Steel, formerly employed by Pullman, was determined to avoid the earlier mistakes [which had led to the Pullman strike]. Most of all he wanted to keep away from company housing, which he thought had brought such woe to Pullman. Hence Gary was more a gigantic tract than a model town.[39]

In reality, the character of the city was planned at a higher managerial level. Gary was to be a community that would avoid labor unrest by tying the skilled workers into a position of dependency through private home ownership and the relative privileges afforded to the "labor aristrocracy" of the period.[40] As to the unskilled workers, so long as they could be prevented from gaining the active support of the skilled workers, the corporation felt that they would not represent a serious threat.

To achieve a community of this sort, in which a united working-class opposition could not readily be forged, the measures adequate in a remote and small company town would not suffice. (Most company towns were relatively small: even Pullman, which was larger than most, barely reached 10,000, while Gary's population would surpass 30,000 by the end of World War I.) Not only was Gary to be a goodly sized city in its own right, it was also within the orbit of metropolitan Chicago. So a directly authoritarian policy would have to be eschewed. Moreover, the corporation did not want to be troubled with the managerial problems of running a city.[41]

The corporation's goal was to have minimum direct involvement with civic affairs while still assuring that Gary would be run in a fashion congruent with its vital interests. Buffington explicitly described this sophisticated strategy to the leading citizens of Gary in a speech in November 1907. Speaking before the exclusive Commercial Club, composed of the city's leading Protestant business and professional men, he explained:

> We know more about the steel business than we do about running a town. We expect the people in this community to show us how to run a town. We shall gladly welcome the day when all the affairs of Gary can be taken over by an organization, in due course of law, with no attempted direction by the Corporation. There is nothing paternalistic in the undertaking of the Corporation in Gary.[42]

In short, the corporation wanted the political life of the community to be dominated by the respectable middle-class elements on which it could confidently rely. In this, it was to prove largely successful.

Building Gary

In the spring of 1906 the corporation began laying out the city, and within a year had erected 500 dwellings, a hotel, restaurant, school, and hospital. It also developed five miles of paved streets and seven miles of paved sidewalks, an electric power station, waterworks, twenty miles of sewers, and fourteen miles of gas mains. Several blocks of land had already been sold for commercial buildings to private entrepreneurs, who had already spent over $.5 million putting up establishments.

Two corporation engineers, A. P. Melton and Ralph Rowley, were placed in charge of the development of the city. Melton, in addition to his job with U.S. Steel, served for many years as city engineer. And Rowley, who was chief engineer at the Gary Works until his retirement in 1938, served continuously on the Gary city council from 1910 to 1935. From 1913 he was council president and effectively controlled the city budget.[43]

One of their main tasks was to lay out the physical contours of the city, which they did in the grid pattern common to most American cities. The grid was rectangular, in blocks 600 feet by 300 feet split down the middle, with 20-foot-wide alleys in which the utilities were embedded.[44] The result of this pattern, which ignored the railroads and other features of the terrain, was an absence of any defined urban center.[45] The main north-south street, Broadway, was an ample 100 feet in width; the main east-west street, Fifth Avenue, was 80 feet. Where they met became the commercial center of Gary, whose "downtown" is little more than the extention of these two streets from their intersection. The combination of a grid pattern and small lot size minimized initial land costs and facilitated rapid development. But with the coming of the automobile, the streets and yards were quickly overcrowded, and easily blighted.

Significantly, Gary followed Vandergrift rather than Pullman in its omission of any civic center. One contemporary observer suggested that "the idea of a civic center ... seems not to have occurred to those who designed the town." This result served the interests of the board of directors who, despite their knowledge of and support for modern architecture, clearly preferred that Gary's working class not engage in too much political activity.[46]

Since the bulk of the corporation's tract was reserved for the Gary Works, the city was allotted a relatively small section of 800 acres under the aegis of the Gary Land Company. And as rapidly as was feasible the Land Company devolved its land to private homeowners and businesses. The city grew southward very rapidly, and, as a result of annexations, by 1909 extended as far southward from Lake Michigan (seven miles) as it did along its original east-west axis. Consequently, by 1914 the amount of land occupied by housing which was never owned by U.S. Steel was four times greater than that which the Gary Land Company controlled.[47]

The fact that the corporation used most of its tract for the Gary Works affected the physical development of the city in other ways as well. Over a third of Gary's developed land is occupied by either industrial or railroad property—more than three times the proportion of most cities. This in turn has resulted in a residential density far exceeding that of most cities of its size, and in relatively large numbers of multiple-dwelling units. Also, by reserving almost all of the shoreline for the Gary Works, the corporation essentially cut the population off from ready access to Lake Michigan.[48]

Besides its desultory city planning and provision of utility services, the corporation made a series of generous donations of land for civic and social purposes, with the notable exception of parks. Land was donated for Gary's two hospitals, a public library—in 1910 Andrew Carnegie gave an unusually generous $65,000 for the building—a federal building and armory, a public auditorium, schools, and, in 1907, a City Hall (and then again in the 1920s for the current City Hall). In addition, the Gary Land Company provided land for a YMCA, Judge Gary personally paid for the building, and the corporation thereafter provided for its maintenance and personnel. Overall, by the onset of the Depression the corporation and Judge Gary together donated over $5 million in land and cash to the city. As one historian later acerbically commented:

> Paternalism and repression bore their finest flower in the magnificent libraries donated to the steel communities by Andrew Carnegie—libraries whose swimming pools and lecture programs could scarcely be appreciated by the men who were doing their eighty-four hours a week in the roaring mills nearby.[49]

Both land and financial support were freely provided to the local churches. According to H. S. Norton, Buffington's personal assistant who was made head of the Gary Land Company (and who went on to become president of the local chamber of commerce and the top leader of the Gary Republican Party), by 1923 the corporation had given over a quarter of a million dollars in cash to the local churches; and later it provided almost twice that for a magnificent Indiana limestone Methodist Church, built in a gothic style. The only direct control which the corporation placed on the land it sold was that it not be used for the sale of alcoholic beverages. (Gary himself insisted for years that prohibition was vital to reducing crime and immorality in any community.) But two bars were reluctantly permitted in the Land Company's tract—the corporation explaining that given the city's proximity to Chicago, the kind of absolute prohibition practiced in Vandergrift wasn't feasible. So saloons took root in the remainder of the city, and by 1911 they numbered 238. Soon the saloons became one of the central institutions around which Gary's new ethnic petty bourgeoisie grew.[50]

In 1909, when the first steel began to come out of the Gary Works, the town had already become a functioning city of 12,000 people. On the fifteen miles of paved streets and twenty-five miles of cement sidewalks were "six hotels, three dailies and one weekly newspaper, two public schoolhouses, several substantial church edifices, ten denominations represented in church organizations, and many well-appointed stores and shops." Even though the mills were not yet completed, the Gary Works employed 4,200 workers, served by 46 lawyers, 24 physicians, and 6 dentists.[51]

A third of Gary's population consisted of homeowners, since the corporation built housing for both its managerial personnel and its skilled workers. By 1907 it had constructed 260 brick units (at monthly rentals of $23-$42) for company officials, and 190 four-to-six-room frame units (at monthly rentals of $14-$20) for its crafts workers. The corporation very quickly sold off its housing by providing mortgage money at favorable terms to its employees, since comparable housing outside the Land Company's tract was even more expensive. (Overall, rental costs in Gary ran significantly above those of Chicago.) A congressional report summarized the situation:

> As a result of the rapid growth of the town real estate prices have advanced greatly, and this has affected the rates of rental. The chief beneficiary of this rapid increase of land values has been the [Gary Land Company], which owns all the land in the immediate neighborhood of the steel plant. The result of the high real estate prices and rentals has been that a large part of the population, particularly the unskilled laborers, are living a long distance from the plant in poor and badly crowded accomodations.[52]

The corporation made one small effort at housing its unskilled workers, but its fifty four-room wood-frame houses for this purpose were quickly torn down when the laborers doubled up in order to afford the rents.[53] Given the low wage level it was paying its unskilled workers, the corporation was not able to provide them with even minimally decent housing unless it was prepared to subsidize the housing at a loss, as they themselves acknowledged:

> The housing provided by the Corporation is perhaps better suited to the needs of the skilled workmen than to the wages of the unskilled laborers [who are] largely foreigners without families. . . . These men earn low wages, out of which they seek to save the utmost amount possible.[54]

Consequently, U.S. Steel made the decision not to house the mass of its workforce.

Thus, low wage rates for unskilled labor combined with U.S. Steel's decision not to subsidize housing for its workers in the Pullman pattern stimulated the growth of Gary's small business community, since workers had to live somewhere. South of the Gary Land Company's holdings an immense real estate boom unfolded and many small businesses thrived. Indeed, the local petty bourgeoisie, grouped around the Knotts brothers, who became major real estate operators, even went so far as to contest successfully with the corporation over the priorities of urban development. With temporary control of the local government in their hands, the real estate speculators and saloon-keepers were able to obtain the franchise for Gary's trolley car system— and build it southward down Broadway so as to maximize their land values. U.S. Steel, on the other hand, wanted the trolley line to run on an east-west axis along Fifth Avenue, in order to enhance the value of their own land, and in addition maintain control of development and land usage. They also wanted to house their workers close to their various plants.[55]

Thus, from the very outset, U.S. Steel found that while its power in the community was immense, it was not absolute. Limited in its actions by considerations both of profits and of political hegemony, the corporation necessarily had to compromise with the local small business community. That compromise left the Gary Works under the exclusive control of U.S. Steel, but the community in the hands of a heterogeneous group of local entrepreneurs who, whatever their immediate divergencies with U.S. Steel, could be counted on to fervently support the free enterprise system in the face of any labor insurgency from below. This initial compromise between the corporation and the local business community has been maintained in its essentials to the present day. And the kind of city Gary turned out to be is in substantial measure the result.

3
Early History, 1906-1928

Before World War I black people were an insignificant factor in the community life of Gary. Among the 6,000 itinerant construction workers who actually built the Gary Works there were 250 blacks, but they were far outnumbered by Croatians and Italians. The bulk of these construction workers had moved on when the job was done; only a handful of the black men brought their families and settled down in the city.[1]

Table 3.1
Population Composition of Gary 1910-1930

	1910	1920	1930
Total population	17,000	55,000	100,000
Percent: white	49	61	59
Foreign born	49	30	23
Black	2	10	18

Source: Roger K. Oden, "Black Political Power in Gary, Indiana: A Theoretical and Structural Analysis" (Ph.D., University of Chicago, 1977), p. 184, Table 12.

As can be seen from Table 3.1, the major split in the Gary working class was not along racial lines but between the native-born workers and the "new immigrants," those who came to the

United States from the nations of Eastern and Southern Europe (in contrast to "old immigrants" whose lands of origin were in Western and Northern Europe). As in American manufacturing generally, the majority of the Gary Works employees were foreign born (see Table 3.2): a survey in 1912 showed that 25 percent were native-born whites, another 2 percent blacks, and 11 percent "old immigrants"; the rest were "new immigrants," most of whom had been peasants in their country of origin and a majority of whom could not even speak English.[2]

Table 3.2
The Role of Immigrant Labor

Immigrants as a percentage of	1890	1910
Total population	9	14
Total employment	22	21
Manufacturing employment	32	60
Steel industry employment	38	65

Sources: Simon Kuznets, "The Contribution of Immigration to the Growth of the Labor Force," in *The Reinterpretation of American Economic History*, ed. R. W. Fogel and S. L. Engerman (New York: Harper and Row, 1971), p. 397, table I, and Charlotte Erickson, *American Industry and the European Immigrant, 1860-1885* (Cambridge: Harvard University Press, 1957), p. 190.

These "new immigrants" were healthy and vigorous young peasant men, both taller and heavier than their native-born counterparts according to a 1914 study.[3] Carl Sandburg described them more poetically:

> And some had bunches of specialized muscles around
> their shoulder-blades as hard as pig-iron, muscles
> of their forearms were sheet metal and they looked
> to me like men who had been somewhere.[4]

During the early years of the twentieth century most of the "new immigrants" were either unmarried or had left their families behind in Europe. For example, as late as 1919, there were 10,000 Poles, 1,000 of whom were women, and 6,000 Yugoslavs, 600 of whom were women.[5] The men worked in American industry for years before either bringing their wives to the United States or returning to their native lands. The costs of producing these active workers were assumed by the nations from which they came; the immense benefits of their labor power accrued to American capital.[6]

The radical disproportion between the sexes meant that initially there were few children among the "new immigrants." While in 1910 one-third of the U.S. population was under age 15, only one-tenth fell into that group in Gary. Nor were there many older people: 85 percent of the immigrant steelworkers were under age 45. The consequence of this demographic phenomenon was that there was available a workforce of unskilled labor whose subsistence wage was less than that necessary to support an entire family. In the absence of unionization or minimum wages, it was feasible for U.S. Steel prior to World War I not to "pay to the average common laborer in its employ sufficient wages to enable him to support a normal size family in health and decency."[7]

The result, however, was not the rise of a militant working class. While such Marxist theorists as Lenin were confident that "uniting workers from all countries in huge factories and mines in America" would further the process of international proletarian solidarity, others, such as the Italian Antonio Gramsci, suspected that the absence of a common culture would prove an obstacle to the creation of a serious radical labor movement. Gramsci's worries proved accurate; the mélange of workers from different lands were not readily transformed into a class-conscious proletariat. As Herbert G. Gutman points out:

> A recurrent tension also existed between the native and immigrant men . . . fresh to the factory and the demands imposed upon them by the regularities and disciplines of factory labor. That state of tension was regularly revitalized by the migration of diverse premodern native and foreign peoples into a . . . fully industrialized society.[8]

Among the ethnic groups represented in the Gary Works in

its early years were Poles, Serbians, Croatians, Montenegrans, Italians, Hungarians, Slavonians, Russians, Germans, Jews, Swedes, Bohemians, Macedonians, Norwegians, Welsh, Greeks, Turks, Armenians, Finns, Belgians, Danes, Japanese, and French. As the years passed, they were joined by at least as many more nationality groups.

The United States Steel Corporation actively encouraged social and ethnic diversity in its mills, both to hamper unified working-class activity and to assure itself adequate reserve supplies of labor. Members of different ethnic groups were placed in the same labor gangs so as to block them from even speaking to each other. A similar policy was followed in the community. As one old priest recently reminisced:

> U.S. Steel encouraged the establishment of these new nationality parishes by giving a direct money grant to build a church-school building. The Corporation hoped that these parishes would stabilize the work force by tying the immigrant to Gary and by giving the immigrant a place to maintain his culture. With an established neighborhood for each nationality, the Corporation believed that other immigrants would follow, thus providing an inexhaustible supply of unskilled labor for the mills.[9]

The central aspect of the corporation's labor policy was to foster an unbridgeable chasm between its "new immigrant" workers and the rest of its employees. For the "new immigrants" there was only harsh toil and discrimination in the mill and the community, while for the native-born workers there was a policy of paternalism.

"Old immigrants" were treated much like native-born workers: at the turn of the century, both received equal pay for equal work, while "new immigrants" were, on the average, paid 10 percent less for the same jobs.[10] All the managerial, professional, and clerical jobs in the Gary Works were reserved for native-born Protestants. Native-born whites and "old immigrants" were given virtually all of the jobs as foremen and the vast majority of the skilled craft jobs. But only a tenth of the "new immigrants" obtained skilled jobs: overwhelmingly, they were consigned to the unskilled and semiskilled tasks.

This distinction resulted in very different lifestyles available

to the two groups. A skilled crafts worker in the Gary Works in
1910 could expect an annual income of $1,100, double that of an
unskilled "new immigrant." The skilled steelworker earned
enough to provide for his family without placing his wife or
children in the labor market. Even though steel was a notoriously
cyclical industry, the skilled worker's job was relatively secure,
since if there was not enough work to go around, management
would lay off common labor to assure some work for the skilled.
These workers were concentrated in such shops as electric power
and repairs, where the work was far less arduous than in production. Their accident rates were less than half that of the non-
English-speaking steelworkers. In addition to having access to
company housing, a large minority of the skilled workers were
at least nominal beneficiaries of the corporation's policy of
making stock available to its workers. According to David Brody,
"there was money enough for a healthy, varied diet; for furniture, clothes, and small pleasures; and for insurance and some
savings."[11] By means of this policy of careful paternalism, the
skilled men were developed into a labor aristocracy, dependent
economically, culturally, and ideologically upon the corporation.

In striking contrast with this life of relative decency were the
circumstances of the "new immigrants." Poverty was only the
beginning of their misfortune. Their working conditions in the
mills were grim. Although the average American manufacturing
work week was sixty hours, the "new immigrant" steelworkers
put in six twelve-hour days each week. (On the other hand, even
in prosperous years, the average laborer could anticipate about
two months of unemployment.) The work was so physically
taxing that "old age at forty" was the popular expression of the
day. And it was frightfully dangerous: each year a quarter of the
unskilled workers were injured or killed on the job.

Wage levels were so low that if the "new immigrant" had a
family his wife and children were obliged to enter the labor
market to work to supplement his income. Alternately, if he saved
up enough to purchase a house, his "wife [was] a drudge and
slave[d] incessantly for her household," which was filled with
paying boarders.[12]

The infant mortality rates among the children of the unskilled workers were over double those of the skilled workers. Even at the end of World War I—after real wages had increased one-third from their prewar level—two-thirds of the children of Gary's foreign-born workers had no milk, fruit, or eggs in their daily diet. Over half of them had no vegetables, a government study found, and one-third lacked any meat.[13]

It is scarcely surprising that many men were destroyed by these conditions. As a physician practicing among steelworkers summed it up: "The non-English speaking Poles and Bohemians . . . are the scapegoats of the whole metallic manufacturing industry. Their sick and disabled make them the leading nation-alities in our dispensaries, county hospitals, and other charitable institutions."[14] Others returned, broken men, to Europe. In at-tempting to assess the circumstances of the steel industry laborers it is essential to realize that almost half of the "new immigrants" left the United States entirely. As yet, social historians have not been able to determine accurately how many of these men returned impoverished and how many with the stake necessary to buy farms in their homeland, but probably there were more of the former than the latter. Nor do we have the information to follow the typical patterns among the immigrants who moved within this country from city to city, or who drifted from one industry to another.

So we do not know if those who remained for a lifetime in the Gary Works were representative; probably they were among the more fortunate. And even among this group it is hard to precisely determine their fate. Some historians who are deeply influenced by the notion that the United States offered unusual opportuni-ties for personal advancement have suggested that with time the "new immigrants" advanced to skilled jobs and their children left the industry for middle-class occupations. The weight of the evidence now available, however, points in the other direction: it seems that the bulk of the "new immigrants" who remained in the Gary Works remained at lowly jobs throughout their lives. Nor were their children apt to move out of the proletariat, even if they did often succeed in achieving craft positions.[15]

Despite their poverty, "new immigrants" who remained in Gary bent every effort to obtaining their own homes (even if these homes were mere shacks), and by World War I a third of the foreign-born workers were homeowners. Residency patterns replicated the division of the workforce, however: in its early stages, residential segregation occurred between the native American and foreign-born sections of town.[16]

However, in late nineteenth- and early twentieth-century urban America, there were very few genuine ethnic ghettos, and Gary was no exception.[17] The typical urban housing pattern more accurately could be called one of ethnic clusters; this was equally true for blacks and for "new immigrants." Before World War I in the northern cities, neighborhoods had pluralities of a particular ethnic group, but rarely had blocks which were uniformly of one nationality.[18]

The northern part of the city was divided into two districts. The west side was the residence of the city's white Protestants, largely business and professional people and corporation executives, who lived in luxury apartments or owned capacious homes worth $10,000-$20,000. On the east side resided white-collar elements, foremen, and many of the craft workers. The majority of these were native-born Protestants too, but there was an admixture of "old immigrants." Their housing was largely two-story frame houses with some three-story apartments. The far south of the city, Glen Park, was somewhat like the east side in terms of occupation and income, but its population was heavily "new immigrant." It was this district to which upwardly mobile ethnic workers aspired.[19]

Gary's central core, noted for its numerous saloons and bordels, was the abode of the unskilled immigrant masses. Here were the structurally unsound and shamefully overcrowded boarding houses and the small shacks purchased by mill laborers. In 1920 only a handful of the native-born workers lived in this district, but two-fifths of the "old immigrants" and three-fourths of the immigrants from eastern Europe were to be found here, along with almost all of the blacks and Mexicans. There were particular ethnic enclaves within it, but it would be most accurate to describe it as a polyglot, not a ghetto:

> It is where the distinctive flavor is to be found in Gary; it is where aliens and newly made Americans congregate in their national

cluster. Here are the Serbs, here the Croats, there the Mexicans, there the Poles, and here, there, and everywhere are the Negroes. . . .

This is the old world. Streets are narrow, houses of every type of shack, bungalow, and tenement; stores have exotic names and advertisements; cafes have distinct national airs, featuring tamales, ravioli, or whatever the favorite dish may be; national club houses display strange and interesting posters in their mysterious windows. . . .[20]

Before World War I the small black population lived interspersed among the "new immigrants" in the central district, mainly within a few blocks on either side of Broadway between 15th and 19th streets. A few black families resided in the northern districts of Gary, though they would be evicted in the 1920s. The city's first Jim Crow housing was built during World War I by the Gary Land Company. H. S. Norton, head of the Land Company, declared that his purpose was to give "special opportunities" to the city's blacks; their protests that he was introducing racial segregation into the workers' district was ignored.

World War I set in motion a profound internal transformation of the Gary proletariat. One immediate effect of the war was an expansion of the need for steel labor to fill military orders—at a time when nearly a quarter of the workers at the Gary Works were drafted and European nationals left the country. For example, almost 500 Serbs left Gary to fight for their national independence.[21] Consequently, the industry looked to southern blacks as a way of meeting its sudden labor shortage.

In the early years of the twentieth century, the American black working class was minute. Although one-third of all southern Appalachian coalminers and two-thirds of all Birmingham, Alabama steel district workers were black, the size of the black working class in the South was constricted by the industrial underdevelopment of the region. And while the North also had the beginnings of a black working class, only in rare instances were blacks employed above the ranks of common labor.[22]

With World War I, there was a rapid expansion of the black proletariat, and as this occurred, blacks began to be concentrated in the larger northern cities which were the focal point of manufacturing. The pattern of black urbanization was similar to that of the "new immigrants": the larger the population, the more heavily black as well as immigrant was its composition (a relationship which grew more pronounced as the century advanced) (see Table 3.3).[23]

Table 3.3
The Concentration of Blacks in Large Cities

Population in 1970	Percent black
Over 500,000	26
250,000-500,000	20
100,000-250,000	15
50,000-100,000	8

Source: U.S. Bureau of the Census, *Race of the Population of SMSAs [Standard Metropolitan Statistical Areas], Urbanized Areas, and Places of 50,000 or more: 1970* (Washington, D.C.: Government Printing Office, n.d.).

By 1920 960,000 blacks were employed in manufacturing nationwide, and by 1930 they numbered 1.1 million. This growth was particularly marked in such major industrial centers as Chicago, which by 1920 had a manufacturing force that was one-sixth black. In that year blacks constituted one-tenth of the steelworkers in Gary and Chicago and were the largest single group in Chicago's meatpacking industry.[24]

An even more fundamental consequence of the war was the drastic change in the situation and consciousness of the "new immigrants" in the mills. No longer did they consider themselves transient in the United States; the large majority now expected to remain permanently in the steel industry. And thus they attempted to unionize. As Herbert Gutman points out, their circumstances as proletarians "had become a way of life for them and was no longer the means by which to reaffirm and even strengthen older peasant and village lifestyles."[25] Only among the minority of "new immigrants" who expected to return to Europe was there a significant number who refused to participate in the strike activities.[26]

The Steel Strike of 1919 was one of the most important strikes in American history. As labor historians Boyer and Morais point out:

> If steel were organized, the great bulwark and fortress of the open shop, the symbol of the nearly 20,000,000 unorganized wage earners, if steel were organized, it was generally agreed on both sides, all American industry would soon be unionized. It was a crucial strike and recognized as such.[27]

Despite the ardor and militancy of the mass of the "new immigrant" strikers, however, three months of battle ended in complete defeat, leaving industrial unionism in America to wait until the New Deal period. The workers were unable to withstand the combined economic power of the corporation, government intervention on behalf of the industry, and the refusal of the majority of the crafts workers to participate fully. The unwillingness of the skilled workers to support the union was partly a consequence of their relatively favored economic position and partly due to their prejudices against the "new immigrants." The black workers, too, "lined up with the bosses," in the words of chief strike organizer William Z. Foster, because their limited prior experience with unions was that of severe discrimination or outright exclusion.[28]

After World War I

The city of Gary flourished economically in the postwar period. While the 1920s saw the average American city increase its population by 20 percent, Gary's population virtually doubled to reach 100,000, and with the significant exception of its black and Chicano communities, represented a viable urban environment (see Table 1.1). The vigor of the steel industry provided the underlying basis for the expansion, and private entrepreneurship was responsible for the city's growth. As early as 1916 Randolph Bourne commented on how rapidly Gary was maturing as a community:

With a well-built business section, lines of residence streets, handsome public buildings and churches, electric cars and taxi-cabs, Gary has a settled air of community life unusual even for an older town. It has the aspect of a commercial rather than an industrial center. It is the focus of the county trade, and the extent of its business and middle-class residential districts is somewhat larger than in neighboring towns.[29]

Bourne proved to be an astute observer, as during the 1920s Gary developed into the commercial and cultural center of the entire Calumet region. With the completion in 1926 of the 400-room Gary Hotel, the city, with a total of 1,800 hotel rooms, enjoyed the status of convention capital of the state. There were thirteen movie houses, and the capacious new Masonic and Knights of Columbus headquarters. Indeed, it was during the 1920s that virtually every major structure in Gary was built: the largest office building, the Gary State Bank Building (at the key intersection of 5th Avenue and Broadway) was completed in 1928; the twin Gary City Hall and County Buildings were con-structed at a cost of $3.7 million; and the municipality invested over $7 million more in new sewers and streets.[30]

In 1929 Gary had 1,300 retail stores directly employing 4,000 workers and generating annual sales of $48 million. In short, the city was prosperous. Its economic health was so great that, while the government was engaging in an ambitious program of expanding the urban infrastructure, it was simultaneously able to maintain a lower than average municipal debt and an ef-fective property tax rate that was only 80 percent of the national urban average.[31]

For its large stratum of upper-middle-class and native-stock Americans who were hegemonic over the local political economy, urban life was sweet. This group possessed

valuable buildings and lands in the dull and narrow business streets down town. In their vaults were bulky deeds to rich farms, gilt-edged railroad bonds, state and federal securities of low but unquestioned yield. . . . [They] dwelt in spacious homes . . . where they soared above rows of tumbledown shacks inhabited by raggedy white folks and coloured factory hands; or else they lived far back from the road in pretentious new houses along the peace-ful boulevards skirting the town.[32]

In part, even the working class shared in the affluence of the capitalist boom. The "new immigrant" steelworkers, whose prospects for a better life had seemed utterly crushed by their defeat in the Steel Strike of 1919, participated, to a degree, in Gary's "golden age." The work shifts in the mill were reduced from twelve to eight hours; and a significant minority among the previously unskilled workers achieved skilled craft positions.

A study of American cities conducted in 1930 concluded that in terms of its overall level of social welfare, Gary was near the American urban average (if one excepted the wealthy "bedroom suburbs"). By this time a full two-fifths of Gary's families had achieved the status of homeowners. Of course, the housing of the working class was hardly sumptuous. A study of 1,500 homes—of which many were the better sort owned by middle-income families—revealed that 4 percent were "unfit for habitation" and another 20 percent in need of major repairs.[33]

Moreover, in the main the homes of the "new immigrant" workers were built on lots which were only 40 by 140 feet (half the currently permissible minimum width). This resulted in a relatively high population density for a city of Gary's size, a tendency that was intensified by the relatively large number of multiple-dwelling units and the virtual absence of recreational land. (Parks occupy less than 3 percent of Gary's total area.) For the unskilled workers who were too poor to purchase their own homes, the housing situation was even worse: either they remained boarders or rented such housing as one of the 1,200 midtown area shacks that lacked both sanitation and running water. As for the blacks and Chicanos, the additional burden of racial discrimination in the housing market added to their generally inferior economic situation. Thus, only a fifth of black families were able to achieve homeowner status by 1930, and black renters found themselves paying about 20 percent more than whites for inferior facilities.[34]

The role of U.S. Steel in housing construction changed drastically after the war. While prior to World War I the corporation had constructed 1,250 units of housing and had advanced another $4 million in building loans to employees, in the postwar period it phased itself out of the city's construction activity, leaving private business to meet the estimated 4,000 wartime housing-unit deficit and the immense additional need caused by the city's doubling population in the 1920s. During this decade over 14,000 new residential buildings were constructed, among them 1,800 multiple-dwelling units. (By 1930, 9 percent of Gary's population was housed in such units—which gave the city the appearance of a far larger metropolis.) Altogether, more new housing was built in the 1920s than in the following two decades combined: from 1923 to 1929 the Gary Building Department issued permits for $79 million in new construction, while from 1930 to 1939 the total was only $8.5 million.

The result of this housing boom was that Gary enjoyed a younger housing stock than it would ever again achieve, made possible because local builders had access to ample capital. In 1922 alone, according to H. S. Norton, who also served as president of the local chamber of commerce, large East Coast insurance companies lent $3.5 million to local real estate interests. Since the rate of new construction in Gary multiplied fivefold through the decade, the total sum of external mortgage money available to the city's contractors must have been immense.[35]

As a number of immigrants moved to Glen Park, blacks found themselves increasingly concentrated in certain neighborhoods. Corporation executives, who predominated in local banking, real estate, and governmental circles, encouraged this trend.[36] When the decade began, the 5,300 blacks who composed 9 percent of the population had been substantially integrated with the "new immigrants." But when it ended, the 18,000 blacks who made up 18 percent of the population were substantially ghettoized. By 1940 Gary had one of the most racially segregated housing patterns in the entire country.[37]

During the 1920s a variety of other community developments effectively segregated blacks into a separate and unequal place in urban life. This period saw not only a sharp increase in housing segregation in Gary, but the marked growth of Jim Crow patterns in public accommodations, recreation, and education. The rising structural racism in the community was complementary to developments in the Gary Works.[38]

The steel industry continued to actively recruit black workers even after the war, going so far as to send agents to the South to locate potential employees. Until 1923 the industry faced a labor shortage because of the unwillingness of native Americans to work under the harsh mill conditions. But once black workers alleviated this temporary labor shortage, steel management took momentous initiatives with respect to its new workers. Beginning in 1924, the year the Immigration Act finally ended the historical pattern through which American industry had assured itself of an adequate source of common labor, heavy industry determined to place both numerical quotas and job ceilings on its black employees. This was the decisive year for the fate of the emerging black proletariat; unable to prevent the passage of the Immigration Act, steelmakers acted to assure themselves of a new permanent pool of unskilled workers from a different source.[39]

In so doing the industry was simply following its traditional policy of encouraging ethnic splits and conflicts among its workers.[40] The steelmakers also adopted the southern manufacturers' policy of strict racial segregation to prevent unionization. U.S. Steel itself (through its southern subsidiary, a leading employer in the Birmingham steel district) had long imposed stringent limits on how far blacks could rise in the job hierarchy. As one local observer summarized it:

> The Negro of Birmingham fills the industrial position which elsewhere in great manufacturing towns is filled by a low class of whites. . . . The white laboring classes here are separated from the Negroes, working all day side by side with them, by an innate sense of race superiority. . . . It excites a sentiment of sympathy and equality on their part with the classes above them, and in this way becomes a wholesome social leaven.[41]

Bringing this policy up north to the Gary Works simply meant focusing an old policy on a new target, namely, northern white workers.

The available data, while fragmentary, indicate an actual retrogression in the 1920s in the relative position of blacks in the Gary Works job hierarchy. From 1918 to 1928, the proportion of blacks holding skilled or semiskilled jobs declined from 30 percent to 20 percent.[42]

Similarly, the twenties saw the erection of numerical quotas for black steelworkers. When interviewed in 1937, W. S. McNabb, the head of industrial relations at the Gary Works, admitted that the proportion of black employees deliberately had been stabilized at 15 percent, beginning in 1924.[43] Steel industry management was quite open about this policy. As the superintendent of one large Calumet region steel mill stated: "When we got [up to 10% black] employees, I said [to the employment manager], 'No more colored without discussion.' I got the colored pastors to send colored men whom they could guarantee would not organize and were not bolsheviks." The employment manager of another Calumet steel mill explained their quota system by pointing out: "It isn't good to have all of one nationality; they will gang up on you. . . . We have Negroes and Mexicans in a sort of competition with each other. It is a dirty trick, but we don't have the kind of work that will break a man down." Developments of this sort throughout American heavy industry meant that blacks and Mexicans increasingly did the unskilled work. Not only in steel, but also in the meatpacking industry, blacks began to lose ground in their share of jobs in the mid-twenties. Around this time numerical quotas were also instituted in the farm equipment and automobile industries.[44]

The containment of blacks at the bottom of the job hierarchy enlarged the relative opportunity for other workers to advance. Thus, while the skilled jobs in steel were still dominated by native-born Americans, the "new immigrants" (and their children who were beginning to enter the mills) began to make modest inroads into the skilled craft positions during the 1920s.[45] In 1928 blacks and Mexicans constituted almost half of the unskilled workers but only 2 percent of the skilled workers in the Gary Works. At the same time, only a quarter of all the white workers were still relegated to unskilled jobs; a full half of them had achieved skilled positions (see Table 3.4).

In recent years, as the political climate of the country has changed, industry executives have become more discreet about the public expression of such motives. And to the extent that the policy has been successful and white workers have internalized cultural norms of racism toward their black fellow workers, there has been less need for management to develop the structural basis for such prejudices. But as late as 1945 a Calumet steel executive was willing to observe: "Negroes are nice, simple people. I don't approve of using them for skilled work—not that they couldn't do it, but we have enough competition within the skilled groups. Let the Negroes scramble for the unskilled jobs."[46]

Table 3.4
Racial Employment Patterns of Gary Works, 1928
(in percent)

	Skilled	Semiskilled	Unskilled
White	47	27	26
Black	5	16	79
Mexican	2	19	79

Source: Paul S. Taylor, *Mexican Labor in the United States: Chicago and the Calumet Region* (Berkeley: University of California Press, 1932), p. 36, table 3, p. 157, table 22. These figures are for both the Chicago South Works and the Gary Works, but they were both under the common management of the Illinois Steel Company of U.S. Steel and had common employment patterns.

It was employer racial discrimination, not a lack of job skills or illiteracy, which consigned workers in the 1920s to an inferior job status. The weight of the evidence is that the black steelworkers were as well suited to modern industry as the "new immigrants" who were beginning to move ahead of them. In Gary, they were as apt as the "new immigrants" to have had prior urban living experience and to have worked in modern industry; they apparently maintained comparable turnover and absentee rates; and they were more likely to be literate, to send their children to school, and to have been to school themselves.[47] In short, this period saw the steelmakers create a new permanent stratum of black workers to serve as their common labor reserve and to continue in a new way the tradition of "divide and rule."[48]

4

Later History, 1929-1966

The Depression hit Gary hard. Between 1929 and 1935 retail sales, the expression of mass purchasing power, declined by 40 percent. One contemporary observer described Gary as follows:

> Machines throwing men out of work by the thousands. Half of the blast furnaces of [U.S. Steel] closed down, and no more of those sudden glorious crimson flare-ups springing of a sudden into the mighty skies overhead. . . . The dismal emptiness of stores unrented. Failures, bankruptcies, foreclosures; merchants big and little; the chains cutting their throats into the bargain.[1]

Gary was a part of the general urban collapse that saw new housing starts fall to a third of their 1920s' level. Since only a handful of new buildings were constructed, the physical plant of the city began an aging process which has continued to the present day. By the end of the 1930s a fifth of Gary's white-owned houses were classified as substandard by the Census Bureau along with over half of the black-owned ones. Among the 80 percent of black families who continued to rent, two-thirds lived in apartments which either required major repairs or lacked plumbing facilities.[2]

The Depression was a disaster for the steelworkers. A positive wage differential was maintained relative to other manufacturing workers, but it was of little consolation in the face of massive layoffs and across-the-board wage reductions. Even those fortunate enough to keep their jobs were generally working on only a part-time basis. Not until 1937 did the average steelworker's week rebound to forty hours.[3]

The black community was especially hard hit: in 1930 black unemployment rates in Gary were almost double those of whites, reflecting the situation nationwide (at the depths of the Depression in industrial cities half of the black population was unemployed). Black workers were differentially furloughed in industry after industry, so the Depression decade saw blacks lose a full third of their share in manufacturing jobs. The economic catastrophe was so great that the black family—which had survived slavery and the migration north during and after World War I—began to disintegrate. The 1930s saw a 33 percent increase in the proportion of female-headed black families, in contrast to a 20 percent increase among white families.[4]

The steel industry was no exception to this pattern. Foremen continued to have discretion over layoffs, and blacks and Mexicans were the first to go. The proportion of blacks in the steel industry fell from 13 percent in 1930 to 10 percent in 1938.[5] Those who were lucky enough to retain their jobs remained at the bottom of the work hierarchy throughout the Depression. At the Gary Works, for instance, black workers were concentrated in such arduous and dangerous jobs as those in the coke oven and blast furnace departments, and could not hope to be promoted above a semiskilled position. As one observer put it:

> It is not surprising that the Negro was highly represented in the blast furnace area of the industry. This part . . . contains a great deal of the hot, dirty, heavy work that Negroes were thought to be eminently qualified to perform.[6]

In addition to the central political effect of splitting the workers, confining blacks to the lower jobs in the blast furnaces had a direct economic payoff to U.S. Steel. The wage differential between skilled and unskilled was gradually declining in other production shops; but in the blast furnaces the wage gap did not diminish.[7]

Mexican workers in Gary suffered even more than blacks. In the years immediately preceding World War I, a small number of Mexican workers had come to the Calumet region as part of the work crews of southwestern railroads with terminals in Chicago. Taking advantage of the wartime labor shortage, many of these workers transferred into the packinghouse and steel industries, so that in 1920 there were 1,200 Mexicans in Chicago and 160 in Gary. The main surge in Mexican labor followed the passage of the Immigration Act, so that by 1930 100,000 Mexicans worked in the midwestern industrial cities. The 3,500 Mexicans in Gary provided over 6 percent of the labor force of the Gary Works, living in conditions much like those of the "new immigrants" of the prewar period.

The Mexicans who came to Gary were overwhelmingly young men from rural origins without wives or families. They settled in the central district, mainly in a cluster between 9th and 15th avenues east of Broadway, but in several other small areas as well. In no case did they achieve a majority on any block, although in several cases they were the largest single ethnic group. Very few could afford to buy homes; most of them resided in boarding houses. While not subject to the extremes of Jim Crow laws that blacks were encountering in the 1920s, there were some serious efforts to discriminate against them. It required a battle to reverse the local movie theaters' policy of providing a separate section for Mexicans, and local real estate interests narrowly limited their housing location choices.[8]

Then in the Depression the Gary Works management introduced a requirement that workers produce proof of American citizenship, which very few Mexican workers could do. Massive layoffs were followed by a pattern of disease and malnutrition which reached epidemic proportions. The corporation also actively participated in the deportation of 1,500 Mexicans (part of a national movement which was responsible for the repatriation of .5 million Mexicans). The leader in Gary's deportation movement was none other than H. S. Norton, who proclaimed: "The kindest thing which could be done for these people would be to send them back to Mexico. . . . They do not assimilate and they are unhappy here. They want to go back."[9] The desire to return, given the economic conditions in Mexico at the time, was induced. As one of the Calumet area Mexicans who was repatriated in this process recalls, after being removed from the welfare roles, the unemployed were offered free transportation to Mexico: "So actually they weren't forcing you to leave. They gave you a choice: starve or go back to Mexico."[10]

In contrast to the wartime situation, sociological trends in the American working class during the 1930s were in the direction of increasing homogenization. This was clearly the case in steel. By the early 1930s the substantial majority of steelworkers were native-born whites. During the Depression decade a full 90 percent of those entering the industry were native born, many of them second-generation steelworkers. And all of them— foreign born, native white, or black—were undergoing a process of immiseration which could be checked only by their own collective efforts.[11]

During the Depression era the American proletariat developed two new sources of power, one economic and one political. The Congress for Industrial Organizations (CIO) was organized through a coalition of liberal and radical trade unionists, and one of the central battle grounds for mass industrial unionism was the steel industry.[12] In politics, the working class developed close ties to President Roosevelt and the New Deal. Locally, this meant a city government whose police would no longer simply serve as strikebreakers, and nationally it meant the passage of labor law legislation which provided the benevolent neutrality of the courts and state apparatus for the workers' organizing drive. As a Gary steelworker summed up popular attitudes: "We're a New Deal crowd and we want what we voted for. We think this is our chance to get a real New Deal, and we are determined to get it."[13]

The increased political activity of the working class, which underlay the national government's concession in permitting union organizing to occur without repression, was also what made it possible for the Steelworkers' Organizing Committee to achieve hegemony among the steelworkers: the two fronts of advance were necessarily and inextricably tied to each other.[14] The successful outcome of that contest, in which the United States Steel Corporation was for the first time bested by its wage slaves, brought with it genuine and impressive gains. Wages made an unprecedented leap forward. By 1939, after the recognition of the union by U.S. Steel, their relative differential over the average pay of other manufacturing workers increased to one-third. For the first time workers fully shared in the productivity gains of the industry. In the period between 1935 and 1939 hourly earnings and output both rose by 27 percent. Moreover, there was no speedup.[15]

More impressive than the sheer size of the gains was their distribution. The CIO, with the core of its strength among the foreign-born and black workers, gave its highest priority to those at the bottom of the workforce. In its wage increase of November 1936 U.S. Steel was forced to abandon its traditional policy of a flat percentage increase, and admitted that it was doing so in the face of the labor insurgency in its mills. With the recognition of the Steelworkers' Union in March 1937 came a second raise; this increased the average wage by 10 percent, and that of common labor by 19 percent.

The biggest beneficiaries of this radically egalitarian policy of the CIO were the black workers in Gary and throughout the nation's steel industry. The relative pay of black steelworkers between 1935 and 1939 rose from 79 percent to 85 percent of their fellow white workers.[16] Similar wage gains were made in other industries organized by the CIO. One careful estimate indicates that the overall effect by 1940 was to raise the pay of black compared to white workers 5 percent above what it would have been in the absence of unionization.[17]

Another major achievement of the early CIO was the institution of seniority clauses in the newly won employment contracts. The demand for the creation of a formal seniority system was raised by both black and white workers to reduce the arbitrariness and corruption of the traditional system by which work assignment and layoff decisions were discretionary with the foreman. For black workers who were the most likely to be discriminated against, the institution of seniority was particularly welcome.[18]

In the early days of the Steelworkers' Union blacks were substantially overrepresented on the local union bargaining committees which negotiated these gains. This circumstance was in large measure due to the Communist Party, which exercised its influence to advance blacks into positions of union leadership.[19] However, the expectation that this egalitarian thrust would lead to a union push for new promotion opportunities for blacks in the mills was not realized. In part this was due to the fact that a sharp business downturn occurred almost immediately after union recognition, and rather than new jobs opening up, existing ones disappeared, not to reappear until World War II loomed on the horizon. (Between August 1937 and February 1938 steel-workers' average weekly wages fell by 37 percent.) And in part this failure was because promotion opportunities often rested not only on seniority but also on the shop one was in and on discretionary decisions by supervisors. Given the widespread racism among white workers, union leaderships were rarely prepared to battle to redress racially discriminatory decisions of management.[20]

Notwithstanding its limits, the extraordinary nature of these early CIO achievements can best be appreciated by contrasting them with what followed. During and after World War II the secular decline in work hours in the industry came to an end. Moreover, the seniority system was elaborated along racially discriminatory lines, and no further flattening of the occupational wage differentials took place in steel. Indeed, an actual retro-gression occurred in relative black wages over the years: by 1969 they had fallen 2 percent, to 83 percent of the white average. A similar retrogression took place throughout manufacturing as a whole: from 1940 to 1967 the wages of black industrial workers fell relative to those of whites by 1 percent.[21]

The failure to continue the prewar progress reflected the broader changes in the structure of the society, but it also resulted from the destruction of the trade union left and its replacement by a leadership which rejected a strategy of militant struggle at the point of production.[22]

World War II

As employment was stimulated by military spending prepara-tory to World War II, blacks and Mexicans found themselves the last to be recalled by industry, including U.S. Steel. In 1940 the Gary Works was operating at 90 percent of capacity. But although blacks constituted only one-fifth of Gary's population, they accounted for one-third of the city's unemployed. It wasn't until American entry into the war that the labor shortage became acute enough to bring blacks back into the employed labor force. As Harold Baron indicated in a recent article, the war mobilization of much of the existing labor force together with an almost 20 percent growth in nonfarm employment from 1940 to 1942 were "the pre-conditions necessary to enlarge the demand for black labor."[23] For blacks in Indiana, World War II created an historic opportunity. Indiana's total manufacturing employment doubled between 1939 and 1943 and black employment in manufacturing rose by 50 percent in 1941 and an additional 82 percent in 1942. Steel industry employment rose by a third in the Calumet region between 1940 and 1943. Exhausting local labor reserves, U.S. Steel welcomed back the same Mexican workers it had been so eager to see depart a few years before, and even looked to Puerto Rico for additional workers.[24]

Overall, World War II saw the most striking progress ever made by black labor: while the real wages of the American white workers rose by a third from 1939 to 1947, the real wages of black workers during this period rose by 73 percent. The key advance took place in the war industries of the major industrial cities, where total black employment tripled between 1942 and 1944. (For example, black employment in the Chrysler auto factories, largely located in Detroit, reached 17 percent of the total by the end of World War II.) In the Gary Works, out of 28,000 employees at the end of the war, 6,400 were black. With the end of the war, however, progress of the black workers in the steel mills ended as well. While generally full postwar employment meant that few black workers actually lost their jobs, the return of demobilized white workers who reclaimed their positions resulted in black workers finding themselves "bumped down" in the mill. The demands of the Communist Party that black steelworkers be granted super-seniority at the end of the war were denounced as "racism in reverse" and rejected by the Steelworkers' Union.[25]

The experience of women during and after the war paralleled

that of blacks. During the war, the labor shortage became so acute that beginning in mid-1942 large manufacturing concerns began to employ female labor on a large scale, especially in the war industries, and by 1944 a third of Indiana's industrial workforce was made up of women. A full tenth of the Calumet steel production workers were women. They were employed mainly as laborers on the ore docks and storage yards, in the coke plants and blast furnaces, and in the rolling and fabricating mills. Where the labor was particularly arduous, as with loading, the steel corporations used black women. But as soon as the emergency passed, women were excluded from the industry. As one steel manufacturer succinctly asserted in the aftermath of World War II: "We have tried to rid our plants of female labor."[26]

The period following World War II saw three trends that were decisive for Gary. The first was a break in the traditional correspondence between manufacturing growth and urban development. The second was the relative decline of the steel industry itself. And the third was the continuing blackening of the mill workforce and the city's population. Together, these developments structured the context in which Richard Hatcher was to win election to the mayor's office.

Urban Decline

Once World War II ended and the postwar reconversion to a civilian economy began, a new trend became dominant in American cities. While the process of suburbanization had long characterized American urban development, it was not pronounced until after World War II. The mass production of the automobile, the development of the highway system, and the development of trucking for manufactured goods (in place of the limits of rail transport) in the 1920s made the modern form of suburbanization technically feasible. But the Depression and World War II deferred the unfolding of this process. Housing patterns could hardly shift radically in a period in which there was virtually no new residential construction and since new factories were not built during the Depression neither could manufacturing locations.

During the war itself new manufacturing construction took place largely on the preexisting sites, so that if anything, there was a slight increase in the concentration of manufacturing in the older industrial centers. Similarly, government housing for wartime industrial workers concentrated in the urban centers. Thus Gary, in addition to some government-sponsored steel-making facilities, received an allocation of 800 units of public housing during World War II.[27]

But after the war the underlying tendency toward suburbanization rapidly became dominant. The consequence is that, ever since, the older central cities have undergone decline—and Gary has been a part of this trend. Thus between 1947 and 1963 the share of the nation's jobs in central cities dropped off from two-thirds to one-half of the total as new industrial plants came to be built outside city limits. Similarly, suburbanization of the population—with two-thirds of all new housing units since 1950 built in the suburbs—reduced average central city density from 7,800 per square mile to 4,500 per square mile by 1970.

While Gary had a modest population gain (see Table 4.1), the city's share of the population of the metropolitan region declined sharply as the bulk of new housing was built in the surrounding

Table 4.1
Gary, Indiana, Population, 1940-1970

Year	Total	Percent foreign born	Percent native white	Percent black
1940	112,000	16	66	18
1950	134,000	11	60	29
1960	178,000	—	—	39
1970	175,000	6	41	53

Source: Roger K. Oden, *Black Political Power in Gary, Indiana: A Theoretical and Structural Analysis* (Ph.D., University of Chicago, 1977), p. 184, table 12.

suburbs. While most of the city's residents continued to work in the city, by 1960 about half of those living in its suburbs worked elsewhere and no longer participated in the central city's economy or political life.[28]

The physical separation between the suburban core of manufacturing and the urban centers manifested itself rapidly in the postwar housing market. While government intervention was stimulating an expansion in the private homeowning market, this expansion took place in new suburban tracts (from which black families were effectively excluded). Banking industry policy contributed to this development. By the early 1950s, real estate loans in the older central cities fell off sharply as banks made their housing loans to the suburbs. In Gary private builders began to have difficulties in obtaining bank capital.[29]

By the 1960s throughout the nation new urban housing was being built at a rate of only 1 percent annually, a rate of replacement well below that required to prevent an overall aging of the cities' housing stock. In Gary, this fell to 0.5 percent a year by the time Hatcher became mayor; fewer than 15 percent of Gary's housing units (as opposed to 33 percent of those in the surrounding suburbs) were under a decade old. With half of the housing built prior to the Depression, a Public Health Service survey concluded that Gary had "a significant rat problem" which should be "expected to increase."[30]

In short, a qualitative transformation took place in the relationship between American manufacturing and urban development. Whereas in the period before World War II, the business cycle and urban prosperity moved together, after the war they no longer did. The long postwar boom, which lasted through the late 1960s, took place independently of—and indeed even in contradiction to—developments in the nation's urban centers. By the late 1950s, Gary, which had not even existed prior to 1906, had become an older, declining city.

The weakening of the central city business districts was a major symptom of, and a further contributor to, this decline. In 1950 suburban shopping centers were nonexistent; they now absorb virtually half of the consumer sales dollar. By the 1960s retail sales in central business districts were often declining.[31]

And these downward trends were exacerbated in the central cities with large black minorities, where the flight of capital was even more pronounced.[32]

Gary, it will be remembered, had been the Calumet region's shopping center before the war. But by the late 1950s the weakening was evident. While the retail sales sector of the local economy was employing more than 12,000 workers and sales were split between white and black consumers, already there was a radical drop-off in sales to suburban residents and a full quarter of the purchases of local residents took place outside of the city limits.[33] Year after year the absolute level of local retail sales dropped off, as more of the better off residents departed for new suburban locations, and by the late 1960s sales were almost exclusively to local black residents. By 1970, Gary provided only 8,000 jobs in retail sales.[34] Whenever possible, even black residents did their shopping in the suburbs, where prices were lower. Gary merchants, facing a poorer set of consumers, rising costs for taxes and insurance, and astronomical rates of thefts and forfeitures on credit sales, found themselves charging higher prices than their suburban counterparts and still making lower profits. The result was that store after store simply went out of business and was not replaced, so that currently Gary's downtown provides a desolate vista of boarded-up storefronts.[35]

As this process continued throughout the 1950s and 1960s, professional services also fled. Until the mid-60s there was a waiting list for professional office space in the prestigious Gary National Bank Building (which constituted about one-third of Gary's office space). By 1968 the waiting list had disappeared, and four years later the building was one-fifth unoccupied. Throughout the 1960s the lawyers and doctors of the city moved to suburban locations; as one leading attorney put it, their clients "are uncomfortable about coming to town." Thus, in a complete reversal of the traditional pattern, inner-city residents in Gary are now often compelled to commute outside of town to avail themselves of such services. In the late 1970s even the hospitals have been attempting to leave the city—although in this case Mayor Hatcher has been able to apply some pressure on the Department of Housing and Urban Development to block federal grants for such a move.[36] Thus the collapse of Gary as a viable urban environment took place consequent to larger tendencies in the political economy which are beyond the power of local government to control.[37]

Impact of the Steel Industry

Before World War II urban growth in America was primarily dependent upon manufacturing. Later, commercial and governmental activities, relying upon that manufacturing base, took over the leading role. But Gary as an industrial city remains dependent upon the steel industry, and as its growth flagged, the underlying economic welfare of the community rapidly declined.[38] The anomaly is that the city began to decline while the steel industry was still flourishing. This is directly consequent to the private character of American business, since as a free enterprise U.S. Steel was not compelled to reinvest its profits in the city, but could make new capital investments where the rate of profit was maximized. And while this was true to the interests of those who owned the corporation, it was antagonistic to the people of Gary.[39]

While wages rose rapidly in the steel industry in the 1940s and 1950s, after the end of the Korean War the steel companies no longer continued to increase employment. On the contrary, a gradual decline in the number of steelworkers began. So, while in its earlier years the steel mills of Gary were able to employ all of the available labor in the community, by the late 1950s a considerable pool of labor power, largely black, had been created. Without alternate sources of employment, a mass of permanently unemployed and semiemployed labor grew in the city. Thus, while in 1950 the average per capita income in Gary was 118 percent of the national average, by 1972 it had fallen to 98 percent.[40]

This decline took place notwithstanding the fact that steel remains, relatively, a very high wage industry. What had happened was that an ever larger wage gap had developed within the working class between the workers in highly organized basic production industries in the oligopoly sector and those in the nonunionized, competitive sector. In addition, many of the best paid skilled white workers moved out of Gary to surrounding suburban locations.[41]

It should be pointed out here that government employment in Gary could not take up the slack of a stagnant manufacturing sector. In 1949 the city employed 700 workers (exclusive of school personnel). In 1974, after the Hatcher administration had been specially favored with federal programs—including a large Model Cities Program and a Concentrated Employment Program—and after the vast expansion of public service employment which characterized the 1960s, the number more than tripled, to reach 2,400. Nevertheless, this total was only one-tenth the number provided by the private sector. What this means, of course, is that while the private manufacturing sector is in disarray, advances in government employment for blacks will not solve urban poverty or the economically depressed conditions of the mass of black people. Whatever advances Mayor Hatcher was able to implement in terms of affirmative action in the hiring of minority group members by the city were overbalanced by the failure of the steel mill to grow.[42]

Gary in this respect exemplifies a larger trend in the economy: nationwide, since the 1950s the free enterprise system has not created new, well-paid jobs at a rate fast enough to employ the growing labor force. On the contrary, the mass of the new jobs have been low-paid clerical, sales, and service jobs in the tertiary sector. Currently, as the productive core of the American manufacturing economy declines (and as government employment ceases to be increased to pick up the slack) the real standard of living of the American working class has turned downward.[43]

Black Employment Patterns

In recent years, especially as a result of propaganda charging that affirmative action programs in employment have given black workers special privileges, the idea has spread that the economic impoverishment of the black community is rapidly being overcome. In the academic literature, this notion takes the form of an argument that after World War II employment discrimination on the basis of race has been overcome and that therefore the lot of the black community is gradually merging with that of the white.[44] From the more extreme formulations of this position, one would think that the bulk of the black people were entering the middle class and that only a few pockets of poverty are left.

This idea is simply false: between 1945 and 1973 the median family income of blacks went from 53 percent to 58 percent of the white median and thereafter actually has fallen off.[45] It seemed plausible only because of advances of black female labor out of domestic service and into lower tier white-collar jobs which, due to pressures of the civil rights movement, opened up in government employment. Then in the 1960s this trend extended to the major private employers of clerical labor in the northern metropolises, largely because employers found it difficult to fill their rising needs for such workers from the diminishing pool of urban white females.[46] It is these jobs which enable the statistically correct, but misleading, conclusion that while in 1940 blacks held only one-sixth their proportionate share of white-collar jobs, they had achieved parity by 1970. When we look at the types of jobs held by black males in comparison with those held by white males, a quite different picture emerges. Thus, for instance, from an examination of the relative occupational profile of black workers in the steel industry before World War II and in the current period it is obvious that only modest progress has occurred[47] (see Table 4.2).

Even in the absence of complete statistical data, it seems fair to conclude that the entire postwar period has seen no major progress in the position of blacks in the steel industry job hierarchy, despite a large increase in the proportion of blacks in the industry's workforce. In 1940 this was 5.9 percent of the industry total; by 1960 it had reached 13.2 percent; and it has gone up significantly since then.[48] But since the total employment in the industry has declined substantially, the number of these relatively high-paying jobs has not increased sufficiently to meet the need. Young black men in large numbers are thus kept out of the productive sector of the economy and consigned permanently to unemployment. It is little wonder that some of them become demoralized and turn to antisocial activity.

Table 4.2
Distribution of Black Male Workers in the Iron and Steel Industry (in percent)

	1938	1969
White collar	—	2.0
Skilled	12.5	10.2
Semiskilled	38.3	56.9
Unskilled	49.2	40.0

Sources: Richard L. Rowan, "The Negro in the Steel Industry," in *Negro Employment in Basic Industry*, ed. Herbert R. Northrup (Philadelphia: University of Pennsylvania, 1970) p. 31, table 13, and U.S. Equal Employment Opportunity Commission, *Equal Employment Opportunity Report, 1969* (Washington: Government Printing Office, n.d.), Vol. I, p. 238.

In 1966 the Gary Works employed 17,900 males, of whom 5,200 were black. Among the 3,200 white-collar or foremen's jobs, only 100 were held by blacks. Thus, while only 2 percent of the black Gary Works employees held white-collar or managerial positions, a full 25 percent of the white workers did so. And among the blue-collar workers, the whites on the average held better jobs than the blacks (see Table 4.3).

While the Steelworkers' Union has some power to affect the corporation's policies with respect to its blue-collar employees, U.S. Steel exercises unilateral control over white-collar and foremen's jobs, and its policy has been to give such opportunities to only a handful of black workers. According to corporation figures, in 1968 only 22 out of 1,011 foremen in the Gary Works were black, and these supervised largely or entirely black crews. Moreover, the corporation has systematically favored whites for promotion, promoting them over blacks even when they have less seniority and less education.[49]

Table 4.3
Numerical Distribution of Blue-Collar Employees
in Gary Works in 1966 and 1974

	1966		1974	
	white	black	white	black
Skilled	4,000	900	5,600	1,500
Semiskilled	3,600	2,500	3,800	3,600
Unskilled	1,200	1,200	1,000	1,800

Source: Data obtained from Equal Employment Opportunity Commission, under Freedom of Information Act.

This pattern of racial discrimination is industry-wide, as demonstrated by each of the several civil rights lawsuits against American steel mills that have reached a final decision. For instance, in a recent case, the Lackawanna plant management of Bethlehem Steel admitted pursuing a policy of generally excluding blacks from supervisory positions by basing promotions on "essentially subjective determinations." Moreover, in some cases they shifted white employees from traditionally white departments to other supervisory positions, thereby further limiting the number of black supervisory personnel.[50] Similarly, the assignment of new hires, which is solely under management control, has followed a consistent pattern in the postwar period, placing mainly white workers in the well-paid craft jobs in the nonproduction maintenance and repair divisions. The 30 percent higher accident rate among black steelworkers is mute testimony to their differential assignment to the most dangerous production jobs. Throughout the country black workers constitute the vast majority of the coke oven jobs, which are virtual death sentences. The lung cancer rates for these workers are ten times those of steelworkers as a whole.[51]

Finally, and most decisively, the skewed job placement pattern of the corporation has become entrenched through the steel industry seniority system into a lifetime pattern of lesser opportunity for the black workers. The peculiarities of this system have been described elsewhere.[52] It is sufficient to understand that instead of operating on a plantwide basis, seniority is by department. This means that the black workers, once they have been tracked into inferior "lines of promotion," are locked into particular areas, with extremely limited possibilities for transfer and promotion. The result is that black steelworkers with equivalent years of service actually earn about 15 percent less than their fellow white workers![53]

So far at least, suits under the Civil Rights Act of 1964 have proven ineffective in altering this situation. After the successful conclusion of one major lawsuit in Baltimore, fewer than 1 percent of the black steelworkers actually succeeded in changing jobs in their mill. The effect of the "consent decree" negotiated out of court between the companies, union, and government essentially precludes black steelworkers from bringing new employment discrimination cases even though its terms do not substantially change traditional employment patterns. Hailed by the industry and union leadership, it was bitterly opposed by insurgent rank-and-file groups and civil rights organizations,[54] and effectively forestalls any likelihood of substantial improvement in the black steelworkers' relative employment situation in the foreseeable future.

Race and the Steelworkers' Union

U.S. Steel, pursuant to its strategy of "divide and rule" toward the working class, keeps the black people of Gary at the bottom of the occupational structure. The position of the city's 10,000 Chicanos lies halfway between that of the blacks and whites. When Hatcher became mayor about 90 percent of Gary's Chicano population still held manual jobs (mainly in the steel industry) and still suffered from discrimination in jobs and housing, a condition which made them, along with the Jewish population, the major nonblack source of Hatcher's support. Despite lower educational levels than blacks, the Chicanos' relatively better position in the steel mill job hierarchy results from the fact that discrimination against them is less intense.[55]

The white workers, on the other hand, found themselves increasingly in a position in which their opportunities appeared to be in opposition to those of their black fellows. The posture of the Steelworkers' Union national leadership in collaborating with the industry in the discriminatory seniority system would scarcely be possible were there not a profound popular racist impulse among a considerable fraction of the white steelworkers.

The reality is that with a limited number of jobs and promotions available, arbitrarily excluding black workers increases the likelihood for whites to obtain them. This is palpably evident to most white workers, and it provides a powerful material basis for encouraging their racism. Thus, if jobs in the Gary Works were redistributed to be racially equitable, about one-quarter of the white workers in skilled job classifications would have to drop down to semiskilled and unskilled positions.[56]

In his analysis of imperialism, Lenin pointed out that a labor aristocracy of workers in the imperialist nations was morally corrupted by sharing crumbs from the high profits extracted from the capitalists' colonial possessions; similarly today, in the United States, many white workers see their immediate self-interest as entailing opposition to the special measures necessary to overcome the structural heritage of racism. Needless to say, condemnations of this as immoral, and demands that white workers sacrifice their petty privileges on behalf of equalization of conditions within the ranks of the workers, are futile.

But in fact, the "advantage" enjoyed by the white workers as a whole is quite limited and problematic. For instance, all other factors being equal, a racially equitable distribution of wages would lower white steelworkers' wages by 5 percent. Moreover, the amount of wages paid in the industry is not a "zero sum game," in which whatever goes to blacks comes from white workers. The alternative, for black and white workers jointly to obtain a larger share of the value they collectively produce through a unified class struggle, requires militant unity in order to extract additional concessions.

Not to understand and emphasize this underlying reality is to accept both a permanent racial division of the society and the corporation's continued hegemony over the community. It is thus profoundly erroneous to conflate the contradictory and limited interest of the white workers of Gary in supporting racism with that of the corporate elite. Management, as we have seen, is fundamentally responsible for the oppression of the blacks in Gary and remains hegemonic over the process of production in large measure because of it. That liberal academics—who conceive of the capitalist system as permanent and in the interests of the mass of the American people—make such a confusion between the racism of the powerful and that of the powerless is understandable. But it is troubling that many radical analysts have also effectively adopted this ideological perspective and lost sight of the qualitative distinction between company racism and that of white workers.[57]

The most comprehensive formulation of this approach appears in Paul A. Baran and Paul M. Sweezy's *Monopoly Capital*, which argues that in addition to capitalists, social strata that include white workers, who "taken together . . . constitute a vast majority of the white population," are joint beneficiaries of racism. This analysis leads them to the conclusion that it is the anarchy of capitalist society rather than the capitalists' political domination of the society which reinforces racism.[58]

The insurgent rank-and-file forces in the Steelworkers' Union, who have recently captured control of the union's Calumet district, electing militant Jim Balanoff as district director, have adopted a different approach, arguing that racial discrimination is against the interests of the workers in the industry and must be actively combated in the spirit of the early CIO if the gains won by unionization are to be protected in the current period of industry decline. Pointing to the fact that the recent period has seen a significant speedup and a reversal of the secular decline in industry accident rates, these forces place the burden on the entrenched national union leadership, which has adopted a posture of collaboration with rather than struggle against the industry.[59] Wages in steel during the decade of the 1960s rose at only 1.3 percent annually, compared to 3.5 percent for manufacturing production wages generally.[60] These diminutions in the advances made by the steelworkers are integrally linked to the unwillingness or inability of the union to develop a militant black–white unity among its membership. The Balanoff forces aver that this kind of class struggle approach is the absolute prerequisite for realizing the full possibilities of union organization. And judging from the ability of insurgent candidate Ed Sadlowski to garner a majority of the votes among the steelworkers employed in the industry, this approach has broad appeal in the current period.[61]

Hopefully, the emergence and maturing of such new forces within the working-class movement, and institutional victories by them within the existing mass production unions, will usher in a new period in which the black liberation movement will have a powerful ally. But during the period under discussion in this book, the trade unions were at best neutral toward the aspirations of the black community of Gary. And as we shall see repeatedly, the profound racial fissure in the community effectively precluded the Hatcher administration from making changes necessary to improve the city.

The Blackening of Gary

All of these trends occurred in a context of a city which was progressively turning black (see Table 4.1). The postwar process of residential suburbanization permitted a large number of white residents of Gary to purchase new homes in the suburbs and move out of the city entirely, while new black and Latino residents kept moving into the city. This increasing segregation resulted in a sharp rise in racial isolation in the city's schools. Because black families were younger and had more children, the proportion of black students rose even more rapidly than did their overall share of the population. Thus, in 1960, when they made up only 39 percent of the residents, blacks constituted 54 percent of the school children. Between 1951 and 1961 the proportion of black children in Gary attending de facto Jim Crow schools increased from 83 percent to 97 percent.[62]

It was this blockage of opportunity for the black community—in schools, housing, employment—which in the 1960s turned the civil rights movement into a mass force. The young attorney Richard Hatcher could "seize the time" in this movement and strive for local political power because a half century of social and economic evolution of the city had created a majority of black working-class people. But as many other reformers, insurgents, and revolutionaries have discovered both in America and throughout the world, it is one thing to be elected to public office and quite another to exercise sufficient power to right injustices and create a better future for the people. In Gary, too, the historical legacy of the community—and the ongoing power of the existing class relationships—would narrowly constrict the options at the new government's disposal. Indeed, these forces so closely bound in the new mayor that, in the absence of a great popular and coherently organized movement for fundamental social change, his effectiveness was slight. The remainder of the book analyzes several key examples of how Hatcher's efforts to bring about social equality in Gary were frustrated, and in so doing explores the limits of political reform of contemporary capitalism.

II
Case Studies
in Local Public Policy

5

The Police Department

The major achievement of Mayor Hatcher's administration has been a significant reduction in police repression of the black community. This advance, which contradicts the pessimistic view that black urban power is essentially of only symbolic significance, has hardly been noted, let alone analyzed. This is the result, I think, of an ideological bias in pluralistic concepts of power. Generally, bourgeois social scientists perceive the normal police functions as simply crime control and the maintenance of order, and thus they insist that acts of police brutality are rare and exceptional.[1] Liberal pluralists are more realistic: they acknowledge widespread police repression in central city ghettos, but treat it as a deviation from proper police functions.[2] But police brutality is commonplace.[3] The most careful effort to quantify the frequency of such unlawful police acts concludes: "we must accept the estimate that several million Americans have been physically mistreated by the police—perhaps a million black people alone."[4]

It is difficult for the pluralists to blame the political elites for police brutality, given their belief in the classless and neutral character of the state. Instead, they place the main burden on the psychological attributes of the white police. Specifically, they attribute to the police manifestations of authoritarianism and racism supposedly endemic to the working class from whose ranks they are said to be recruited.[5] This, too, is a biased approach.

The notion of American "working-class authoritarianism" was developed in the context of a vigorous Cold War intellectual assault on Marxism,[6] and recent research has largely discredited this idea.[7]

The class reality of the police is quite different from the pluralist model. The police in Gary, as in other urban centers, come predominantly from the petty bourgeoisie. In fact, a significant result of Hatcher's gaining control of Gary's City Hall is that he began to break up this class orientation and formation, as political power within the police department began to shift from the white petty bourgeoisie toward the black working class.[8] We can understand it better through a detailed discussion of the historical evolution of the Gary Police Department.

"Sin City" and Middle-Class Vigilantes

Ever since the United States Steel Corporation built Gary in 1906, substantial corruption and brutality have characterized the city's police department. From its earliest days, Gary earned a reputation as a "sin city"—a tough industrial town with high rates of violent crimes, widespread illegal organized vice, and endemic local government corruption.[9]

Whereas the "new immigrant" workers early on accused the police of persistent brutality and arbitrary arrests and the criminal justice system of corruption, middle-class opinion held that the turbulent character of the steelworkers made it necessary to obtain tough police to maintain public order. Accordingly, the city's first Republican mayor, Roswell O. Johnson, appointed the chief inspector of the Gary Land Company, the wholly owned subsidiary of U.S. Steel, as his police chief.[10]

The police concentrated on Gary's working-class districts. Most arrests were for consensual crimes, most of those arrested were foreign born, and a disproportionate number of the others were black. The court system followed suit: the lower the defendent's class origins, the more severe the sentence for the same offense. Consequently, many immigrant workers became fiercely antagonistic toward the police. Fights between workers and police occurred frequently, with at least one major riot prior to World War I.[11]

At the root of this antagonism lay the servile attachment of the police to the interests of U.S. Steel, for which they provided an armed guarantor of labor control. Until the New Deal, with its attendant rise of the Congress of Industrial Organizations (CIO) and the transfer of local political power to the Democratic Party machine, Gary's police force functioned as an auxiliary of U.S. Steel. For several decades the police worked in unison with middle-class vigilante groups to break strikes, harass labor unions, intimidate the black community, and prevent public meetings by radical groups.[12] So intense was the hatred engendered among the workers that even a decade after recognition of the Steelworkers' Union, they still considered it shameful for a man to join the police department.[13]

The middle class tended to follow the lead set by U.S. Steel executives. H. S. Norton, head of the Gary Land Company, working in tandem with Gary Works' mill superintendent William P. Gleason, effectively dominated the local Republican Party and commercial life. He also served as president of the Gary Commercial Club, an organization that "included most of the leading business and professional men in the city and soon became the most lively, active, and powerful group in Gary."

The first meeting of this august body had as its keynote speaker Eugene Buffington, president of U.S. Steel's midwest division, and Norton's and Gleason's boss. Buffington articulated the corporation's philosophy of local government: its role was to make steel, not manage a municipality. The latter task, he indicated, was appropriately devolved on the members of the Commercial Club.[14]

David Brody has described this type of relationship in the steel communities as follows: "The more substantial merchants and professionals recognized a kinship with the plant officialdom. They lived in the same sections, frequented the same clubs and churches, and shared its outlook on industrial and business matters."[15] Thus, when a crisis loomed, the corporation could count on the fervent support of this upper-middle-class stratum.

As World War I loomed, Gary Works' superintendent Gleason and Mayor Johnson worked together to stimulate popular support and to intimidate antiwar radicals among the millworkers. A Gary Patriotic Committee "composed of leading professional people" emerged as a vigilante group. And when local socialists tried to hold a public protest meeting in August 1917, Mayor Johnson sent the police *en masse* to prevent it. Soon the vigilante committee, reorganized as the Loyalty League, took to making nighttime visits to the homes of families of dissidents to ascertain if they were participating in the war bond activities organized by the Gary Works' management. On May 4, 1919, a march to memorialize the victims of the Chicago Haymarket Affair—radical activists of a generation earlier who were framed and executed for demanding an eight-hour day—was broken up by the Gary police and local vigilantes, among them H. S. Norton himself.[16]

After the war, the Loyalty League joined the local police to break the great Steel Strike of 1919, which had closed down the Gary Works. The new mayor, Republican William Hodges, explained to the *Saturday Evening Post*:

> With my regular police force and such assistance as we had [from the Loyalty League] there were thirty of these rioters here in this building inside of fifteen minutes. Incidentally there were a good many of them laid out in that little row on the street. I have heard a report that one diligent deputy with the cranking lever of a flivver laid out eight of those people before all the arrests were made. We didn't really need to arrest them very much.[17]

The diligent *Saturday Evening Post* reporter also provided vivid descriptions from the vigilantes of how they dealt with the immigrant strikers. Throughout the nation's steel towns, local police deputized loyal company employees for strike duty. In the event, however, they were not enough, and federal troops had to intervene to win the day for the steel companies.[18]

The vigilantes, whose core consisted of native-born Protestant, upper-middle-class business and professional men, had as reserves heterogeneous lower-middle-class elements. In part, the common religion, ethnicity, and culture of these shopkeepers, minor mill functionaries, and even some "labor aristocrats" explains the formation of this reserve mass base.[19]

It is easy to see why the men of the Commercial Club went along with the corporation. Yet, we must also explain the collaboration of a substantial portion of the petty bourgeoisie—often themselves "new immigrants"—who essentially were excluded from managerial jobs in U.S. Steel and the leading businesses and professions. While their nationality lay with the millworkers, their class interest lay with the more substantial capitalists.

As militant labor leader Mother Jones acerbically noted during her participation in the 1919 steel strike, this part of the Gary vigilante force was composed of "the little shopkeepers dependent upon the smile of the steel companies." Moreover, in contrast to the vast majority of Gary's "new immigrants," who were from the countryside in their lands of origin, almost all of the ethnic shopkeepers were from the cities. Also in contrast to the Gary "new immigrant" workers, these petty bourgeois generally brought from their countries of origin both prior merchant experience and some capital.[20]

When an immigrant without such prior resources began his own small business, he typically earned even less than a common laborer. So those who succeeded often did so by a willingness to defraud their ignorant countrymen. A large proportion, for example, had strong ties to organized crime. Criminal activity did not provide an alternative to legitimate business pursuits: the same individuals simultaneously engaged in diverse forms of entrepreneurship. Profits made illicitly—whether in kickbacks, pimping, gambling, liquor, or fraud—were simply invested in the family firms, their origins quickly forgotten. Blacks, however, could not follow this path of upward mobility; of sixteen black businesses begun in 1911, more than half went bankrupt within two years.

This kind of ethnic petty-bourgeois advancement, especially in the liquor trade, was closely tied to the political machine. City Hall, regardless of the predilections of Judge Gary, soon became deeply enmeshed in the illegal sale of liquor, in effect licensed through the police department in return for financial and political support. Moreover, U.S. Steel policy tolerated widespread corruption. Thus, when Mayor Johnson went to prison in 1925 for violating prohibition (to be pardoned soon after by President Coolidge) he received a public expression of sympathy from superintendent Gleason. Along with the bootleggers and the mayor, several policemen, the Lake County sheriff, the county prosecutor, and a judge were indicted by a Federal grand jury for conspiring to elect public officials hostile to the prohibition laws. It was charged that they had assigned various city districts to certain bootleggers, driving out their competitors, and that they had been able to see to it that bootleggers who were given prison sentences never served them. Gary's elite thought these escapades too trivial to deny Johnson renomination after his return in 1929. In 1932, however, while serving his new term in office, he was again indicted, this time for having embezzled city funds to construct a summer cottage for himself.[21]

The other main method of "new immigrant" advance to petty-bourgeois status involved a much more intimate relationship with the corporation. Until the Gary Works systematically centralized personnel practices during the Depression, the foreman hired unskilled workers. The ability of a "straw boss" to provide workers with jobs enabled him to advance his own income and status, for workers commonly had to pay bribes for jobs and promotions.

Often labor procurement and supervision accompanied the boarding of single workers. To keep their jobs, "new immigrants" often had to board—at inflated rates—at their foreman's home. The foreman's intermediary role fostered corruption: in addition to working their men to the limit, they had the job of assuring that the "new immigrants" voted Republican and that of participating in measures to curb trade union activity.[22]

As part of this small and mean system of private aggrandizement, the owner of the boarding house might exploit his own wife as well.

> Among the newer immigrants . . . the number of women is very small. The few who accompanied the immigrants are enslaved as wives of boarding houses, and their lot is most wretched. . . . To cook, wash, do the chores, and to keep open house for twenty or thirty men was no small task. The boarders work day and night

and it is meals at all hours. The wife is the only one who watches over the fire, gets ready the water for the men to wash, and prepares the food. Night men come home at any hour in the morning, and the women must be there to wait on them.[23]

When World War I began, a full third of the married foreign-born women of Gary had lodgers in their homes—a proportion that closely corresponded to the third of all foreign-born home-owners. The majority of the "new immigrant" women who came from working-class families too poor to own homes were in the general workforce, even when they had small children. So, too, were most black women, for only 2 percent of Gary's black families were homeowners. Sometimes, the women's responsibilities included having sexual relations with the boarders, for prostitution brought particularly lucrative returns in demographically imbalanced Gary. The "new immigrant" women supplied the bulk of the prostitutes of industrial America, and some owners of boarding houses waxed affluent off this trade.[24]

Thus, Gary's entire petty bourgeoisie had numerous ties of mutual interest and ideology to the ruling class and its political structure, including the police department. In effect, they were united in their common support for the American system of enterprise and their common pursuit of the extraction and realization of surplus value from Gary's industrial proletariat.

Ongoing Corruption

The direct subordination of the Gary Police Department to U.S. Steel continued until the mid-1930s, when the New Deal Democrats plus the successful organizing efforts of the CIO began to change Gary politics. As late as March 1933, for example, a meeting of 1,000 Gary Works employees sponsored by the Communist Party was broken up by a combination of local police and specially deputized men drawn from the American Legion. Yet after the Democratic Party won the mayor's office and the corporation capitulated to the CIO's organizing drive, the police department ceased their direct repression of the trade union movement. Thus, a few years later, when the Steelworkers' Organizing Committee set up a picket line to prevent nonunion members from entering the Gary Works the city attorney ruled that the picketing was legal. The police were told to arrest for assault and battery anyone trying to crash the picket line, and only those carrying paid-up union cards were to be allowed to pass through. The line contained 1,000 pickets.[25]

The rise to power of the Gary Democratic Party during the New Deal, of course, did not end the integration of organized crime, the police, and local businesses. Rather, it changed the form and focus of this union, as gambling passed under the control of the cronies of the Chicago Democratic Party machine. The pattern of crime continued into the post-World War II period, with prostitution, gambling, and street crimes concentrated in the now-black central slum.[26]

Periodic reform drives petered out, and organized crime flourished under the benevolent protection of the ethnic machine. The police preferred assignment to the vice squad since it offered the best opportunities for graft. In 1950, for example, the only prominent black who enthusiastically supported the local police was Gary's "policy king," the chief of the illegal gambling syndicate. Jobs on the police force were purchased from city councilmen for $1,500.[27]

Police corruption was tied directly to City Hall, where it was considered normal for mayors to retire as millionaires after a four-year term. City Hall acted as a silent partner to organized crime, which provided a substantial portion of the machine's virtually limitless appetite for cash. While a portion of that money built the personal fortunes of its leaders, much was redistributed. The black community regularly received hundreds of thousands of dollars, distributed through black precinct committeemen, to buy elections. Ultimately, Hatcher's insurgency took on additional popular appeal from the deep resentment among blacks against "plantation politics." His promise to drive organized crime out of Gary's ghetto and end police corruption became a significant factor, although less salient than his color, in building his popularity among blacks.[28]

Hatcher, it will be recalled, won in 1967 both because of the growing black electorate and because the machine's disarray led to a split in the white vote. The disarray followed upon the imprisonment, for income-tax evasion, of former mayor and machine boss, George Chacharis. After much waffling by the Justice Department, his indictment resulted in the internal factional strife that provided Hatcher's opportunity. With a black mayor in office, the character of Gary's police department began to change.[29]

Hatcher vs. City Hall

When Hatcher won the Democratic Party primary in 1967, the police chief, a lifelong Democrat, began sporting a Republican campaign button. But police activity was not restricted to the confines of lawful electioneering. During the primary, police officers attempted to prevent the opening of polling booths in several black precincts by physically barring the entrance. Anticipating this development, Hatcher's campaign organization succeeded in opening the polls (the votes in which represented his margin of victory) by hiring armed black criminals from the Chicago ghetto to confront the police; fortunately no one was killed. It was only after the failure of this effort that the Democratic Party machine resorted to the massive vote fraud scheme we have already described.[30]

The hostility of the Gary Police Department did not stop after the election. Thus, rather than follow the normal pattern of assigning policemen as mayoral bodyguards, Hatcher deemed it more prudent to assign this task to the private individuals who had protected him during his candidacy. Moreover, for the first couple of months of his tenure there was virtually no police patrolling of the city; two-thirds of the forty-five patrol cars rapidly became inoperable due to such vital parts as batteries and tires disappearing while the cars were under the exclusive control of the police. Later in the year, several of the officers from the stolen car detail were indicted for auto theft, yet none were convicted and one was actually given a promotion by the Gary Police Civil Service Commission.[31]

This pattern of conflict between the police and City Hall has occurred in virtually every city in which a black mayor has taken office. A good place to begin to understand the function of the police in the larger class and political system of the nation is by observing that the most intransigent opposition to black mayors from any urban group has been located in the municipal police departments.

The Police, Capitalism, and the Middle Class

From its beginnings in the first years of this century, the police department in Gary protected the interests of capital, large and small, in direct opposition to the interests of the working class. This pattern has occurred in most industrial cities. In the major Western capitalist nations modern police forces arose not primarily to control crime, but rather, in the context of "prolonged popular resistance to government," as a mechanism for the defense of bourgeois power in class struggles with the lower orders. Without that impetus, the propertied classes tolerated extraordinarily high levels of public violence and saw no need to create a police force.[32]

The United States offered no exception. As one prominent observer summarized it: "The emergence of a municipal police force [in the United States was] not so much the result of mounting crime rates as of growing levels of civil disorder."[33] Like the National Guard, the police force in America was developed primarily as a strikebreaking force, and one designed to prevent working-class insurrection.[34]

Although we lack an adequate history of the American urban police, the example of the Buffalo force during the late nineteenth century indicates that it was neither population growth nor the incidence of criminal acts which correlated with increases in the size of that department. Rather, increases corresponded to the magnitude of labor strife. Even their organizational model—a platoon instead of a patrol system—was more suited to riot than crime control. Robert and Helen Lynd's classic study of Muncie,

Indiana describes how the major expansion of the police department in 1935 resulted not from an increase in street crime, but from trade union organizing in the local General Motors plant. Even today, manufacturing cities generally have the largest police forces per capita, perhaps as a residue of past labor struggles.[35]

Similarly, the massive increment in urban police strength and heavy weaponry during the past decade reflects fear of black ghetto insurgencies far more than it does a desire to protect the poor from criminals. Police budgets have expanded dramatically, despite unambiguous findings of social scientists that the number of police has no perceptible relationship to the incidence of criminal assaults.[36] Indeed, the new focus of municipal police forces in preparing for ghetto rebellions parallels not only earlier police developments, but the rearmament of the National Guard in the late nineteenth century. Then units were equipped and trained for riot duty: according to a study of public control in that period, "in the employment of Gatling guns the militia surpassed the United States Army. The Gatling was a light, inexpensive and effective weapon for use against crowds."[37]

Thus the desire to protect private property, and toward that end more specifically, to repress labor insurgency, historically has stimulated the expansion of police power. By serving this function the police above all have served the interests of the American ruling class. In so doing they have been in complicity with the extra-legal violence of such "distinctly American institutions" as lynching and vigilantism.[38]

In addition to their historical role, an examination of the class position of the urban police reveals the large gap which separates them from the working class. The family backgrounds of urban police, both currently and in the past, are for the majority those of white-collar workers, skilled craftsmen, and foremen, that is, lower middle class. Few come from the mass of factory laborers. A study of the police in Gary, Indiana in 1950, for instance, revealed that almost a third of the members had fathers in the "labor aristocracy," while one by the International Association of Chiefs of Police shows that almost two-thirds of police come from families whose male heads "held jobs at or above craftsmen or foremen."[39] Moreover, police officers who achieve the rank of detective or above disproportionately come from "higher class origins" than those who remain at the patrolman level.[40]

The police in the United States enjoy a substantially superior position in the economic structure than do manual workers. The median weekly pay of police is one-and-a-half times that of factory operatives and a fifth above even crafts workers and foremen. The pay is regular and guaranteed, and the pensions handsome in comparison to those of most workers.[41]

A marked if indeterminate proportion of the police are actually small entrepreneurs of a kind, mostly by way of corruption. Many receive substantial sums of tax-free income from their ties both to organized crime and legitimate business, pushing them up to petty-bourgeois status.[42]

Students of American local politics have long emphasized the singularly high level of police involvement, in contrast to that of the average municipal employee, with the ethnic political machines that have dominated so many city halls. In this respect, police behavior resembles that of local merchants doing business with the city government.[43]

Finally, the conservative political ideology of the police points toward the protection of the elites, rather than responsiveness to the working class; indeed, the police include a significant minority with proto-fascist politics. In this respect as well, they manifest a correlation with the lower-middle-class strata who have often provided the main mass base for right-wing extremism.[44] For instance, a Gary police reporter in 1964—with very close ties to the police based on his father's twenty-one years on the force—stated that all of the policemen he talked to had voted for Wallace.[45]

By properly viewing the urban police as part of the lower-middle-class social strata, rather than accepting simplistic comments about police "racism," we can provide an adequate explanation of why urban police departments are so hostile to the advent of black mayors in their cities: these mayors present an assault on the *class interests* as well as the ideology of the police. In particular, a reform black mayor threatens the job security and privileges of the white police.

Crime and the Community

To fully understand the intensity of the conflict between the black community and the police it is also necessary to outline the perspective of the black community toward the problem of crime, and its notions as to the appropriate role of the police department in crime control. Crime was a major public issue when Richard Hatcher ran for mayor in Gary. As we have seen, because of his record as an active and militant leader in Gary's civil rights movement, all factions of the local machine bitterly opposed his election. Every effort was made to discredit him as a dangerous subversive. Thus, in his opening campaign speech the incumbent mayor stated:

> Any violence occurring in the next few weeks must be laid at the feet of those preaching the doctrine of division, using their outside agitators and advisors, and manipulated by interests foreign to democratic principles. . . . Gary has no room for people who wish to be catapulted into public office on the rocket ship of violence, using the fuel of race hatred.[46]

While ineffective in the black community, this propaganda evoked a deep response among numerous whites. Not only did most of them refuse to vote for Hatcher, but a political atmosphere was created which predisposed many to hold him culpable for local street crime.[47]

In reality, Gary's black community was terribly concerned about the high crime rates in their city and desirous of ameliorating the problem. For the large majority of victims of street crimes (and perpetrators as well) are black. Half the arrests for crimes against the person, and two-thirds of the arrests for crimes against property, regularly take place in the small central section of the ghetto. In one recent year twenty-six of twenty-eight residents arrested for murder were black, and so too were five-sixths of those arrested for auto theft, both among adults and juveniles.[48]

Generally, one's personal fear of criminal attack is actually proportional to the real danger.[49] Throughout the 1960s the fear of both black and white Gary residents of personal victimization rapidly intensified, so that by the middle of Hatcher's first term in office most people felt the streets were unsafe except in the presence of a policeman. Currently, many white suburban dwellers simply refuse to enter the city (with catastrophic consequences to the downtown business district), and many blacks refuse to leave their homes at night for fear of burglaries in their absence.[50]

This situation is hardly restricted to Gary: a recent national poll of larger American cities found half of the population afraid to walk in their neighborhood at night. In the black ghettos, the fear is even more pervasive. A government survey of a public housing project in Washington, D. C., for instance, "found that more than half of the residents never went out at night alone; 40 percent had stopped visiting friends in the project because they were afraid to walk there at all."[51]

All of this increases resentment against the police.[52] Black ghetto dwellers, in particular, are indignant that corrupt police operate in their communities in such a fashion as to facilitate organized crime and narcotics. Although invisible to the white majority, it is painfully evident to the mass of the black population who are resentful that municipalities have customarily tolerated a far higher level of criminal activity in the ghettos.

Hatcher: A New Deal?

Hatcher campaigned for office on a four-point program for police reform: an end to police corruption; professionalization of the police; legal measures to create a civilian review board; and a substantial increase in minority-group policemen. His success in implementing these reforms has been mixed and their effect on reducing the amount of crime in the city has been too small to measure. But their effect on the police department itself has been substantial, and, in the view of most of the white police, adverse.

The hostility among the Gary police to Hatcher represented, in addition to widespread personal racism, a reaction to his determination to extirpate endemic corruption from the department. With his own police chief, Hatcher could somewhat limit organized gambling activities, and during his first year in office, there was a thirteen-fold multiplication in gambling raids. Soon gambling and prostitution became far less visible in the community, as operations were shifted out of the city limits. As this process occurred, the police became far more militant in their demands for substantial pay raises.

In addition, following the pressure from his black constituents, Hatcher demanded a more vigorous battle against street crime. His first term of office saw a substantial increase in the proportion of the municipal budget devoted to the police department. The bulk of this increase went for new equipment, so that by 1974, for instance, the number of patrol vehicles reached 160.[53] A combination of increases in the size of the force and more efficient personnel deployment patterns resulted in doubling the amount of street patrolling over that of Mayor Katz's administration.

While Gary police reports indicate declines in criminal acts, such figures are not trustworthy in view of the generally poor correlation between patrolling and crime reduction. And Hatcher's former public safety director, William Johnson, told me that he believes that the real incidence rate has increased. In any event, there is no way to know for certain. The local statistics on auto theft and murder—generally considered the most accurate of major crime indices—show an auto theft rate seven times and a murder rate three times the American average when Hatcher assumed office. The rate of increase of each of these categories for the five years prior to his election and the five years following it are similar. Over the decade involved the absolute numbers of auto thefts and murders in Gary tripled.[54]

Hatcher's administrative reforms, regardless of their impact on public safety, meant additional work for the Gary police. But a greater source of incumbent police hostility, in terms of importance to his attack on police corruption, was Hatcher's vigorous and effective campaign to recruit black police. One of the police prerogatives is the ability to pass one's job on to one's children. Police are recruited from the local population, and about a third come from police families. Given the historical exclusion of blacks from police work, there are virtually no black police from police families. As with the so-called labor aristocrats in some of the building trades, members of the police department view their jobs as virtually hereditary: an influx of black police recruits is thus perceived as destroying a vested property right.[55]

Gary is typical of the national underrepresentation of blacks on police forces, state as well as local. (In Chicago, after an increase in black police militancy in the mid-1960s, the proportion of black police officers was actually reduced.[56]) Indeed, so blatant is the inequality that several of the larger municipalities have been sued by the Justice Department for racial discrimination in police department hiring and promotion practices.[57]

Hatcher's biggest accomplishment with respect to the police department has been to substantially blacken its racial composition. Gary's first black policeman had been hired in response to organized pressure from the black community in 1912. From that point on, rather than following a straight line of progress, the history of Gary's black police has ebbed and flowed with the political climate. Thus, during the New Deal, integrated police teams patrolled the entire city, but in the early postwar period black police were segregated and assigned only to ghetto patrols.[58] In the late fifties, when one-third of the city's population was black, only 5 percent of its police were black. Over the next few years, in response to increased civil rights agitation, the proportion of black police doubled.[59]

But black officers continued to suffer discrimination on the job independently of their modest numerical gains: an example was assignment to patrol cars in poor repair.[60] Applicants from Spanish-speaking backgrounds continued to be effectively excluded from the force by a rigid height requirement. Moreover, black numerical advances were strictly circumscribed by discriminatory hiring patterns in the Gary Police Civil Service Commission. Thus, while half of those who passed the written examination in 1966 were black, only one-quarter of the cohort actually appointed were black.[61]

Hatcher was able to make a striking change in this pattern. Each year since his election has seen a majority of new police drawn from the ranks of minority groups. By 1972 a full third of the department was of black or Spanish-speaking origins, and it is now in its majority black.[62] As part of this racial shift, Hatcher was able to end the Gary tradition of purchasing entry into the department. The initial socializing experience of police work was no longer one of corruption.[63]

Hatcher's power to appoint the police chief also gave him significant leverage over the department's activities. But since Indiana law, like that of most states, forbids lateral entry into the department, his ability to alter its command structure has been far more limited. After his first term of office, only one of twenty-four sergeants and one of the higher officers were black. As Hatcher's administrative assistant, Charlotte Johnson, bitterly complained, "It's impossible to control them, because it's the same people as before." A clique of high seniority white officers thus has retained effective control over many aspects of the department, continuing their traditional patterns.[64]

This lag in blackening the higher ranks of police forces despite the efforts of black mayors is also typical of the nation's cities. In Detroit, only 61 of 1,200 sergeants are black; in Newark, only 2 of 29 captains are black; in Washington, D.C., only 32 of 268 policemen holding the rank of lieutenant or above in 1975 were black.[65] But as Hatcher's administration goes into its second decade of power, a combination of attrition and a deepening entrenchment of blacks over the city's entire administrative apparatus essentially has resulted in black control over all levels of the Gary police.

The blackening of the police force, moreover, has had a significant effect on the problem of police brutality—a widespread cause of conflict between the black community and the police department. After the New Deal transition of local political power, police brutality largely shifted from ethnic to racial minorities. In 1950 for instance, the following incident took place in the Gary police station:

> They had brought in a small Negro man, and when the detective sergeant, who was a huge, muscular man, asked him what he had been doing that afternoon and the man said something that was obviously considered false, the sergeant slapped him across the

side of the head with such force that the man was knocked off his feet.[66]

In other incidents during this period a black man was kept secretly jailed for sixteen days during which time his nose and ribs were broken. Four black suspects were arrested, and one of the policemen involved said: "We took them down to the station and really worked them over. I guess that everybody that came into the station had a hand in it and they were in pretty bad shape."[67]

Such practices, common to Gary and many other parts of the country, were long a major political concern in the black community and a focus of civil rights struggles. As a result of this struggle in Gary, Hatcher's immediate predecessor, Mayor A. Martin Katz, essentially ended beatings at the station house.

Thus, even before Hatcher took office, there had been a substantial reduction in police brutality against blacks, a change analogous to that won by the white working class a generation before. Hatcher's main contribution was to initiate a new patrol pattern with respect to ghetto youth, under which the amount of "hassling" young men who were simply hanging around on the streets was sharply reduced.[68]

This advance should not be overestimated, however, for the Gary police have continued to kill criminal suspects under circumstances suggestive of murder. In the most flagrant of these incidents, on February 27, 1971, a teenaged Chicano suspect was arrested and placed in a patrol car with his arms handcuffed behind his back. He arrived at the station house dead of nine bullet wounds. The police claimed they believed he was reaching for a gun, but no weapon was recovered. The officers were exonerated by the Gary Police Civil Service Commission and continue to patrol in the community.

Hatcher refused the public investigation demanded by indignant community groups on the grounds that it might prejudice the hearing then pending before the Civil Service Commission. Instead he sent copies of the police department's investigative report to the Lake County Prosecutor's Office and the United States District Attorney, neither of which has ever acted on the matter. As Public Safety Director William Johnson wryly observed, if police had "perpetrated a murder, there's really not much that the police department can do."[69] In evaluating this failure, it is well to keep in mind that while a firm juridical basis exists to prosecute instances of police brutality, nowhere in America have either internal review processes nor those of the criminal justice system been employed to do so, except in the most extraordinary circumstances.[70]

Moreover, civil service regulations (which protect police everywhere but in the South) are apt to effectively shield police officers far more than other municipal employees from disciplinary measures. Historically, the development of police civil service protection (viewed by many academics as part of progressive reform reducing police corruption and "political influence" over police departments) has served to insulate local police departments from popular control.[71] As Mayor Hatcher noted with some exasperation, the effect of independent administrative boards "means that you cannot make concise decisions as a chief executive of a city like Gary, because all these decisions are tempered by what this board . . . will do."[72]

Gary's police civil service law dates back to 1939. It was the first, and for many years the only, independent police civil service commission in Indiana. The direct result of the initiative of Gary's last Republican mayor, Ernest Schaible,[73] the Gary Police Civil Service Commission was a last ditch effort to put the local police "above politics": that is, to insulate them as much as possible from control by the New Deal coalition sympathetic to the CIO.[74]

Hatcher's police chief considers the board "an albatross" in his efforts to break the resistance of the white police and reshape the department in accordance with the mayor's priorities. And in the short run it served to defer complete black control over the Gary police. But over time Hatcher has gained full control over the commission, as did the petty-bourgeois ethnic Democratic machine which preceded him.[75]

The overall effect of Hatcher's administration and the blackening of the Gary Police Department has been to reduce police brutality and repression in the black community. Yet it would be foolish to deny that in many ways the larger structure of society results in a continuation of a fundamentally repressive role of the urban police in the black community.[76] Thus during Gary's ghetto riot in July 1968, Hatcher brought in the state police to enforce a curfew, engaged in a mass arrest policy of dubious legality, prepared to bring in the National Guard if necessary, and, in general, took "the same steps that any white mayor would have taken, even though he had a greater understanding of the causes of the riot."[77]

As I drove down to police headquarters on the night of the street disorders with Hatcher's administrative assistant—through streets patrolled by police armed with submachine guns—he told me that his sympathies lay with the rioters and that were it not for his official position he would be a participant, not a controller, of the events. But, he went on to add, Hatcher had no choice but to act as he did. The implication was, in part, that a failure to do so would lead to the supervening of Hatcher's authority by the governor; but also implied was the belief that no government could permit such behavior.

Another sign leading to the conclusion that a black mayor is largely irrelevant to structural changes of local police functions is that during his reelection campaign in 1971, Hatcher quietly dropped from his platform the call for a civilian review board. This followed upon a public declaration by the police chief of his opposition to such a body, on the grounds that it would simply "be another attempt to hamper the police in their efforts to properly uphold the law."[78]

After the election Mayor Hatcher and his police chief continued to call for stronger crime control measures, and for greater police latitude to undertake such measures. Thereafter, when a teenager fleeing from a vehicle containing stolen merchandise was shot by the police on the grounds that he refused to halt and "flashed a knife" (which was never found), the police chief publicly supported the officers involved, saying: "Anyone who commits a felony has to realize that he risks losing his life. . . . Any other way and criminals will be able to act without the fear of the ultimate consequences and they'll be running wild."[79] The chief also called for the issuance of machine guns to the police.

Despite this contradictory evidence, I believe that a rather hopeful conclusion is in order. It is true that in the short run police departments seem little changed as a result of the advent of black mayors. Nevertheless, my opinion is that a process of social change is resulting from the blackening of the urban police, which has the long-term potential of altering their class orientation. Fundamental to this change is the fact that the black police are drawn overwhelmingly from the working class and are representative of the predominantly working-class character of the black community.[80]

Not only are the class origins of the black police significantly different than those of their white peers, so too are most of the other factors involved in determining their class interest. In contrast to the white police, the advent of large numbers of blacks on urban police forces is a result of historical struggles by an oppressed group; the ideology of black police is rarely that of the right wing. Moreover, the black police are entirely separate from the white petty-bourgeois political bloc associated with the ethnic machines. Whereas these machines served to reinforce the dominant class structure of their communities and legitimate it in the political sphere, the insurgent black mayors cannot be viewed realistically as an expression of their local business community. Local "black bourgeoisies" are simply too small and underdeveloped a social stratum to provide the basis for co-opting black police *en masse* into the ranks of the possessing classes. And given the deep antagonisms between the white petty bourgeois and the black police, this route of integration is also blocked.

Thus, there is a tendency for the black police to orient themselves toward service to the black community. It is the class orientation of the black police which makes it possible to explain the otherwise apparent paradox reported in a detailed study by Peter Rossi: "the higher the levels of reported police abuse the more satisfied are blacks with police services."[81] Once the black community believes that the police force is not randomly brutalizing them, but is instead actively and aggressively campaigning against street crime, it is likely to be far more sympathetic to policing activities in the black community.

A popular black mayor seen as controlling the local department apparently tends to stimulate such a belief. Similarly, black community confidence in the police department also seems to increase from the kind of blackening of its racial composition that has been occurring in Gary. Some preliminary evidence, moreover, seems to suggest that more black police may actually result in decreases in crime rates; if so, this is probably because of increased citizen cooperation with police investigative work in the ghettos.[82]

It thus appears that municipal black power has unleashed a gradual process of internal transformation of police interaction with the black community. In this process, a police force that traditionally has been used indiscriminately in the ghetto begins to become more responsive to that community. Since the black community wants aggressive crime control, that is what it gets.

Just as the New Deal transition of political power in Gary resulted in a marked change in how the police treated the white working class, so too a diminution of generalized police repression of the black community is a result of the higher level of political organization and autonomy that has emerged in Gary's black community. This reflects the historical development of the city, characterized by a kind of public order which changes only as a result of mass political struggles.

Thus whereas in cities where the police are dominated by ethnic machines and black officers are a distinct minority, the traditional class orientation of the police may continue; it would be wrong to assume that this pattern will continue in cities with black mayoral control and largely black police departments.[83] On the contrary, there is every reason to anticipate that the police department of Gary, and of other cities in an analogous situation, will substantially orient itself toward the black community. Since the black community is overwhelmingly working class in character, and ever more politically autonomous and coherent, the prognosis is that its local police department will finally come to serve the class interest of that community.[84]

6

The Limits of Housing Reform

When the black people of Gary elected Richard Hatcher on a platform which called for radical amelioration of the city's housing crisis, two courses of action theoretically were open to the new municipal government to improve the housing of inadequately housed families. One was to increase the production of new rental units for lower income families; the other was to develop a program which would maintain and rehabilitate the existing housing stock. Hatcher tried both of these approaches, in addition to continuing the city's conventional urban renewal program. His overall impact was minuscule relative to the size of the problem.

Because Gary's housing problem is typical of the failure of the private housing market in the United States to provide shelter for its cities' poor, we need to see the situation in terms of the broader political economy.

The Quality of Housing in the United States

The most important development in the American working class in the period after World War II has been the giant leap forward in living standards for those industrial workers who achieved unionization during the New Deal period. Instead of

the split between a mass of unskilled and a small minority of
skilled crafts workers, with blacks among the former, postwar
prosperity has resulted in splitting most blacks and a distinct
minority of poor white workers from an actual majority of the
working class.

This new split has its most evident and most important manifestation in home ownership. The American ruling class historically has wanted its workers tied to private home ownership,
and we have seen how—within the limits imposed by the poverty
of the mass of its workforce—the United States Steel Corporation
encouraged such ownership in Gary's early years. After World
War II, this process of encouraging home ownership was adopted
by the federal government, as part of its generally expanded
role. And with the remarkable growth of the economy from the
outset of World War II until the Vietnam War, the policy was
quite successful.

Currently, almost four-fifths of all trade union members in the
United States own their own homes, two-thirds of American
families are homeowners, and a majority of even those families
with annual incomes below $6,000 own their place of abode.[1] In
the postwar period, government support for housing, largely in
the form of various tax benefits, has reduced the cost of home
ownership by 15 percent over what it would be in a "free
market" situation.[2] It is estimated that the effect has been to
increase the proportion of American working-class families who
own homes by as much as one-third.[3]

Thus in the thirty-year period following World War II private
home ownership in Gary went from two-fifths to three-fifths of
all families (and this during a period in which many better off
families were leaving for private homes in the suburbs).[4]

Not only did an additional fifth of Gary's population achieve
home ownership, the general size and quality of this form of
housing improved as well. This great shift of the core of the
industrial working class into private homes, along with a marked
improvement in other aspects of their standard of living, constituted a kind of affluence previously unknown to any proletariat
in world history, and provided the material basis for the long
period of class collaboration which marked the Cold War.

But what happened to the housing of the substantial minority in Gary (including half of the black families) who remained too poor to purchase homes? Conventional conservative wisdom has it that this, too, radically improved during the postwar period as a consequence of the process known as "filtering."[5] Put simply, filtering means that as better off families move into new suburban homes, the units which they previously occupied become available to the poor, who in turn vacate the worst urban housing. Abandonment and demolition of units in the poorest slums, then, is a consequence of an absolute improvement in housing for those still renting.

Considerable evidence can be brought to bear in support of this thesis, which is partially true. In the United States between 1950 and 1970, all of the objective indicators available show substantial improvements in the quality of housing available to the poor. For instance, among the bottom third in annual income of all families in 1950, 57 percent lacked complete plumbing; by 1970, the proportion had fallen to only 12 percent.[6]

But it is somewhat facile to conclude from such evidence that progress is being made in improving housing for the poor. It is well to bear in mind Karl Marx's aphorism on the subject: a peasant hut in the woods is adequate housing until a king's mansion is built next door, at which point it becomes a hovel. What is adequate housing is determined by the standard of civilization, an historical and moral measure, rather than any so-called objective standard. And between 1950 and 1970 a chasm opened up between the income of homeowners and that of renters. In the former year, on the average, owners in the United States had an income 20 percent greater than the average renters; in the latter year the gap reached 50 percent. The same development took place in Gary.[7]

Thus one result of expanding working-class home ownership is a radical increase in the gap between the group living standards of owners and renters, as the pool of renters becomes concentrated along the lower end of the income distribution spectrum.[8]

Moreover, it is not quite so clear from the space and plumbing indicators that central city housing quality has improved in the postwar period. First of all, housing exists in an environment. If the environment exhibits a marked decline in safety (as is the case in Gary's slums) that surely must be weighed as a negative factor in the desirability of the housing. The same holds for all the other conditions of central city life in the present period: racial segregation in the public schools, declining job opportunities as new employment is generated elsewhere, and so on. The relative undesirability of Gary housing has in fact become reason for suburbanization. As one realtor put it:

> In the suburbs, sales are very brisk—$27,000 homes are going as though you were selling them for $10,000. In Gary, which is feeling the effects of changing neighborhoods, soaring taxes, pollution and deteriorating schools, sellers take a beating.[9]

Second, it does not necessarily follow that because central city dwellers have achieved more capacious residences the absolute quality of their housing has improved. It is quite possible that even if the very worst units are being removed from a pool of housing stock that the average quality of the units is simultaneously deteriorating. This can occur, for example, if the overall average age of the housing stock is increasing or if maintenance expenditures have fallen so low that the typical unit is in worse repair than previously. Precisely this course of events took place in Harlem, where the initial housing stock was of superior quality.[10]

I believe that both of these factors are operative in Gary (and in most older central cities) to such an extent that the overall quality of the housing is in actual decline. Despite the fact that Gary is a relatively new city, its housing stock is somewhat older than is true for the nation. While about two-fifths of all American housing was built before the Depression, in Gary this is true of half of all dwelling units.[11] And due to the very low replacement rate, the overall age of the housing maintains a slow but steady rise. Thus, between 1960 and 1970 the proportion of housing units which were over twenty years old increased from three-fifths to two-thirds.[12]

There is also good reason to believe that private maintenance expenditures in Gary have dropped off to the point that the absolute quality of the housing is in decline, as is painfully evident from an even perfunctory examination. For instance, the west side of Gary is the site of luxurious private homes built to house U.S. Steel executives and the most prosperous business and professional people of the city—many of them are virtual mansions. This section of town remained white until the end of the 1960s. Yet despite being the focus of the most intensive effort at housing preservation in the city, this neighborhood's housing stock rapidly and radically deteriorated. The numerous boarded-up windows illustrate the fact that their present owners simply cannot afford to maintain them.

To the extent that spontaneous housing market forces have failed to improve the situation of the mass of renters in Gary, other means to achieve that end can be imagined. One simple one would be a massive redistribution of income to the poor. If this were accomplished by structural reforms in the national political economy, there is no reason to doubt that the "free market" would rapidly respond by providing improved housing to a group able to pay for it. It is outside the scope of this book to address the barriers at a national political level to this outcome, other than to point out that at a minimum it would require a kind of working-class political organization and consciousness which does not seem in the immediate offing. Instead, we will trace the history of federal government efforts to find a solution within the context of the free market in housing.

Federally Subsidized Housing

In 1937 the federal government, as part of its public works programs designed to combat the Depression, adopted legislation to supplement the private housing market by building subsidized low-income housing. This program was supported by a part of the capitalist class, especially manufacturers of building supplies, as well as workers in the construction trades. The criticism of the rest of the business community was muted, since the law was "structured so as to avoid any actual government competition with business. Homes would be built only for those who could not possibly afford to buy them on their own."[13]

To qualify for federal public housing a city had to set up a local public housing agency, although only a minority even among larger cities did so.[14] Gary acted rapidly, setting up the Gary Housing Authority in 1938 and submitting its controversial first plan to the city council in January 1939. The project was supported by the Republican mayor, whose administration managed to overcome the opposition of that part of the business community who regarded the measure as "socialistic."

According to the official history of the Gary Housing Authority, the intervention of the United States Steel Corporation was decisive in overcoming local opposition. Corporation spokesman H. S. Norton—who was also president of the Chamber of Commerce—testified that the project would not undermine the private housing market because it was intended for people who could not afford private home ownership. "Furthermore," he added, "the construction of 600 to 700 living units would provide homes for many of our steelworkers earning less than $1,000 a year—and there are many such."[15]

As Norton so candidly stated, this support was not entirely unselfish. Since the housing was to be paid for by the federal government it would not lead to an increased local property tax burden for U.S. Steel, allowing the corporation to appear as a proponent of its workers' welfare in accordance with its traditional paternalistic policies. And by supporting the provision of cheap housing for its poorer workers, it could reduce pressures for increased wages.[16] It is also likely that U.S. Steel was already looking ahead to the forthcoming expansion of production for military preparations. During the following year there was a vast increase in steel employment, and with the outbreak of World War II local employment expanded phenomenally. But there was not sufficient housing for the migrants attracted by new jobs: in 1941 the Gary market had only 437 units (fewer than 1 percent of the total) available for either rental or sale![17]

In place of its original motivation, public housing in Gary as elsewhere "emerged as a legislative device to build housing for defense workers."[18] During the war 787 units of public housing were built; after its close public housing construction virtually ceased. Better off tenants were expelled for exceeding income limits and encouraged to buy suburban homes, and in the conservative Cold War political climate public housing was reduced to a welfare program for the poor. No further public housing was built in Gary until the Korean War, during which boom another 500 units were constructed. Thereafter local opposition—which now included many whites seeking to exclude blacks from their neighborhoods—successfully blocked any further public housing until Hatcher became mayor.

Although Hatcher, with assistance from the federal government and the local business interests supporting urban renewal, was able to overcome this roadblock, he did so in the context of a collapsed private housing market. (It will be recalled that after the Korean War ended older industrial cities such as Gary were effectively "redlined" by their financial communities, who found suburban investment more profitable.[19]) While during the 1950s as many as 1,300 units of privately financed housing were built in Gary annually, in the 1960s this rate dropped off sharply, to fewer than 300 units a year. This catastrophe had already taken place by the time Hatcher achieved office. In a speech during his first year of office he summed up the situation as of 1968:

> Between 1960 and 1965, 859 units of multifamily new construction were built. In the same five year period, 830 units were demolished. Thus the net addition to the rental housing stock averaged about six units per year—a not very impressive figure.
>
> This year . . . there were a total of 182 units of private construction underway, but our rate of demolition of nonrepairable and structurally unsafe dwellings are running at a rate of almost 200 units a year. Thus, old buildings are being destroyed as fast as new ones are constructed. I am afraid that, absent some sudden and unexpected change, we cannot expect the private sector to be very helpful.[20]

Over the past decade, private housing construction in Gary has essentially ceased, running at about 50 units per year. Thus, federally subsidized low-income housing, intended only as a minor supplement to the free market, has come to constitute the entirety of new housing in Gary, Indiana.

The 862 units of public housing built over this decade obviously has been desultory in relation to the local need.[21] While determining the local "need," as we have already seen, is no simple task, the absence of an objective standard hardly precludes us from making a sensible judgment on the matter. The minimum estimates are those put forth by the various federal commissions studying the problem; these generally place the proportion of those needing better quality housing at one-tenth of all families. Probably a better standard is one which takes into account the situation of poor families whose incomes are so low that purchasing private housing results in great economic hardship. (Over half of renters with annual family incomes of less than $7,000 are currently paying more than 35 percent of their income for housing.) If we take this factor into consideration, a full fifth of American families should be considered "housing deprived."[22]

Actually, Gary was already relatively well served by public housing at the time Hatcher became mayor. The 1,400 units constituted almost 3 percent of the local housing stock—double the national average. In the early 1960s a bare 0.2 percent of the federal budget was allocated to public housing subsidies. Only one-tenth of those officially defined as "poor" by the government have public housing, and only 6 percent of families with incomes below $5,000 receive any form of federal housing assistance. Despite the large increase in government housing expenditures in the late 1960s, the average public housing tenant is relatively poorer than was the case a decade previously. (For instance, the percentage of public housing tenants on welfare rose during the decade of the 1960s from 35 percent to 70 percent.)[23]

The irony of this situation, which we will look at in more detail when we examine the tax structure of the city, is that direct federal tax subsidies to families with incomes below $5,000 for purposes of housing cost about $2.5 billion a year, but indirect federal tax benefits for families with incomes above $15,000 a year (in the form of tax deductions for expenses associated with mortgages and local property taxes) are $4.2 billion.[24] In short, as with all government "transfer payments" to the poor, the scale is mean and grudging in comparison both to the need and to government benefits for the well-to-do.[25] When Hatcher became mayor the average income of the public housing tenants in Gary was $2,500; yet only a third of the population with annual incomes below $3,000 had access to public housing. Since the government income cut-off point for public housing in Gary was $5,200, there were 8,500 families who qualified economically for such housing, yet only 1,400 received it.[26]

The total addition to Gary public housing under Mayor Hatcher effectively met only one-tenth of the local need. Given the vast disproportion between the scale of the housing problem of the poor and the subsidy provided by the federal government the result could hardly be otherwise. If the people desperately needing such housing in Gary were to be served, federal housing expenditures for subsidized housing would have to multiply tenfold: to $20 to $30 billion a year. Lacking a major restructuring of national political power there is no prospect for this kind of development.

Urban Renewal

Public housing for the poor was not the only form of government subsidized new construction in Gary: the other program that had a major impact on the community's housing stock was urban renewal. In Gary, as in most cities, the effect of urban renewal on the local housing situation has proven distinctly harmful. From its origins through 1977, the net result of urban renewal in Gary has been to reduce the number of housing units by 2,400.[27] The program has thus more than counterbalanced the total benefits of both public housing and the private housing market during Hatcher's tenure in office. To understand how, it is necessary to clear away some popular misconceptions about urban renewal.

From its outset, urban renewal has been class-biased legislation, in that its function has been to aid economically that fraction of the capitalist class whose profits depend upon downtown central city sales. As we have already seen, after World War II powerful market forces (stimulated by federal government tax and transport policies) led to rapid suburbanization, a process which in turn resulted in a relative decline in central business districts. After the federal enabling legislation of 1949 those cities with older housing stock and a larger concentration of poor and black inhabitants moved most rapidly to initiate urban renewal programs.[28]

Urban renewal functioned to remove poor people from the core of the city in the hope of making downtown more economically viable. Thus by 1972, 1 million people—almost two-thirds of them black—had been forced to relocate as a result of urban renewal programs.[29] Far more units were demolished in the course of the program than were built to replace them as densely crowded central city tracts were replaced by commercial structures and luxury housing subsidies were granted to those cities which initiated urban renewal programs. As early as 1961 the federal urban renewal program had contributed $1.3 billion to 574 projects.[30] Once a municipal redevelopment authority was in operation, it could declare an area blighted, condemn it, and automatically purchase all the sites in the area at "fair market value." Jerome Rothenberg summarizes the redevelopment process:

> Land assembly is followed by demolition of structures in the site (clearance) and preparation of the land for development. . . . [A]ny families displaced as a result of this clearance are relocated elsewhere. . . . The next step is the sale or lease of the area to a private redeveloper; but sometimes part of the area is given to a government agency for construction of public housing or other public purpose. Under the private redeveloper, the area is typically subjected to significant change in land use—often high-rise or large-scale housing projects for people in the upper-middle-income bracket, and . . . modern commercial centers.[31]

Despite the federal subsidies, which approximate two-thirds of the difference in cost between the original purchase price and land preparation cost by the urban renewal authority and the below-market subsidized price at which it is sold to the developer, cities were slow to take advantage of urban renewal. As late as 1963 (fourteen years after the federal government initiated urban renewal), only two-thirds of larger cities had begun even one such project, and only a minority of smaller cities had done so.[32]

The New Haven "Model"

Gary began its first urban renewal project in 1960. But before discussing the politics that surrounded the initiation and course of redevelopment in that city, it will be useful to make a slight detour and discuss urban renewal in New Haven, Connecticut. New Haven was the first city to initiate a major urban renewal program. Also, because the most important pluralist study of local government—Robert Dahl's *Who Governs?*—devoted major attention to that city's urban renewal program, it is hardly an exaggeration to state that the dominant popular conception of redevelopment comes from Dahl's rendition of events in New Haven.[33]

In sharp conflict with populist "power elite" approaches, Dahl argued that after the New Deal reforms local government was no longer the instrument of a ruling class. Instead, power is in the hands of governmental leaders who in turn are responsive to the mass electorate; the economic elite is both split internally and relatively passive politically. Dahl uses his study of urban renewal in New Haven to advance the pluralist thesis that the state is not subject to ruling-class hegemony. To demonstrate this in the case of New Haven's urban renewal program requires some subtlety, particularly since Dahl agrees that the capitalist class in New Haven is "frequently influential on specific decisions, particularly when these directly involve business prosperity"; that urban renewal involved such prosperity; and that municipal leaders will not undertake significant policy initiatives against their united opposition.[34]

Moreover, Dahl concedes that the local government officials "took the major outlines of the socioeconomic structure as given," there was no working-class demand for redevelopment, members of the capitalist class made up the largest group of those involved with redevelopment, and "downtown property owners and construction contractors" gained the most directly, at least initially. A mere fifty property holders owned almost a third of the assessed value of the city's real property. What then, is left of Dahl's pluralism beyond its nomenclature? As best as I can tell, it is that the business community, on its own, would not have initiated or carried out urban renewal—their support was a necessary condition, but not a sufficient one. What was also essential (and what Dahl argues the historical record of redevelopment reveals) was the initiative of the mayor. The mayor and his administration thus get the credit for the program: they put together the supraclass popular coalition which made urban renewal possible.[35]

More recent investigation—using the original data on which Dahl based his conclusions as well as additional sources—suggests that Dahl's account is probably inaccurate in attributing to the mayor even this much autonomy, underestimating the extent to which a concensus had already developed among larger capitalists in New Haven on behalf of the program well before he took office. At most, Mayor Lee catalyzed redevelopment.[36] The other weakness in Dahl's analysis is that he explicitly refuses to take into account which groups benefited and which lost, an omission that undermines his theory: when the outcome of the program is taken into account, it is obvious that redevelopment in New Haven was sharply class biased.

Before the federal government passed its urban renewal legislation, the effect of government housing programs in New Haven was to add 300 units to the housing stock. Between 1949 and 1957, during the initial stage of redevelopment covered by Dahl's study, the effect was a net reduction of 2,900 units.[37] And in the period from 1957 to 1969:

> Redevelopment has demolished about 5,000 living units of the poor in New Haven . . . but has built only about 1,500, of which about 793 have been luxury housing and 445 middle-income, with only 12 low-income public-housing units, and 257 for the elderly. . . . All the rest of New Haven's public housing, and not too much of it at that, was built before Redevelopment, under earlier administrations.[38]

The accompanying social devastation wreaked upon New Haven's poor and the fabric of that city's urban life is brilliantly detailed by architect-planner Harris Stone, who was employed during that period by New Haven's redevelopment program.[39]

Urban renewal is, in short, a program on behalf of a fraction of the capitalist class (namely, larger commercial, banking, real estate, and construction groups in the central cities), organized by the state apparatus, and carried through at the direct expense of those displaced by it (namely, small businesses and poor workers). Local business interests operating through political machines sought to reverse through redevelopment the colossal forces which were undermining central city economies and their personal profits. These groups were prepared to destroy their cities in order to save them: for instance, Gary's redevelopment plan called for "the relocation of no fewer than 40,000 persons."[40]

Redevelopment in Gary

In the light of the devastating effects of early urban renewal programs on local black populations, and the sharp response of political opposition to "Negro removal" during the civil rights movement, federal agencies supervising the disbursement of funds came to insist that something be done for the poor. In practice, that something was the creation of new public housing into which those who were displaced could be relocated. Despite the efforts of local chambers of commerce to separate the two programs, by the mid-1960s it was apparent that cities that wished to obtain federal grants for their urban renewal projects would have to overcome local opposition to public housing. Thus, in many cities chambers of commerce moved from bitter opposition to public housing to reluctant support.[41]

Precisely this sequence of events unfolded in Gary. Its local urban renewal enabling legislation, passed in 1955, carefully insulated it from direct popular control. A five-man board of trustees was created, two of whose members are appointed by the mayor, two by the president of the city council, and one by the judge of the Lake County Circuit Court, with staggered four-year terms. In turn, these trustees appoint five commissioners, and the commissioners in turn choose the executive secretary, who runs the Redevelopment Commission.[42]

Under these circumstances, it was hardly surprising that after his first term in office, Hatcher was still operating with the same executive secretary chosen in 1960. The individual concerned was reputed to have close ties to the Gary banking community, and he absolutely refused to help in the mayor's reelection campaign. By the time he was replaced by someone more congenial, urban renewal in the city had essentially ended.[43]

By the time Hatcher became mayor, about 1,500 units of housing had been demolished by redevelopment; only 132 new units (occupied by black middle-income families) had taken their place.[44] The sequence of events of the first renewal project was classic. This project was announced in 1957, but the demolition of the structures on the chosen tract in the Pulaski neighborhood was not completed until 1963. From the moment the area was designated for redevelopment, the housing stock underwent radical deterioration. Even prior to the Redevelopment Commission's official condemnation and purchase of the land, owners stopped making repairs. Plumbing, heating, and electrical systems were simply not replaced and some units became uninhabitable. Many families thus found themselves compelled to move out of the neighborhood even before the redevelopment process formally began.

Between the time of commission acquisition and actual demolition housing conditions continued their catastrophic course downward. For instance:

> Frozen pipes were a nemesis because the only way the staff could combat this hazard was to temporarily move families who lived in houses [in the area] to where one or more units were vacated on site when suitable units became available; or to maintain a 45-degree temperature in the vacated units. It was impossible to maintain a 45-degree temperature in the majority of the units because most of them had no central heating, but had been heated by space heaters. It was impractical to place space heaters in vacated units because of vandalism or theft.[45]

For poor families compelled to continue to live in the neighborhood until demolition and relocation, this process often meant several years of housing conditions far more appalling than would have been the case in the absence of governmental intervention in the market.

For the petty bourgeoisie with businesses in the neighborhood, the process spelled economic collapse. (The twenty-five businesses in Pulaski shared $30,000 for all their moving and relocation costs.) Losing their neighborhood markets, many of these entrepreneurs simply ceased to exist.[46] The process was an economic disaster for many small property owners in the urban renewal area as well. An attorney managing one such structure in the ambit of Gary's redevelopment program vividly described the process:

> In Gary they started publishing reports of redevelopment areas and outlined them geographically. Gentlemen, within four and five years, those areas looked like bombed-out Berlin at the end of World War II.
>
> I will give you an example. I handled this particular condemnation case . . . I would say this [six-unit house] had a true cash value four or five years ago of $25,000. . . . They couldn't get the people who were tenants there to stay . . . so she boarded up the building.
>
> If you saw the building on the day that the Redevelopment Commission made the offer to her, they made an offer of $1,200. . . . Everything in that building was ripped out. The floor joists were ripped out. Just a completely vandalized wrecked building, and this is what happens . . . to nearly every building in the redevelopment area.[47]

The hundreds of displacees—96 percent of whom were black—also largely were losers, except for the one-fourth who were fortunate enough to be able to move into Gary Housing Authority low-income units. (Families relocated by urban renewal were placed at the top of the waiting list for public housing; in Gary almost no one else ever actually got to move in.)[48] Families who did not obtain public housing not only were compelled to move against their will, but generally found themselves "in housing considerably more expensive than their previous homes."[49]

Perhaps the most invidious part of this displacement process has been its repeating nature. A substantial minority of those compelled to leave their neighborhood in Pulaski moved to the area designated as Midtown West, in the main poor black central city ghetto. The influx of additional families contributed to a deterioration of the housing and community fabric of this new neighborhood, which in turn was designated for destruction—

in part because of this induced overcrowding. Thus numerous families found themselves repeatedly displaced by urban renewal, a process which entails the most damaging social consequences.[50]

To achieve this socially dubious effect, the federal government subsidized the project by $2.6 million and the people of Gary paid another $1.4 million, through the mechanism of municipal bonds which must be repaid with interest.[51] It is extremely doubtful that additional property taxes on the new property will ever amount to enough to justify this expenditure of the taxpayers' money. Thus, the beneficiaries of redevelopment are the businesses which actually participated in the process of demolition and reconstruction; the banks and lawyers who processed the bond issue; and the wealthy bondholders who obtained taxfree interest on their investment.

The one other major redevelopment project prior to Hatcher's inauguration was even more abortive: this was the Gateway Project in the heart of the downtown commercial district. The 2.4-acre parcel did not have residents and the city purchased the site and then sold it to a private developer at a net loss of $400,000. The theory behind this project was that it would revitalize the downtown commercial area and "help Gary to become a convention center." Needless to say, there was no mention of the fact that Gary had been a convention center before the Depression nor what factors in the political economy had caused it to cease to be one. Had this historical process been analyzed, it might have been obvious that the effort was completely utopian. Central to the project was a 300-room Holiday Inn, which ran at a deficit from its construction in 1969. It requested and obtained special relief from the local property tax, and ultimately went bankrupt. The building is currently boarded up, with the city hoping somehow to find the money to convert it into public housing.[52]

Closely tied to the Gateway Project was another central business district renewal activity. Indiana state enabling legislation of 1964 permitted the creation in 1967 of the Gary Downtown Improvement Association, which had the power to finance and administer a redevelopment plan for downtown Gary. Composed of the major capitalists with property interests in the city, it directly determined what new construction would take place in coordination with the Gateway Project and other Redevelopment Commission activities. Its four officers were the president of the largest bank, the editor of the Gary *Post-Tribune* (a major downtown property owner, as well as integrally tied via advertising revenues to downtown commercial interests), and the owners of two major department stores.[53]

Despite some ambitious brochures and plans, however, little was actually accomplished. The renewal proposals were all based on expanding the local market by convincing well-off families who had left Gary to return. And since that was unrealistic given the overall context of suburbanization, all that was actually accomplished was the provision of additional downtown parking spaces for commuters.[54] In the event, as in the case of private market housing, the local capitalists considered it too risky to undertake substantial new commercial investments in the face of the economic decline of the city.

Notwithstanding these abysmal initial results, the early 1960s saw increasing support for urban renewal among Gary's capitalists and professional community, of which Hatcher was the beneficiary.[55] On the basis of their desire to continue and expand urban renewal (and with the help of the federal government), Hatcher was able to unblock funds for more public housing and for housing code enforcement. But the cost of this political trade-off was very high. At the end of 1977 the effect of Gary's urban renewal program had been to demolish 2,900 housing units, replaced by 476 new units (of which 220 were public housing).[56]

Hatcher's administration had thus supervised and supported the destruction of a large chunk of the center of the city. There is now a gaping swath in the center of Gary three blocks wide and about ten blocks long. In the heart of the central city, there is a vast empty plain. In this entire tract constituting Midtown West there stands a lonely high-rise public housing project for the aged and a few trees. The local planning agencies, with unconscious irony, now call for the development of this land into a linear park and refer to it as "underdeveloped land." It stands as mute testimony to the disaster of urban renewal in the context of a declining local economy.[57]

By taking a somewhat longer time span than Dahl did in investigating New Haven's urban renewal, it is possible to reach a more sober assessment of redevelopment as a public policy. Since planners, following the priorities of the larger businesses in the community, were concerned with making policy serve private profit, in the early 1960s the Redevelopment Commission officially estimated that 20,000 of the 54,000 units of housing in Gary were either "unsound" or suffering from "major deficiencies."

While we have seen that a considerable fraction of Gary's housing is inadequate, this most expansive method of labeling half of the city as worthy of destruction really served to make it possible to designate any part of the city as a redevelopment area. It is hardly surprising that the commission's grandiose hopes were for a twenty-year cycle of destruction and rebuilding, including "the relocation of no fewer than 40,000 persons and perhaps 1,000 businesses." Their program explicitly stated that a large fraction of the petty bourgeoisie in the affected areas— "pool halls, neighborhood grocery stores, restaurants, taverns, used clothing stores, junk yards, used furniture stores"—would be annihilated in the process.[58]

Initially, many of Gary's larger capitalists were unsympathetic to urban renewal. By the late 1950s real estate, construction, and larger commercial interests were favorable, but others, including U.S. Steel, were not. They saw no direct payoff and feared a rise in their property taxes to pay for the costs of the projects. The Gary Chamber of Commerce refused to support the renewal program until it became clear that the infusion of federal funds was not going to harm the larger businesses not directly involved, when their opposition declined. (The petty bourgeoisie who were directly harmed turned out to be unable to influence policy, and the working class and black population remained essentially quiescent throughout.) By the mid-60s U.S. Steel moved to a position of neutrality toward redevelopment, and in 1968 the Chamber of Commerce actually endorsed the program.

Later, as urban renewal proceeded, the intervention of the federal government increased. While federal regulations required that displaced families be adequately rehoused, Gary's Redevelopment Commission, like many others, was able in its earlier projects to submit false reports and avoid this responsibility.[59] But in the wake of growing popular opposition to the effects of redevelopment, and in the course of "Great Society" reforms that called for increased "citizen participation," the federal authorities gradually began to get more strict in requiring local redevelopment commissions actually to do something for the victims of the demolition process.

Specifically, the federal housing agencies required as a precondition for all federal grants to municipalities that a "Workable Program" be approved that included some ameliorative measures with regard to public housing and building department housing code enforcement. Gary was so remiss in carrying this out that in 1967 the federal government actually put a freeze on the disbursement of funds.

Hatcher came into office at a point when the federal government was already attempting to pressure the city into taking some affirmative action on building new public housing and improving the operations of the building department. Mayor Hatcher worked cooperatively with the Department of Housing and Development (taking advantage of his close political relationship with the national Democratic administration, which wished his venture as mayor to prove successful) to obtain these concessions as the price for continued urban renewal.

Essentially, what took place during Hatcher's first year of office is that the federal officials informed the Redevelopment Commission that the Workable Program for 1968 would not be approved unless it included provisions for these housing reforms, meaning the city would not receive its federal subsidies. The commission then got those businessmen who were most favorable to redevelopment to lobby their fellow businessmen until the Chamber of Commerce took an official position favorable to redevelopment. At that point machine-backed resistance by the city council collapsed. The council agreed to permit new public housing to be constructed, and to fund additional building department inspectors for housing code enforcement.[60]

Hatcher and his staff, of which I was a member, took this event as a victory over the machine and its racism: we had obtained money for new public housing for poor blacks and funds to enforce adequate housing standards for renters. I was assigned the task of preparing the new Workable Program which, upon the pledge to provide adequate rehousing of the displacees, was approved. The federal money was made available, and part of it even reached local black contractors, who for the first time were afforded an opportunity to participate in the demolition contracts. Over the years, the share of these funds going to minority businesses has steadily increased.[61]

It is unclear whether if Hatcher had tried to block further urban renewal he would have been able to achieve even the few hundred units of public housing which were built. I am inclined to believe that with sufficient determination and persistence he could have overcome the resistance of the capitalists and their political machine. But this is speculative, because that policy option was never even considered. Both the mayor and his advisors (with the exception of myself) considered urban renewal to be a positive program and believed its rationale of improving the local economic situation of the city. Furthermore, Hatcher was concerned to achieve results from high-visibility programs to show his constituents that he was doing something on their behalf.[62] As he observed to me at the time, "If even one of these federal programs 'clicks,' we're in." Moreover, the combined urban renewal–public housing program was touted as a great success and doubtless believed to be such by many people in the community.

But in fact, the outcome was most dubious. Even if one assumes that all of the public housing built in Gary during Hatcher's administration occurred only because of the political concession to redevelopment, the overall balance is distinctly negative. In place of the 2,900 units destroyed by urban renewal, the combined new construction due to public housing and redevelopment is 1,120 units. No one can fairly assess this outcome as a triumph of public policy redistribution toward the poor and black people of Gary.

Rehabilitation Programs

If efforts at the production of new low-cost rental units failed, so too did those to maintain and rehabilitate the existing housing stock. On the basis of my experience in the Gary building department, I estimate that roughly half of Gary's black renters live in housing which falls below the minimum standards set by the city's building code.[63] Bringing this housing up to code standard and preventing the rest of the rental stock from falling below it would be the largest single possible step to ensure adequate and decent housing for Gary's poor—one not met by the present private housing market. The reason for this is that despite paying a much larger proportion of their total income for housing than the rest of the population, the amount which the poor can afford in rent is inadequate for landlords to fully conserve the existing rental stock. This is especially true for blacks where as a result of segregation rental costs are particularly high.[64]

The problem in Gary has been further exacerbated by the "redlining" of neighborhoods by local banks and national insurance companies. Higher interest rates on loans and obstacles to obtaining mortgages at all make it particularly difficult for landlords to make improvements in the existing stock, which has led to a city-wide decline in property values.[65]

Rather than acting to overcome this bias, federal government policy has reinforced it. Federal housing legislation exhibits a distinct priority on behalf of new housing over rehabilitation: the government subsidizes the building of ten times as many new units as it does repairs of existing ones, despite some good evidence that the total cost of rehabilitation is less per unit than new construction.[66] This bias may reflect the greater congressional influence of large-scale builders and financial institutions that prefer major new construction projects to smaller scale rehabilitation projects arguably more suited to community groups and petty-bourgeois interests. This bias is reinforced by the federal tax structure. The tax incentives also encourage the construction of suburban single-family units as opposed to urban multifamily ones, and acceleration of replacement of older buildings. Federal tax policy, which leaves municipal governments dependent largely on the property tax for revenue, further accentuates the phenomenon of urban housing disinvestment: a fear of increased assessments tends to discourage landlords from investing in repairs, and the burden of high property taxes leaves less capital available for improving the quality of homes.[67]

Against such structural obstacles to the provision of adequate housing for the poor, all that exists is the housing code, a mechanism which is, as one might guess, inadequate to the task. Gary's not particularly stringent housing code, dating from 1949, sets the minimum conditions for all dwelling units in the city. Enforcement of the housing and building codes is vested in the municipal building department.[68] In principle, these codes set a minimum "floor" below which the quality of housing units cannot fall, and mandate their owners to carry out the necessary maintenance expenditures to achieve this result. In practice, Gary's codes, like those throughout the nation, have proven unenforceable.[69]

Like minimum wage statutes and other laws designed to force capitalists to behave in a manner contrary to the logic of profit maximization, building code enforcement faces systematic efforts by landlords to avoid compliance. Since slum rents are already as high as the market will bear, enforcement of code standards translates into a considerable economic burden for the landlord.[70] Since numerous landlords would find themselves operating at a loss if they obeyed the law, to prevent the abandonment of the building, substantial subsidies, from either the government or large-scale private financial institutions, would have to be provided.[71] Lacking these, Gary's enforcement effort foundered.

Prior to Hatcher's taking office, there was scarcely even a pretense at enforcement, in exchange for which local contractors and landlords were expected to make campaign contributions or pay outright bribes, as is generally the case in machine-dominated cities.[72] Appointment to the building department was a matter of patronage: building inspectors had to have prior consent of the building trades unions. And no blacks were appointed prior to 1964. Despite the radical understaffing of the department, morale was very high. Some patronage workers did not even have to appear except for their paychecks; others averaged a two-hour working day and held second jobs. With the informal perquisites of the job, it was evident that the staff was enjoying a standard of living far above the formal pay scales.

The department was assigned only 1 percent of the municipal budget, which in 1968 amounted to $225,000, enough to support a total staff of only twenty-five. Yet the staff was responsible for not only all the housing units but also the building, electrical, plumbing, and sewer codes for all residential, commercial, and industrial property.[73] Before Hatcher managed to get eight additional inspectors (by federal intervention) the number assigned to housing was so few that we estimated it would take forty-four years to inspect each housing unit.[74] It is no overstatement to say that the department simply lacked an administrative plan for code enforcement. For instance, there was literally no standardized inspection form. In order for a violation to be taken to court, a demolition order to be issued, or a halt to be called to new construction for irregularities, the procedure under the Democratic Party machine required the personal approval of the mayor. Needless to say, it was rarely forthcoming. Generally, upon the payment of a small bribe, the inspector "misplaced" the case record containing the historical record of violations, making enforcement impossible in any event.[75]

During the two years before Hatcher's election, civil rights groups pressured the city to enforce the housing code, and the city took seventy-nine cases to court. But no city attorney was assigned to any of these cases, guaranteeing that procedural irregularities would result in dismissals. In only one case was a fine imposed.[76]

A similar blockage with respect to enforcement of the building code for new construction was a notorious Gary tradition.

> The attention of the Building Commissioner [in the mid-50s] was called to nondescript housing being built in the areas of occupancy by Negroes. His office was aware . . . that individual builders were the major violators of regulations [and claimed] it has been handicapped because of the lack of personnel. . . . Mention was made of the fact that during 1952 and 1953 the Department had taken several cases into court which were continuously postponed. More was accomplished, the Department feels, through its own procedure without court action.[77]

Hatcher assigned to my office the task of investigating the

internal operations of the building department. My staff and I exposed considerable systematic corruption, which forced the resignation of numerous long-time department personnel and the hiring of new administrators pledged to carry out Hatcher's campaign promise of vigorous housing code enforcement.[78] Determined to take every practical step to achieve code enforcement, we began with a series of internal administrative reforms, including standardizing inspections forms and procedures, requiring a full day's work from the inspectors, transferring personnel from other tasks to housing inspection, and quickly filling the eight new positions with sympathetic workers. Instead of simply responding to individual complaints, we adopted a policy of systematic inspection of all units in targeted neighborhoods. Consequently, within six months, we achieved more inspections than in the previous two years.

Since some owners complied voluntarily, increased inspection yielded a modest increase in housing brought up to code standard. The problem, however, was that in the majority of instances where the landlord was intransigent, it was essentially impossible to compel change, despite what seemed like very favorable legislation providing the department with several powerful legal remedies.

The municipal code provides that the city could condemn a structure to demolition without compensation to the owner if it is

> so damaged, decayed, dilapidated, unsanitary, unsafe or vermin infested . . . that it creates a serious hazard to the health and safety of the occupants or to the public; [or if] because of its general condition or location is unsanitary or otherwise dangerous to the health, safety, morals and general welfare of the inhabitants or of the public.

This law requires the city's Board of Public Works to hold a condemnation procedure, which is essentially an internal administrative hearing; to prevent a final condemnation order the owner must appeal to the state courts.[79]

The Board of Public Works, entirely appointed by Mayor Hatcher, assured us that it would issue such an order whenever the building department requested one. Practically, however, it required an accompanying contract to actually demolish the structure, since a vacant slum building is an open invitation to illicit entries, followed by fires and real danger to the entire neighborhood. And that was the snag: the fund for demolition contracts was only $50,000 a year, barely enough to cover those cases where abandonment had occurred spontaneously.[80]

There was another problem, as the landlords full well realized, in that when a building is condemned the tenants are necessarily evicted. In the absence of a substantial number of empty low-cost units, it was simply impractical for the city to dump large numbers of families on the streets.[81]

The second enforcement mechanism was even more elegant from a formal juridical standpoint, and could also in principle be implemented by an internal administrative procedure within the control of the Hatcher administration. The housing code prescribes that after presentation of a described violation, a landlord has thirty days to make the repairs. If he fails to do so, and then fails to abide by a compliance deadline set by the Board of Public Works, the building department itself can have the repairs contracted for at the landlord's expense. It does so by acting as the owner's agent, contracting out the work (with a clause providing that the city "shall in no way be obligated to pay the cost of the work involved"). The contractor can collect against the owner by means of a mechanics lien. In Indiana, the mechanics lien is superior to all other mortgages on the property and is enforceable by the state courts "within one year of its creation."

But this procedure also was unworkable, since no private contractor was willing to bid on such a job. Given the vagaries of court enforcement and the delay in court decisions (which averaged several years), it would be foolhardy to do such work without prior payment, and, of course, the municipality lacked the sums at hand to make loans of this sort. Only with legislation to speed up court procedure plus adequate funding could some real progress be possible.

The third mechanism involved going to the municipal court, a proceeding that has failed in cities throughout the nation.[82] In this sequence, after a recalcitrant landlord is subjected to a Board of Public Works hearing, the case is forwarded to the city attorney's office, which prepares it for the City Court. The latter can issue a court order requiring the repair and fine the landlord.

But the city attorney's office was unwilling to prepare these cases: law department attorneys informed the building department administrators that "legal defects" made court action unfeasible. When I intervened, and demanded in a heated exchange with the staff attorneys that these defects be specified, I was informed that the city attorneys had more important responsibilities than taking to court the cases of "poor, lazy, good-for-nothings" who were themselves responsible for the damage to their apartments.

Thereafter, the mayor's office ordered me not to intervene further in the autonomous functioning of the law department or continue my participation in the building department's activities. The attorneys had threatened to resign as a group if I did, claiming that they were irreplaceable. While complaints from the attorneys (who did not want their work load increased) initiated the process by which I was excluded from effective participation in housing code enforcement, this was not the whole story; at several junctures, my offer to recruit outstanding "public interest" lawyers for implementing various reforms was rebuffed. I believe the mayor was reluctant to initiate a bitter confrontation with Gary's property-owning stratum, particularly in the absence of serious organized mass pressure for such action from the black community.

And it is likely that even if the city had acted vigorously in taking such cases to the City Court, it would have proven futile. Court policy was to routinely dismiss them on alleged technical defects. Even on the rare occasions on which fines were levied, they were trivial in comparison with the cost of repairs.[83]

This resistance by the law department explains the peculiar pattern of cases forwarded for enforcement action by the building department (see Table 6.1). In the latter part of 1968 and early 1969, when there was an effort to carry out enforcement proceedings against landlords violating the codes, the building department prepared a relatively large number of cases. But when it became apparent that the law department would refuse to act, they essentially gave up.

In its *1976 Annual Report*, the building department plaintively calls for meeting two apparently hopeless goals: "1) obtain a minimum of two attorneys to prepare legal work for court hearings; and 2) find an avenue to get flagrant violators of the housing and building codes into court on a continuous basis."[84]

Table 6.1
Cases to Board of Works or City Attorney

1966	1967	1968	1969	1970	1971
109	84	402	180	35	46

Source: Gary Building Department, *Annual Reports, 1966-1972.*

Other enforcement efforts by the building department proved equally abortive. For instance, despite a relatively auspicious beginning, there was no follow-through on a program initiated to suspend the licenses of small contractors found guilty of consumer fraud. Nor was the building department successful in efforts to force the Redevelopment Commission to maintain property it had obtained through eminent domain prior to demolition at code standard. (The Redevelopment Commission naturally preferred tenants to move out "voluntarily" so as not to require relocation, and it was not anxious to be saddled with the financial burden of rehabilitating the very structures it was intending to destroy.) Hatcher ordered the two agencies to work out a compromise. But all the building department was able to achieve in the absence of the mayor's partisan intervention was a settlement under which the redevelopment authorities would make minimum repairs to keep the families dry and supplied with heat.

In short, despite a radically different rhetoric, the actual performance of the Hatcher administration in housing code enforcement was not very different from that under the machine.

The underlying reason was that it was not really possible to achieve genuine compliance. The economic prerequisites, namely massive subsidies for rehabilitation, ample cheap new housing, and large numbers of vacancies for moving displaced families, were simply not available.[85]

Vigorous enforcement efforts in the absence of these factors result in community strife without palpable improvement in housing conditions. Faced with this, the mayor followed a moderate and prudent policy: he permitted his administration to make efforts to achieve code enforcement, but he would not intervene to provide additional support; and when serious resistance from those benefiting from the status quo seemed on the horizon, he quietly backed off.

Conclusion

Hatcher's housing policy represented reform within the existing political economy. Attempts to increase the new housing stock and to preserve the existing housing both failed, and the first decade of Hatcher's administration (1968 to 1978) probably saw an actual decline in the absolute quality of Gary's housing.[86]

Nevertheless, the quality of housing available to blacks actually may have improved over the decade. "White flight" from Gary (doubtless accelerated by the installation of a black administration in City Hall) was so rapid that blacks probably were able to move into previously white neighborhoods with superior housing stock at a rate more rapid than the decline of all the community's housing.[87] In this ironic sense, "filtering" in Gary has led to the simultaneous deterioration of the city's housing and a modest short-run improvement in rental housing at the disposal of the black community. As Gary becomes an all-black city, however, the prospect is for a very rapid absolute and relative decline in the population's housing situation. The failure of housing reform in Gary is thus likely to prove even more damaging in the future than it has in the present.

7

Tax Politics as Class Politics

In general, lack of funds restricted or precluded the possible municipal reforms envisioned by the Hatcher administration. In the context of a declining local economy, it was difficult simply to maintain preexisting levels of public services, let alone initiate new programs. There were, of course, substantial federal funds made available for activities such as urban renewal and a local poverty program, but, in general, the city was, and is, in a tight financial situation.

The problem is particularly acute in Gary because of a cumulative neglect of expenditures for development and maintenance of the physical infrastructure (such as streets, sewers, and parks) and an historic pattern of small budgets, especially for departments dealing with services.[1] As a symbolic example, for the past couple of years, every time I return to Gary for a visit I have to enter City Hall through the basement; the main entrance is closed indefinitely due to a lack of funds to repair crumbling mortar.

Ironically, this municipal impoverishment exists in the midst of splendid wealth. The Gary Works is a fantastically valuable productive facility, one quite able to support a very high level of local government expenditure, were it properly taxed.[2] Indeed, it is no exaggeration to state that for its size Gary is one of the wealthiest communities in the nation. Relying in part upon my experience as director of the Office of Program Coordination during the period, this chapter details the means by which the corporation managed to stalemate our efforts to obtain a portion of that wealth for the municipal coffers, and so protect its profits from redistribution to the Gary working class.

Such an outcome is hardly surprising within a Marxist perspective, in which the fundamental social reality of American society is the class struggle between the capitalist class controlling the economy and polity and the vast mass of the population whom they exploit and oppress. By contrast, by denying the existence of inherently antagonistic social classes, pluralist political theorists are able to conclude that rather than being an instrument of capitalist rule, the state expresses popular sovereignty; its government therefore counteracts capitalist economic power in the private market by acting on behalf of the public interest. (This phenomenon is often referred to by pluralists as "the welfare state.") A central aspect of this process is often claimed to be the use of tax power to redistribute income from the possessing classes to the working people, thus overcoming the most inimical features of the free market.

If such redistribution actually occurred, it would take place through a progressive tax structure, in which the rich capitalists would be compelled to pay a substantially larger proportion of their income and wealth than do the workers. Unfortunately for the pluralists, the overall American tax system is barely progressive. In reality, its effect is to maintain the approximate shares of income which the capitalist market has distributed to the different classes.[3] The tax system works to maintain and buttress the existing class structure and division of wealth in the society, not to reshape it to become more equitable. A Marxist analysis attempts to figure out how—despite the formal ability of the majority to utilize universal suffrage to tax the rich—the capitalist class is able to keep redistribution of income within such narrow limits.

This is a most perplexing question. Notwithstanding rather different social structures and very different levels of working-class organization and militancy, the variations in the distribution of income among the advanced capitalist nations is comparatively small. So too is the effect of different types of governments—whether conservative or reformist.[4] Lester

Thurow seems to suggest that it is a matter of political power; indeed, he asserts that substantial alterations in income distribution within American capitalism would require a social consensus on their behalf on the part of all classes.[5]

This case study of the failure of the Hatcher administration to successfully raise the tax assessment of the Gary Works is a modest contribution to this large theoretical problem. It has the virtue, however, of addressing an aspect of the tax system which has been little studied. While there has been substantial discussion of class biases of the federal tax structure, there has been surprisingly little evaluation of the state-local tax system, even though this is the part of the tax system that is responsible for canceling out the modest progressivity of the federal income tax. This suggests that it is at the level of the state-local taxation that the capitalist class most effectively exerts its hegemony. An examination of tax politics in Gary, Indiana reveals why this is the case.

The Local Property Tax System

Gary relies upon its property tax for virtually all of its locally generated revenue.[6] Approximately two-fifths of this revenue comes from the Gary Works, which in 1971 was assessed by the township assessor at a valuation of $567 million and paid $29 million in property taxes.[7] When Hatcher campaigned for mayor, a central part of his program called for achieving greater equity in the local tax system by increasing the corporation's assessment. This was to lead to both tax relief for individual homeowners and a substantial increase in the provision of social services to the community.[8]

Lacking any realistic prospect of vast increases in subsidies to Gary from the state government, and aware that federal aid to the cities, after the sharp expansion of the 1960s, had clearly peaked, Mayor Hatcher looked to the local property tax as a source of new city funds.[9] The property tax in Gary is levied on industrial, commercial, and residential real property. As we have already seen, the relatively small and declining size of the city's commercial sector essentially precluded this as a practical source.[10] This essentially left two possibilities: increasing the assessments of U.S. Steel or increasing those of the residential property holders.

But when Hatcher took office, the average homeowner in Gary already had an effective property tax that was 50 percent higher than the Indiana average and exceeded the national urban average by 15 percent. In 1970, a typical homeowner with a $10,000 income and home worth $15,000 paid $750 in property taxes.[11] These local taxes were so high that they were a contributing factor to the deterioration of the city's housing stock. As we saw in the previous chapter, disinvestment in Gary's housing was already occurring, a problem which further increases in property taxes (which would have further reduced the funds available for housing maintenance) might well have intensified. In addition, the local population, knowing that Gary's taxes were higher than elsewhere yet municipal amenities inferior, would certainly have viewed major increases as both burdensome and unjust. Nor would this perception have been wrong.

In Gary, as in most cities, the property tax is not only regressive by class, but also racist in its impact. For the poor black renters (for whom such increases would be hidden in their rents), increases would have been particularly onerous. Assessment policies which resulted in affluent white families in the city having their homes assessed at 20 percent or less of their fair market value, while ghetto black homeowners are assessed at 30 percent, are another striking example of the regressive and racist impact of the local property tax.[12]

Both common sense and a process of elimination thus put the Gary Works at the focus of tax reform efforts in Gary. The $29 million paid by the Gary Works in local property taxes in 1971 was a full fifth of all the taxes paid by the corporation in that year.[13] The overall tax climate of U.S. Steel has been one of nominal federal taxes, low Indiana taxes, and low local taxes on its productive facilities.

Indeed, in the period since World War II the tax burden levied by all levels of government on corporations has been steadily declining. In 1954 the federal corporate income tax provided

30 percent of federal revenue; in 1974 it provided only 15 percent. For some industries such as steel, net federal taxes are often nominal:

> A zero tax may . . . occur although there are book profits. The reasons appear to be a combination of investment credits, excessive depreciation, and the benefits for natural resources, the latter being obtained by subsidiaries engaged in that activity and included in a consolidated tax return so that their deductions are applied against the income of the consolidated group.[14]

In 1971 U.S. Steel paid no federal taxes.[15]

State-local corporation taxes have also declined: the share of all state-local revenue obtained from corporations has dropped from 50 percent twenty years ago to about 30 percent currently. Indiana has participated in this national trend. Between 1957 and 1967 the proportion of combined state-local taxes paid by Indiana businesses fell from 37 percent to 29 percent.[16] However, the mixture of taxes varies considerably in different states. Although Indiana's property tax rate is relatively high (about one-quarter above the national average), other taxes run considerably below national averages, resulting in an overall tax burden on corporations slightly below the national average. Thus, the property tax on the Gary Works constitutes 95 percent of all the taxes paid to both the city of Gary and the state of Indiana by U.S. Steel.[17] This is the context which permitted corporation director W. A. Walker (chairman of the board's finance committee) to testify against raises in Gary Works' assessments by pointing out that the Gary Works' property taxes "are the highest we have."[18]

The corporation is clearly determined to prevent any major increase in its property tax to pay for social services for the working class of the city, toward whom its paternalistic impulses have long since disappeared. This stand is buttressed by two additional factors. First, at least some other steel mills in the region and around the country have substantially lower tax burdens. Even though there is no direct price competition between steel companies, for a variety of reasons (such as international competition and the threat of product substitution) they are very concerned with minimizing costs of production. And steel executives are also sensitive to production costs of their rivals, which, if lower than their own, may ultimately lead to a diminished share of the market.

Second, the decline of the Gary economy has left U.S. Steel with an increasing relative burden. In the 1950s the Gary Works paid about one-third of all property taxes collected in the city. By the time Hatcher became mayor, as a result of the continued vitality of the mill and the deterioration of the rest of the city's economic infrastructure, this share had risen to two-fifths.[19]

However, this share has been subject to considerable fluctuation over the past half-century; in the 1920s, for instance, U.S. Steel paid almost half the tax bill, while during the Depression its share fell to one-third.[20] Lacking any means of determining the real worth of property in both the Gary Works and the rest of the community at different historical junctures, it is impossible to state whether U.S. Steel bears more or less of its "fair share" of local taxes than it has at various times in the past. Certainly U.S. Steel executives perceive themselves as unreasonably burdened by recent local tax trends.

My own impression is that it was at the two points in Gary's political history when popular insurgencies gained some control over City Hall—that is, in 1934 when the New Deal coalition gained the mayoralty, and in 1968 when Hatcher's black coalition did so—resulting in greater potential for expanded social services in the community at the expense of capitalist profits, that the corporation demonstrated the most interest in containing municipal expenditures and protecting its traditional valuation on the Gary Works.

From Gary's origins in 1906, U.S. Steel exercised its political power to keep its assessments low, provoking loud cries of complaint from the small business community elements whose interests diverged from those of the corporation. As early as 1908 *The Northern Indianian*, the mouthpiece of these interests, waged a campaign on the subject.[21] Under a series of articles entitled, "Is U.S. Steel Among the Rich Tax Dodgers?" the paper posed the question of whether U.S. Steel paid its proportionate share of local property taxes.

According to *The Northern Indianian*, in 1907 the mill was assessed at $1,573,000. An additional $1,726,000 was assessed for the value of all the land and buildings owned by the Gary Land Company, although it was well known that the land alone had cost the corporation over $7 million. Thus the assessor (who was an employee of U.S. Steel) claimed that between 1907 and 1908 the corporation had invested $693,000 in improvements. But U.S. Steel's own *Annual Report* indicated that during this time it had invested $24 million in the Gary Works. The result of this assessment process was that in 1908 U.S. Steel paid only $75,000 in property taxes instead of the $600,000 an accurate assessment would have yielded.[22]

By 1916, according to the eminent intellectual Randolph S. Bourne, underassessment of the Gary Works was already a local tradition. "The plants of the steel corporation," he wrote, "the most valuable property in the community, were habitually undervalued in the assessments."[23] There is good reason to believe this particular tradition in Gary has been enduring.

The 1971 property tax of $29 million paid by U.S. Steel was based on assessed real worth of $567 million. *The Wall Street Journal* explained how this figure was determined:

> Calumet Township Assessor Tom Fadell says his biggest customer in effect presents its own tax bill. That customer is the U.S. Steel Corp., which supplies its own evaluation on its taxable property there. . . . U.S. Steel won't furnish the township figures on capital investment or depreciation schedules used to arrive at that value because, the company says, such data would aid competitors.[24]

In his Senate testimony the following year Fadell was compelled to admit that he had neither seen U.S. Steel's books (despite the law which provided for access to them), nor carried out a physical inventory of the machinery and equipment. At the end of his testimony, the chairman of the hearing, Senator Edmund Muskie, summed up his understanding of Fadell's testimony: "So what you are saying is that . . . in effect what you get is self-assessment by taxpayers. What they submit is pretty much taken at face value."[25]

Fadell, however, vigorously defended the accuracy of this

assessment, reiterating all of the corporation arguments about high property taxes. Fadell was a protégé of former mayor George Chacharis, Gary's Democratic Party machine boss. He "was a struggling lawyer in 1958 when Chacharis took him under his wing and got him elected assessor. From this advantageous base, Fadell managed, within a few short years and on a $12,500-a-year salary, to assemble a small business empire."[26] Fadell and Chacharis continued to work closely together thereafter, first to try to block Hatcher's insurgency in 1967, then to try to prevent his reelection in 1971. Chacharis even came to Washington during the Senate hearing to watch Fadell testify.[27]

Chacharis, a poor immigrant boy from Greece, had made his way in Democratic Party politics simultaneously with advancing himself in the employ of the United States Steel Corporation. While mayor, Chacharis held occasional meetings with the Gary Works superintendent "to hammer out decisions in face-to-face conferences."[28] At this intersection between corporation, township assessing practices, and Gary city government, Chacharis, and more recently, Fadell, demonstrated the kind of mutual accommodations and brokering that is the genius of American politics.[29]

The Legal Basis for Reassessment

In Indiana, there is a little-known statute, passed by the state legislature in 1905, which gives the city controllers the power to examine property tax returns and assessments.[30] I saw this unutilized law as a possible means to compel the corporation to pay more local taxes. For while the township assessor was a leader on the local Democratic Party machine that had long maintained an amicable relationship with U.S. Steel, the city controller was a key personal appointee of Mayor Hatcher. If the city controller's powers included oversight over the tax assessment roles, it might be possible to ascertain the true value of the Gary Works.

The statute made sense. It was the city government that would be short of revenue if property was inadvertently omitted from the tax assessor's rolls, and in the course of his duties the city controller might well come across such property. The power to notify the assessor of such property thus would permit a correction of the error and a corresponding increase in municipal revenues. In this case we believed the "missing" property of the Gary Works would yield quite substantial additional revenues.

There were two problems, however. One was that in 1961 the state legislature passed a law regulating the powers and duties of the township assessor's office, and among its provisions was one that the records upon which the assessor determined the value of pieces of property be kept confidential. The other problem was that it was necessary to interpret the 1905 law as giving the city controller the power to examine the records of both the corporation and the township assessor to determine if there was any property omitted from the tax rolls. Such a power, if it existed, would in effect give the city government the power to make an independent audit of the Gary Works. It was not clear whether the statute could be interpreted so broadly, but such an interpretation would be consistent with the legislative intent of ensuring comprehensive inclusion of all property on the tax assessment rolls. There was no case law on this matter, but we believed that there was a good chance of prevailing with careful legal preparation.

There was substantial internal opposition in the Hatcher administration to attempting such a bold initiative. Those of us who wanted to invoke the law were met with the objection that any effort to pressure U.S. Steel would result in its eventual removal from Gary. We finally prevailed upon the corporation counsel to write a memorandum in which he asserted that in order for the controller's office to determine whether assessment of property was properly made we had to examine the corporate books. Armed with this and the reluctant consent of the city controller, Maurice Baptiste, we were able to prevail upon Mayor Hatcher to give us the permission to send a letter to the superintendent of the Gary Works on July 9, 1968. In this letter, for the first time in Gary's history, the city government asserted the right to examine the property books and records of U.S. Steel.[31]

Not convinced that the mayor's commitment to this matter was firm, a colleague leaked the news of the letter to the Chicago press. The next day the *Chicago Sun Times* carried a reply by a U.S. Steel representative which asserted that the corporation was in compliance with Indiana law regarding its assessments and warned of the effect on the competitive position of "a leading employer in the Gary area."[32] Thus, the steel fist was revealed. In case the citizen missed the point, however, the Gary *Post-Tribune* carried a lead editorial on the subject. After granting that the corporation was assessed at an "unrealistically low" value, it quickly went on to echo the corporation's posture:

> [If U.S. Steel] were forced to pay a greater share of taxes than others, then it would be put at an obvious competitive disadvantage. In time that could lead to cuts in the use of production facilities and consequent cuts in both tax base and jobs. In short, the Gary administration could be preparing to cut off its nose to spite its face.[33]

The next week Assessor Tom Fadell asserted that he doubted that the city controller had the legal power to examine the corporation's books.

On July 19, U.S. Steel curtly replied that it had received the letter and would respond to it "at an appropriate future date," and we indicated our hope that negotiations would commence within a reasonable time. The corporation then called the mayor's office, and a meeting date was set for August 2, 1968. At this meeting, during which I took the only notes, a well-prepared team from U.S. Steel confronted a confused municipal staff, to whom Mayor Hatcher had not indicated his posture.

Corporation executives laid out their position: "We have complied to the best of our ability with the assessment law of this state." While there was no case law on the 1905 statute, its meaning could be determined either by asking the Indiana State Tax Board for an opinion or by obtaining an advisory opinion from the Indiana attorney general. In either case, they asserted, that effectively would be the end of the matter.

Realizing that these bodies were apt to rule against the city, especially if the matter were posed as a legal question divorced from a real controversy, we replied that we would rather have a court determination in a real case. I started to raise the issue of whether the corporation would consider itself bound by an adverse ruling in either of the bodies it suggested, but Mayor Hatcher interrupted to assert that it was "premature" to discuss this question. Corporation executives immediately took advantage of this, indicating that they felt that both parties had reached an understanding that there would be further discussions before any action was taken in the dispute.

At this point the senior corporation official present spoke for the first time. In an informal manner, addressing the mayor as "Dick," he explained how he was in competition with other branch steel plants, all of whom were trying to get national management to underwrite housing projects in their respective cities. He was doing his best to get U.S. Steel to put 500 moderate-income units in Gary. And, to be perfectly candid, our allowing news of this dispute to become public at such a juncture had "had an unfavorable effect on [the] internal corporation politics" about who would be the recipient of this favorable treatment. He wished, he went on, to minimize activity in the press about the matter.

While this desire to avoid publicity seemed to me to present an opportunity to negotiate for something in return, Mayor Hatcher immediately agreed, stating that he was sorry that the matter was made public in the press. The corporation spokesmen stated that while it was appropriate for the press to be informed, it should not be "out of the proper sequence." The mayor agreed. With these comments the meeting broke up, never to be publicized. The senior corporation official courteously came over to shake hands with me and tell me that he was pleased that I had recently come to Gary and hoped that I would enjoy living in the city.

Shortly thereafter a development occurred, however, that changed the character of the dispute in a manner most advantageous to the city. In the course of the Office of Program Coordination investigation of the building department, it came to my attention that a major provision of the building code required that prior to any new building or structural changes in an existing building, two sets of specifications and blueprints for the construction work, along with a permit fee of 0.5 percent of the value of the work, be filed with the building department. These requirements had not been enforced prior to Mayor Hatcher's term of office. As I was discussing this matter with one of the long-time employees in the department, he blurted out in annoyance: "Why don't you make U.S. Steel obey these rules, too, if you're so smart? Why just go after the small contractors?"

Of course, his comment was meant rhetorically, but I instantly dropped all my other work to investigate just this question. It turned out that the building department had never inspected any construction work undertaken by the Gary Works, and had no plans or specifications on file. Instead, the corporation dealt directly with the city controller's office, sending a check four times a year, along with a cover letter that simply asserted that it covered the value of the construction work done in that period. Essentially the corporation determined on its own account, without any outside examination, what its construction work was worth.[34]

For 1967, the year before Hatcher became mayor, the corporation paid the city $24,416 in fees, in effect, claiming to have invested only $12 million in new construction in the Gary Works that year. But U.S. Steel's *Annual Report* for 1967 listed $574 million worth of new construction. If the Gary Works had received only one-tenth of this sum (and it probably had obtained double that since it constituted one-fifth of U.S. Steel's total production capacity), the city had been short-changed $100,000 in permit fees.[35]

Along with this information went another vital discovery. Indiana law provided that building permit officials should give the township assessor "the names of all persons to whom such permits were issued within the previous month . . . and any information which may be available regarding the cost of such improvements."[36] If such accurate information about the real value of new improvements in the Gary Works were in the hands of the township assessor, this would force a readjustment upward of the mill assessment. In short, by refusing to let the city government inspect construction and determine its real worth (via both specifications and a fee schedule), U.S. Steel was also clearly attempting to avoid giving them information that could be used for tax assessment purposes.[37]

Needless to say, Assessor Tom Fadell was hardly pleased at the prospect of such additional information. At a 1972 U.S. Senate hearing on the matter he stated: "We wouldn't pay any attention to their building permits even if they took them out."[38] Since the existence of such public information would in fact have a powerful impact on the assessment process, Fadell's position merely reveals the machine's real orientation toward the corporation and its interests.

An Unjoined Legal Battle

On September 9, 1968, the mayor gave us permission to act on the 1905 law. We were permitted to mail out a letter following up on the August 2 meeting in which we refused the proposal of requesting further administrative opinions as to the validity of the 1905 law. Instead, we renewed our request under the law that the records "concerning personal property of your corporation located within the city limits of Gary as of March, 1968 . . . be made available to us . . . not later than October 1, 1968."[39]

With the posting of that letter a legal struggle began. But as the city lacked the internal legal capability to contest the matter in court, it needed outside counsel, which the mayor made no effort to obtain. The result was that when, on September 27, U.S. Steel filed suit in the Indiana courts for a declaratory judgment to have the 1905 statute declared void, the city was not prepared to pursue the matter in a serious manner.[40]

The corporation counsel was therefore compelled, at the October 10 hearing for a preliminary injunction, to agree to a temporary restraining order while preserving the city's legal position for a later adjudication on the merits. But despite the city's inadequate preparation, the hearing indicated that the corporation position also had weak spots, of which a capable legal team could take advantage.

The corporation made several points in its testimony on behalf of the temporary injunction: 1) that no property was omitted or improperly assessed; 2) that the normal process of assessment via the township assessor was adequate; 3) that the 1905 law was superceded by the 1961 law; 4) that since the 1905 law did not provide for the confidentiality of records (as did the 1961 statute) it should be viewed as implicitly repealed; and 5) that it would be "burdensome" for the corporation to assemble the necessary scattered and coded data. In addition, they testified that the books and records had been examined with respect to tax returns.[41] But, as we have already noted, the township assessor has since admitted in testimony before a U.S. Senate hearing that he had never actually seen U.S. Steel's books nor carried out an inventory of the machinery and equipment.

In his testimony on behalf of the city, Assistant Controller Arnold Reingold pointed out that: 1) in view of the magnitude of the corporation's contribution to Gary's revenue picture it was vital that the municipal government ascertain that no items were omitted from its assessments, and that a variety of calculations suggested the possibility that there were such omissions; 2) the argument with regard to confidentiality was spurious, since the city would be bound to respect it in precisely the same manner as the assessor; 3) the procedure would not be particularly "burdensome," as certified public accountants had long developed procedures for doing audits without interfering with ongoing corporate activities. Reingold pointed out that if as the corporation asserted it provided the assessor with the requisite materials to do a fair and complete audit annually, it could hardly claim simultaneously that the records were so scattered as not to be readily available.[42]

So while U.S. Steel got a temporary restraining order, we were not convinced that the matter was resolved against us. With a determined legal offensive and a public political campaign to emphasize the corporation's efforts to prevent an independent audit, we believed we had a chance to get a higher assessment. However, the city agreed to further postponements in the setting of a trial date. The case remains pending until the present day, leaving the corporation the victor without a fight.

At this time we also managed to get an offer of free outside legal counsel from a major civil rights organization. I arranged for their senior attorney to come to Gary in December 1968 and meet with Hatcher's key administrators to discuss an overall legal strategy with respect to all problems relating to U.S. Steel. At that meeting, which I taped, we agreed that rather than pursue the 1905 statute, we would resort to the legal tactic of instituting a taxpayers' suit against both the corporation and the township assessor. However, with respect to the building permits, Corporation Counsel Clarence Greenwald was emphatic in asserting that there would not be any need for litigation, and that he would be able to resolve the matter by personal discussion with corporation officials.

On February 6, the civil rights attorney returned for a second meeting, armed with extensive preparatory work by his legal staff. The mayor seemed pleased at the prospect of obtaining this crucial outside legal assistance. In a memorandum to the mayor and corporation counsel summarizing the content of the February 6 meeting, I indicated that the mayor had agreed that this attorney would in effect serve as special counsel on all matters concerning the U.S. Steel Corporation, and we would keep his organization informed on the progress of negotiations. Moreover, in the discussion about the taxpayers' suit against U.S. Steel this attorney suggested that Mayor Hatcher himself could be the chief counsel for the group.

Shortly thereafter (after I had resigned my position in Gary), however, the mayor dismissed this outside counsel. He never made any effort to replace it, nor did he ever take any of the steps to enable the city's law department to carry out effective legal action against U.S. Steel. In doing so he is able to claim that he is vigorously contesting with U.S. Steel and is only constrained by circumstances beyond his control.

In testimony to the Senate Subcommittee on Intergovernmental Affairs three years later, Mayor Hatcher stated:

> We had a choice, of course, at that point when U.S. Steel refused to comply voluntarily . . . of either going into court and attempting to do something about this, or of trying to work out an "arrangement" with the company—which is the course we did follow.

> The problem with going into the court route is that the City
> of Gary is at a decided disadvantage with respect to the legal
> personnel, manpower and expertise required to successfully pros-
> ecute such a case. . . . Beyond that, the hiring of . . . outside
> counsel, of course, is a fairly expensive proposition and in most
> cases not provided for in our budget.
>   *Senator Gurney:* Perhaps I should ask you this question. . . .
> Wasn't it the city's decision that they didn't want to litigate
> this thing . . .?
>   *Mr. Hatcher:* It was our feeling that it would be easier for the city
> to attempt to work out an arrangement or negotiate it rather than to
> fight it through the courts.[43]

Since the mayor had access to capable and free outside counsel,
it would appear that the policy decision turned on an unwillingness to engage in an all-out struggle against U.S. Steel.

The Central Issue

Underlying the seemingly minor issue of construction permits
was the far more momentous one of Gary Works' assessments. It
was this nexus that most participants would rather were left
unexplored. For instance, the corporation counsel believed that
the city was within its rights with respect to the building code
permits. But he viewed this as a means of obtaining the modest
additional revenues to be achieved by enforcement and not
as a lever for forcing a reassessment of the Gary Works. Thus,
despite the city's strong legal position and the seemingly aggressive beginnings of enforcement, ultimately no effective action
was taken.

On December 14, 1968, the corporation counsel sent U.S. Steel
a strong letter demanding compliance with the building code
requirements. U.S. Steel replied by sending the city controller a
check for $5,400.50, accompanied by a letter that asserted that
the sum was for one-quarter of the contemplated expenses of
1969. Regarding permit fees for 1968, the letter indicated that
the check covered that as well, because it was based upon the

1969 budget "adjusted to care for added or deleted work made during the year 1968."

Since the letter included a clause asserting that acceptance of the check would constitute agreement that it was an adequate payment, the corporation was asking us to consent to an agreement that the value of all construction in the Gary Works over the two-year period came to $10 million. In reality, it was probably ten times that amount. The corporation counsel refused to accept such a stipulation, which would waive the city's rights, and returned the check. In the course of later negotiations it was agreed that pending a final resolution of the matter the city would accept U.S. Steel's quarterly payments but reserve its rights.[44]

Thereupon the corporation contacted the mayor and set another meeting for January 30, 1969, to which it again sent its leading officials to meet with the city's top-level staff, and at which I again took notes. Corporation Counsel Clarence Greenwald laid out the city's position, stating that the key question was not the fees themselves, but whether the corporation could violate the building code—which had a variety of functions, such as raising revenue and controlling local construction so as to assure the public safety. The corporation spokesman responded by agreeing they had to obey the law, but asked what the city would gain by enforcing it against them, since a private enterprise needs the latitude to operate without undue restraint. He also argued that in 1926 when the law was passed it was understood that the law would not apply to property north of the Grand Calumet River, that is, to the Gary Works.[45] He added that the corporation had demonstrated this in 1946, at a meeting with the mayor, at which a city councilman from 1926, Ralph Rowley, so testified. At that point, the spokesman claimed (on the basis of corporation historical documents not offered to us), the mayor abandoned any further claim of municipal jurisdiction over the Gary Works. No one mentioned at this meeting that Mr. Rowley, who was president of the city council in the 1920s, simultaneously was the chief engineer at the Gary Works.[46] I do not believe that any of the city officials present were aware of whose testimony the corporation was introducing.

The spokesman went on to say that beginning in 1953, after the same question had been raised by another mayor, an informal settlement had been worked out under which the corporation's chief engineer would summarize the costs that were being undertaken and submit quarterly payments to the city controller. Several mayors since had raised questions about this procedure, but in each case both parties were "successful in continuing the same program."[47] Another corporation spokesman told us that over the period from 1953 to 1968 U.S. Steel had tendered a total of $283,000 in permit fees to the city. According to this, new facilities in the Gary Works over that period would have been worth only $140 million, whereas, as we shall see, their real value was probably almost ten times that amount.

At this point, the discussion became heated. When asked why they were reluctant to comply with the city ordinance, the corporation replied that it would be a "nuisance activity," and asked what the city had to gain from introducing an inspection procedure. I replied that one benefit would be information that would be directly relevant to the question of assessments. An angry retort followed: "Is it policing which you are after?" I said: "Yes, insofar as all law enforcement has that quality." Greenwald interjected that he did not want to overrule me but that the purpose was simply to enforce the building code and the question of tax revenues was not relevant. Mayor Hatcher then interjected that he felt that I was correct and that the city was obliged to report to the township assessor the results garnered by building department permit activities.

The moment that the mayor took this hard line the corporation spokesmen became conciliatory and called a negotiated settlement to "avoid a confrontation." One of the corporation executives then suggested that a joint committee be formed to "thrash out the problem." Hatcher agreed, adding that if "after two or three weeks we can't work it out, then each side will have to take the next steps." (In the context of the discussion it was clear this was a threat to resort to court enforcement.) The mayor added that we were returning U.S. Steel's check, because "we can't afford to say officially that U.S. Steel is not under the same laws as everyone" during a period in which we were attempting to improve the functioning of the building department. A committee was then set up that included the corporation counsel and city engineer; I was not invited to participate, and shortly thereafter resigned from the Hatcher administration.

Apparently the committee undertook desultory negotiations. A year later discussions were still under way, and according to the chief investigative reporter of the Gary *Post-Tribune*, "the city's two chief negotiators, former City Attorney Clarence Greenwald and City Engineer Mahlon Plumb, now credit the corporation with 'good faith.'"[48] In January 1972 the committee was still meeting from time to time, and it is evident from the minutes of the mayor's cabinet meeting during this period that the question of utilizing the building permit fees as a means to force reassessment had been dropped from practical consideration. What was at stake was simply how to reach an acceptable fee schedule.

In June 1972, when the U.S. Senate Subcommittee on Intergovernmental Relations held hearings on property taxation in Gary, the superintendent of the Gary Works, J. David Carr, reiterated the corporation's position that the building code was not applicable to U.S. Steel and admitted that the work of the joint committee was proceeding slowly. Not only did he believe that the Gary Works were fairly assessed but he did not understand why there was any controversy:

> *Mr. Carr:* Perhaps I should tell you that these things are discussed quite frequently. In fact, Mayor Hatcher is invited to our plant. He is there at my request. We review the plant. We tour the plant. The city council goes through it. There is nothing. . . .
>
> *Senator Muskie:* Why don't you let them go through your books then, so that they can document the value of what they are seeing? Brushing aside all the technicalities, why are you so reluctant to give the city authorities the information with respect to what you are building within the city limits, what its cost is and at the same time [why are you] so eager to establish the invalidity of a 1905 statute designed only to give the city information. I mean, what is behind your attitude in these matters?
>
> *Mr. Carr:* It is such a minor thing. I will agree with you, extremely minor, since we do deal with so many things in Gary and particu-

larly with the mayor and particularly with city officials where we have a lot of cooperation—and it is amazing to me too, that such a minor thing is blown out of proportion.[49]

Control over the wealth produced by the Gary Works is not a "minor thing." In an ultimate sense it determines what social class runs the society and thus the type of civilization in which the American people live. And in the immediate sense, of the type of city Gary is, it is not a "minor thing" either. Several independent estimates of the real worth of the Gary Works place its proper assessment value at approximately double the $567 million set by the township assessor. For example, Ralph Nader asserted that the corporation installed $1.2 billion of capital improvements at the Gary Works during the period from 1961 to 1971; Arnold Reingold, Mayor Hatcher's special assistant for finance, utilizing a quite different method of calculation, reached a value of $989 million; and my own rough estimates result in a figure of at least $1 billion.[50] It is thus hardly surprising that U.S. Steel engages in fierce resistance to demands of reassessment. Additional annual property taxes of about $30 million are worth some effort to avoid.

Class Power in the Background

This account illustrates that the ability of U.S. Steel to protect its interests from successful structural reforms rests to a large extent on the absence of any effective popular power in the community capable of engaging in serious contestation. No independently organized working-class or black groups existed which were able to launch and sustain the necessary effort, and the fundamental interests of the majority of the people of Gary in this matter did not even effectively reach the political arena. It was only due to my personal engagement that the issue was even addressed.

Undergirding this, of course, is the vast economic power of U.S. Steel. Even without covert conflicts of interest, government officials are frightened by corporate threats of relocation. The evidence is that business does take tax patterns into effect in location decisions,[51] and without full disclosure of internal business records, not legally attainable, it is difficult for public officials to know whether or not the threat is credible.[52] Certainly corporation threats are plentiful. To cite just one example, Mayor Hatcher described the kind of negotiations he had with corporation executives on the subject as follows:

> I don't believe at any time I heard anyone say that the Gary Works would be shut down completely. I don't believe that was ever said. But I do believe there was an implication that certain parts of the process of making steel . . . would have to be transferred to other locales where there would not be this high property tax rate . . . and for that reason, of course, it could be done more cheaply.[53]

From its earliest days U.S. Steel has indicated its willingness to use its power over capital to compel compliance with its will. During the 1909 steel strike, for instance, a corporation executive announced that unless operations could be conducted "with less trouble incident to labor, and more cooperation on the part of the community, the natural outcome would be the boarding up of the plants . . . and moving them elsewhere."[54] And so I conclude that U.S. Steel to this very day extracts an immense and measurable profit from the city of Gary, at an even more immense but immeasurable loss to its people.

8

Environmental Regulation

The effective veto which U.S. Steel has over reform measures that are harmful to its interests is not limited to the municipal government. Resting on its ownership of the means of production in Gary, this power can manifest itself at other governmental levels as well, making it impossible to resolve community problems simply by shifting formal power from the city to state or federal government levels.

This is well illustrated in the case of efforts to combat air and water pollution from the Gary Works. During Mayor Hatcher's tenure, primary legal responsibility for amelioration of this problem was transferred from local to national authorities. While in some ways this increased the possibility of taming corporation resistance to expenditures on pollution control equipment, the overall result has been rather meager. After a decade of focused public concern (in a matter of primary importance to the very health of the population) the corporation has so far avoided taking the full range of measures needed to stop its massive pollution of the environment. Rather, its response has been one of substantial delay and avoidance of compliance, a pattern which there is every reason to believe will continue.

The same motives that informed corporation resistance to higher property taxes apply in the pollution arena: pollution control measures are very costly, resulting in a reduction in net profits. U.S. Steel is able to exercise its political and economic power as a monopoly corporation to prevent or at least limit such expenditures by simply indicating that if it is made to pay for pollution control it will reduce its level of productive investments and thus penalize the working class of the city. When regulatory power is transferred to the federal government, the corporation repeats the same argument: only instead of threatening to invest in another locality, it indicates that it will not invest in the industry at all, or at least not within the continental United States.

This is so credible, moreover, that it effectively inhibits working-class demands for pollution control measures. In the steel towns there is a popular slogan: "No smoke, no jobs." Given the choice workers must make in a capitalist economy of selling their labor power under unfavorable conditions (such as an unhealthy environment) or being deprived of work entirely, it is hardly to be wondered that they choose the former alternative. Knowing that steel mills and other industrial plants have been taken out of production over pollution control costs, people in Gary fear the effect of regulation on their community. Faced with this alternative to an unclean environment, they have not pressed elected officials to fight for pollution control measures.

This sensibility is reflected in City Hall. I can state from personal conversations with the officials involved that such considerations played a decisive role in inhibiting the Hatcher administration from seriously considering the adoption of any strategy of confrontation with U.S. Steel on the pollution issue. Thus, while pollution adversely affects the people of the city and benefits only the corporation (by reducing its costs of production), the political process does not result in reform. Again, the process of pluralistic political bargaining takes place within the hegemony of capital.

Pollution from the Gary Works

The Gary Works is the largest single source of air and water pollutants in the nation: at the time Richard Hatcher became mayor, the mill spewed almost 70,000 tons of particulates into the sky every year plus large amounts of various gases, including sulphur dioxide.[1] As a result of environmental control measures, by 1974 the quantity of particulates emitted had dropped off considerably, to 23,000 tons a year.[2] This was part of a national industrial trend in which the steel industry participated, since a reduction in the total quantity of particulates was by far the cheapest pollution control measure to carry out.[3] It is also the one that is most apparent to the public: there is no doubt that over the past decade there has been a marked diminution in the ruddiness of the Gary skies as the quantity of particulates released by the steel mill has dropped off.

However, it would be most premature to conclude that the public health dangers associated with air pollution have diminished apace. A large part of the reduction has been due to the substitution of Basic Oxygen Processes for open hearth mills, and the former produce smaller particulate particles that are actually more dangerous.[4] And while particulate discharge has gone down, that of sulphur dioxide has actually increased; between 1972 and 1977 the amount of sulphur dioxide as a byproduct of each ton of steel manufactured at the Gary Works went up from 8.9 pounds to 10.4 pounds.[5]

Air pollution in the city of Gary is often double the permissible federal standard, while available evidence suggests that levels of particulates and sulphur dioxide even below the federal standard have harmful effects on the population exposed to them.[6] Adverse health effects from air pollution include not only massive increases in rates of respiratory illnesses and cancer, but others, such as birth defects and increased heart disease.[7] In Gary, according to the local health commissioner, these consequences include a lung cancer rate four times the national average. As the Lake County coroner graphically puts it: "In the autopsies . . . I've seen lungs of people who've lived and worked here in Gary all of their lives. These organs look like the inside of a coal mine."[8]

The city also has a childhood mortality rate which is twice the national average, even though as we have seen, per capita income is at about the national level. Over half of this mortality—an unusually high proportion—is due to respiratory illnesses. The only time in Gary's history that the childhood mortality rate approximated the national average was during the Depression, when the Gary Works functioned on a sharply reduced production schedule.

Even higher levels of air pollution occur within the Gary Works itself, where rates of air pollution may reach ten times the community rates. The result is particularly hazardous conditions for the working class, who pay the price in their health. Some areas of the mills, such as the coke ovens and foundries, are especially unhealthful, precisely the areas in which the black workers have been concentrated by the corporation's racist employment practices.[9] Moreover, the harmful effects follow the black workers into the community. While air pollution from the Gary Works has been detected as far away as New York City, its effects are naturally most deleterious in the immediate vicinity of the mill. Lake Michigan breezes cause a temperature inversion effect which holds polluted air close to the ground; thus in the heart of the Gary ghetto, "steel mill dust and smoke, particularly coke oven emissions, tend to break from a fanned plume to a low rolling plume" which blankets the area.[10] With the black population concentrated in the area of maximum air pollution, it is hardly a surprise that the black childhood mortality rate (even after adjustments for other factors such as income) considerably exceeds that of local white children.

While from the standpoint of bourgeois economics, the impact of air pollution is discussed as an "external diseconomy" or "social cost," it is more realistic to depict it as a class cost, for its burden falls most heavily on the urban working class. As Matt Edel points out, capitalists cut their production costs

> by imposing pollution on the working public in general. Thus, specific pollution may itself be a form of imposing costs on workers by capitalists. Stopping the pollution, like cutting working hours and making conditions at the plants safer, would appear to be the task of organization by the workers as a group, in opposition to the capitalists.[11]

Gary, as part of the "most polluted urban area in the country," bears witness to this objective class conflict over the environment. As the militant district director of the Steelworkers', Jim Balanoff, puts it, "Clean air and clean water are part of our standard of living."[12] Despite this class impact, U.S. Steel has been able to prevent a mass political struggle against its pollution from unfolding in Gary, and the Hatcher administration has had only a minimal effect upon corporation pollution. The reasons for this impasse are worth detailing.

Historically, the corporation has denied any responsibility in the matter. In 1956, on the occasion of the celebration of the fiftieth anniversary of the city, Corporation President Roger Blough came to town and opined that the "main problem stemmed, not from the mills, but from coal-fired home furnaces."[13] This was arrant nonsense. As late as 1967, in testimony before Gary's city council, the assistant superintendent of the Gary Works maintained that the automobile and not local industry was responsible for the bulk of air pollution.[14]

In the face of rising public indignation over pollution dangers, the corporation has gradually become somewhat more tactful in its public comments. Its more recent approach has been to claim major progress in pollution control activities. In 1969, for instance, the chairman of the board of directors asserted that U.S. Steel would soon "have our air pollution problem in the Gary-Chicago area almost totally under our control." And at the 1971 annual stockholders' meeting, Chairman Edwin A. Gott stated, "We have cleaned up the air and cleaned up the water and are in court seeking to know what the standards are, but the problem is a very large one."[15] In fact, the corporation has been in intransigent opposition to local, state, and federal pollution controls, and has misrepresented its position so flagrantly that the Securities and Exchange Commission has been investigating it for possible fraud in its stockholders' reports.[16]

State Pollution Control

Indiana's air pollution control regulation—along with that of water pollution and industrial health and safety—has been woefully deficient. The state passed its first legislation to control air pollution in 1963, creating an air pollution control board within the state health department and including enabling legislation permitting municipalities to pass local pollution ordinances.[17] But to begin with, the board had such desultory funding it was not able to function effectively. In 1970 the agency had a staff of nine, so small that in order to fulfill its reporting requirements to the federal authorities it was unable for a year to undertake any enforcement proceedings at all. Most states do not adequately fund their pollution control agencies. And Indiana has the dubious distinction of a funding level which, on a per capita basis, is only one-third the state average. In 1970 its budget was three cents per inhabitant. The United States Environmental Protection Agency (EPA) estimated that the Indiana agency needs a fivefold multiplication of its budget in order to function effectively.[18]

Equally seriously, the Indiana air pollution control statute is defective. Its definition of air pollution is excessively narrow, and the law can barely be enforced "because of a lack of sanctions and enforcement procedures."[19]

Finally, the Indiana board has no desire to undertake vigorous enforcement. An EPA staff study concluded that "there has been practically no enforcement action," and the concensus among outside observers is that the agency's effectiveness is minimal. In 1970, for example, the Indiana board initiated only seven enforcement actions, all against petty-bourgeois offenders for such offenses as open burning of trash, and only two cease and desist orders.[20] It is likely that this permissiveness reflects the proindustry bias of the Indiana board, which explicitly provided for industry representation. In the late sixties Charles Kay, assistant superintendent of the Gary Works, was a member, replaced at the end of his term by an official from Bethlehem Steel.[21] The state of Indiana has never been an active leader in attempting to control Gary's air pollution. Thus when Mayor Hatcher's activist health commissioner requested that the Indiana Health Department assist him in investigating and evaluating environmental health problems at the coke facilities of the Gary Works, he was refused outright.[22]

City Pollution Control

The struggle for a local air pollution ordinance goes back to 1956, when reform city counsel member Milton Roth attempted to initiate such legislation. The machine mayor reluctantly agreed to set up a study commission but told Roth that while air pollution control might be a "nice idea," smoke and jobs in the community went together.[23] In typical leisurely fashion, the city council took a year to set up the study commission and another year and a half to produce its report. This ascribed only half of the city's pollution to the Gary Works, and recommended a decade exemption for most of the metallurgical processes. Roth believed that this extraordinarily weak legislation was the best possible, and in 1959 submitted an ordinance based on the study commission's recommendations to the city council. The bill was referred to committee, where it died. It is likely that the machine was unwilling to initiate any pollution legislation against the preferences of the corporation.[24]

No more was heard of the matter for almost four years. Then, a few months prior to the effective date of the Indiana ordinance, the United States Steel Corporation publicly declared itself in favor of local pollution control legislation. While there is no direct evidence on this question, it seems reasonable to infer that the corporation preferred to be regulated by the local machine rather than by the Indiana authorities. Immediately thereafter, Mayor Chacharis opined that he too was in favor of a municipal air pollution ordinance, adding that "the city would not want to damage the steel company by imposing a too-stringent pollution ordinance."[25]

The mayor turned the job of drafting the legislation over to a health department employee, who later explained how U.S. Steel had "been more than willing to go along with our local ordinance." The ordinance was a virtual copy of a rather modest Pittsburgh ordinance, and was passed by the city council without debate or amendment.[26] In 1967, when the ordinance had to be amended to comport with federal legislation, the same sequence unfolded, despite the protests of council member Richard Hatcher. Hatcher's objections that he had not had the opportunity even to read the new bill were simply ignored.

A cursory examination of the ordinance explains the corporation's support. It entirely exempted the coke ovens, the largest single source of Gary Works pollution. It also provided that a variance, which is an agreement exempting the beneficiary from full compliance with the ordinance, could be negotiated between the city and any individual polluter. U.S. Steel immediately requested a variance and entered into negotiations with the city as to its terms. A two-and-a-half-year period of negotiations followed, during which time the city chose to view the ordinance as not requiring any compliance at all while variance negotiations were underway.[27]

The terms of the variance agreement finally signed between the corporation and the city in 1965 followed a nationwide pattern of useless action. On the one hand, the city waived its rights to take any legal actions, outside the terms of the variance itself, for an eight-year period. On the other hand, a careful reading of the variance indicates that the corporation could be in compliance while actually *increasing* the quantity of pollutants emitted from the Gary Works. This remarkable outcome was possible because the variance did not require the control of any specific source of pollution nor that the overall quantity of pollutants released from the mill be reduced. Rather the "reduction" was to be based on a metaphysical construct: the amount of pollutants which the corporation estimated it would have produced if the Gary Works had been run at 100 percent of capacity for a full year. Moreover, the "reduction" was to be based only on the equipment in use as of the signing of the variance on July 4, 1965. Any equipment phased out through normal industrial practice and replaced by new equipment would not have the emissions from the replacement equipment counted at all.[28]

On the basis of the variance it was impossible for the city even to determine what was occurring, let alone exercise any regulatory authority, since the annual corporation letters to the city detailing progress under this agreement "tabulate the percentage of potential dust actually removed."[29]

The corporation was also the beneficiary of a local enforcement agency which was effectively nonfunctional in much the same way as the Indiana State Regulatory Board. The municipal air pollution budget was completely inadequate, reflecting the fiscal frugality of the city and its machine that in turn was the result of U.S. Steel's ability to contain its property tax assessment.[30] The consequence of insufficient funding was a poorly paid and inadequate staff, vulnerable to bribery and lacking motivation for aggressive enforcement. The provision of only a quarter-time attorney in the air pollution budget guaranteed the impracticality of any major enforcement procedure.[31]

Developments Under Mayor Hatcher

Thus, when Mayor Hatcher took office, he confronted a legal situation and a local tradition which sharply curtailed his opportunity to initiate major change. But neither did his office show any impetus toward such change. During the period that I attended cabinet meetings the only environmental matter placed on the agenda was the problem of how to remove abandoned automobiles from the streets. Although my Office of Program Coordination was authorized to carry out a study of the health department, which included the air pollution control division, its report advocating specific administrative reforms was ignored.[32] Among other conclusions the report pointed out that no systematic surveillance of air pollution was carried out; all enforcement was dependent upon citizen complaints; and in its five years of existence, only two noncompliance suits (both involving small trash burning) were initiated.[33]

In the absence of pressure from the community, Hatcher's main initiative was the appointment (after the three years necessary to gain a majority of the Health Commission Board) of an activist health commissioner, Dr. Herschel Bornstein. Bornstein, an eminently qualified local physician determined to control Gary Works air pollution, spent his first year in office carrying out major internal administrative reforms, hiring qualified new personnel, and obtaining legal assistance from a public interest group in Chicago.

Bornstein was able to call on the active support of the Environmental Protection Agency, for national regulation of pollution was in this period superceding local regulation.[34] Acting behind the scenes, the EPA concentrated its efforts on a repeal of the section of the Gary ordinance which exempted the coke ovens from any controls. Such repeal, although it would not affect the variance given to the rest of the Gary Works, would permit the city to require emission controls over the pernicious coke ovens.

Throughout 1970—in the context of national public concern and political pressure for pollution control—local community groups campaigned for a repeal of the coke oven exemption. Privately, EPA officials warned city councilmen that a failure to repeal the exemption would lead to the cut-off of all federal funds, which provided the bulk of the air pollution division's budget. While the corporation opposed the repeal on the grounds that the "state of the art" did not provide adequate technological grounds for controlling coke oven effluents, it did not attempt to block repeal by threats of economic retaliation.[35] So in December 1970 the city council did repeal the exemption.[36]

U.S. Steel immediately applied for a one-year variance. The terms of its proposal were that the corporation would spend the year examining the various control systems in use in steel plants around the world, at the end of which time it would submit a concrete proposal for emission control to the air pollution division.[37]

The next development was extraordinary. On his own initiative, on January 21, 1971, the chief of the air pollution division held a hearing on the variance request and summarily denied it. This obviously defective procedure would have led to a reversal in court, and hence a substantial delay before a valid order could be issued. The Gary law requires that before appealing to the courts, one must first exhaust the available administrative remedies, in this case by first appealing to the Air Pollution Appeal Board. Mayor Hatcher had appointed a strong board, chaired by Milton Roth. By the time the Appeal Board's hearing commenced on March 9, 1971, the case was firmly in the hands of Dr. Bornstein and his attorneys. The Appeal Board canceled out the earlier procedural errors by deciding to hold what was in effect a *de novo* hearing.

After some preliminary procedural maneuvers (including an unsuccessful move by U.S. Steel to ban television cameras from the proceedings), a ten-day hearing was held. The extensive expert testimony revealed that *even without the installation of any new equipment,* about half of the Gary Works' coke oven emissions could be eliminated; this would simply require the proper use of the existing plant. The operating management was not making any systematic effort to prevent the escape of gases in the course of the production cycle. Some oven doors did not fit securely, unnecessary amounts of time were spent in pushing the coke into quenching cars, and the doors often were left open unnecessarily.[38]

Additional evidence indicated that the installation of the types of pollution control devices already in use in newly built coke ovens could further reduce the pollution by a large factor. In combination with the proper use of the facilities, the vast bulk of the coke oven emissions—about 90 percent—could be eliminated. Moreover, exchanges between the corporation's expert witnesses and the counsel for the city demonstrated that contrary to earlier corporation assertions there were no technical obstacles to introducing such equipment into the Gary Works. So by the time of its summation, U.S. Steel was no longer relying upon the argument of technical inability. Instead it shifted the burden of its case to the high costs of reducing coke oven pollution. Rebuilding the Gary Works' coke ovens, it was asserted, would exceed the entire net annual profits of the American steel industry.

In rebuttal, the health department insisted that it was not up to the corporation "to decide that it would be useless to take what steps are available to it to control emissions," insisting they submit a plan with "rigid operational controls" and under conditions of unlimited inspections. This last point is of particular significance in Gary, where by tradition the city does not exert its jurisdiction within the mills, and indeed entry without a warrant is impossible.

On August 16, 1971, the Appeal Board handed down a decision highly favorable to the city. Control devices had to be placed in all the coke batteries upon a specific time schedule, with the first battery completed by July 1973 and the last by July 1977. Dr. Bornstein called for the "strict enforcement of the program with prompt and vigorous prosecution for violations." The City of Chicago, observing the Gary precedent, decided to institute pollution controls over the coke plants within its borders. And the corporation appealed to the Indiana state courts.

The case came to trial in November 1971, with the corporation arguing that the Appeal Board had failed to meet both the procedural and substantive requirements for issuing a valid order, and the city that it had amply met the Indiana standard of "substantial evidence." The city also introduced evidence that the corporation had been less than candid in its testimony before the Appeal Board. Specifically, they pointed out that U.S. Steel had already entered into a contract with the Mitsubishi Company of Japan for an essentially smokeless system for charging coke ovens at the time their director of environmental control was disclaiming knowledge of such technology.[39]

On May 22, 1972, the Lake County Superior Court affirmed the order of the Appeal Board. Curiously, U.S. Steel did not appeal further. The Council on Economic Priorities, in its definitive study of steel industry pollution, described U.S. Steel's general practice as follows: "At a few mills where pollution is particularly severe and damaging, U.S. Steel has dragged legal actions through the courts for years rather than agree to timetables for the installation of controls." In this case, however, within a week of the decision, the corporation filed a letter of intent to comply with the health department; all that was left were the details of implementation to be mutually worked out. And a few weeks later, it proudly announced its initiative in curbing Gary Works pollution to the public.[40]

But the implementation plan was rejected by the air pollution division and Appeal Board as completely inadequate, maintaining that it would in effect nullify the board's decision by giving the corporation "unlimited latitude" in how it carried out the order. The corporation remained intransigent. Soon thereafter, Dr. Bornstein resigned due to political disagreements with the mayor, and local initiatives to compel compliance largely petered out.[41]

Federal Enforcement

The initiative passed entirely into the hands of the federal government, which began efforts at controlling the Gary Works air pollution in April 1973.[42] After an unusually complex set of procedural maneuvers and negotiations involving the EPA, the Indiana and Gary air pollution control authorities, and U.S. Steel, a consent decree was agreed upon in federal district court. Among other provisions, this negotiated settlement provided that the corporation would close down heavily polluting open hearth mills "as soon as No. 2 Q-BOP Shop at Gary Works is able to produce consistently 350,000 tons of steel per month, but no later than December 31, 1974." It also called for the corporation to reduce its coke oven pollution radically by a program of "selective repair or replacement of various battery components designed to accomplish maximum battery operation and reduced emission," or, for those older batteries which were the most polluting, actually close them down.[43]

No sooner was this new agreement reached, however, than U.S. Steel claimed it was unable to abide by its terms and demanded further delays. With respect to its remaining open hearth furnaces, the corporation (which had already phased out forty-three and replaced them with more modern Basic Oxygen Process equipment) stated that it was unable to cease production since its replacement equipment was not yet available. In federal court, it demanded that the EPA give it a further time extension or it would close down those operations and lay off 2,500 workers. The court ruled that it could continue to use the remaining open hearth furnaces until new facilities were ready—if it paid a $2,300 a day fine to the government for violating the consent decree. The corporation refused, stating it would not "accede to a daily tribute to government," and shut down the furnaces.[44]

It should hardly be surprising that the 2,500 figure turned out to be corporation propaganda designed to pressure the government to back off on enforcement. In reality, only 500 workers were employed at the open hearth furnaces involved. But the effect of these potential layoffs was to prevent the Steelworkers' Union from supporting the environmental deadline. Their neutrality, along with a deep fear on increased local unemployment, in turn induced Mayor Hatcher to support a further delay in enforcement.[45]

As it turned out, while the corporation officially did furlough 500 men, the majority of them were rehired within two months. Ultimately, about 150 were laid off, most of whom qualified for early retirement.[46] Moreover, the corporation used its Gary experience as a means of attempting to avoid controls on its open hearth mills in Birmingham, Alabama, indicating it would close down there too rather than pay fines to the government. It succeeded in obtaining a variance in Birmingham through this threat, and in return for permission to continue producing from the Birmingham open hearth furnaces waived its objection "in principle" to "tribute" and agreed to pay a nominal daily fine.[47]

Precisely the same sort of delaying process occurred with respect to the coke ovens. Not until the end of 1975 did the corporation close down its most polluting batteries, then refused to bring other batteries into compliance, compelling the EPA to file a criminal contempt suit on December 16, 1976. On June 16, 1977, a settlement obliged U.S. Steel to pay a $250,000 civil penalty and further fines of $1,000 a day for new violations. The corporation refused to pay the latter fines, requiring a further federal suit (January 1978) which was settled on May 26, 1978.[48]

It is evident that the use of interminable legal appeals to delay compliance with air pollution regulations was a deliberate strategy. As the chief enforcement official of the EPA put it: "U.S. Steel had compiled a record of environmental recalcitrance second to none."[49]

Water Pollution

A similar pattern of noncompliance, delays, and legal appeals characterized U.S. Steel's action on water pollution abatement. Gary's water pollution, while not as visible as its air pollution, represents an even more intractable problem. Before the corporation purchased the tract of land on which the city is built, the area comprised the territory of two exclusive hunting clubs for Chicago magnates. After the corporation purchase, one of the lodges housed the engineers who planned the destruction of the local environment, and they consulted no one but the tycoons prior to the leveling of the local dunes, with their magnificent white pines and cedars.[50]

With the acquiescence of the pliant Indiana state legislature, U.S. Steel started a massive landfill, stretching finally to 1,370 acres: "The filled area extends about 1,800 to 2,000 feet into the lake and roughly parallels the original shore."[51] In the construction of the Gary Works radical changes also were wrought on the Grand Calumet River, meandering through Gary on what is now the demarcation between the mill and the city proper. When the Grand Calumet was first surveyed in the 1830s, the survey notes indicated that the river was wide and, although shallow, navigable. Until past the turn of the century lumber and fruit boats proceeded up the river from Lake Michigan and docked in Hammond, the city due west of Gary. There are pictures of three-masted schooners docked in Hammond in 1905; but by 1910 regular commercial navigation had ceased.

As a result of corporation engineering, a previously public waterway became in effect the private property of U.S. Steel. The Grand Calumet now flows west along the corporation's property until it enters Indiana Harbor Canal, which in turn empties into Lake Michigan. Depending upon local weather conditions, between one-third and the entire flow of the Grand Calumet River enters Lake Michigan; the remainder enters the Mississippi River system via the Calumet River in Illinois.[52] Prior to construction of the Gary Works and the other large manufacturing plants in the region, the Gary beach was the center of a fishing industry. Large commercial catches of whitefish and sturgeon "were caught in nets which were pulled up out of the water by windlasses set up on the beach."[53] However, from the outset of its operations, the Gary Works used the Grand Calumet River and Lake Michigan as a disposal system for chemical effluents, and by the 1940s the fishing industry was decimated. Algae growths in southern Lake Michigan, caused by the dumping of large amounts of nitrogen-ammonia and phosphates, destroyed the ecological balance necessary to support fish populations.

The quantities of pollutants involved are immense. Each day the Gary Works discharges between 500 and 750 million gallons of water; by comparison, the entire Chicago metropolis uses 4 million gallons daily.[54] This wastewater has made the Grand Calumet River entirely unfit for any recreational activity; its entire bottom is "composed of minute iron particles." Not even sludge-worms can live in the Grand Calumet; its only life is blue-green algae. Among other pollutants, U.S. Steel discharges 3,100 pounds of cyanide daily into the reddish-brown water covered with oil slicks. The impact of these effluent discharges extends into the lake itself:

> Whereas in the clean bottom areas of Lake Michigan there are many kinds of organisms . . . this area exhibits only a few kinds. Sludge-worms and acquatic scuds are the most numerous, but bloodworms and fingernail clams are sometimes abundant.[55]

The Public Health Service has charged that the Gary Works is contributing to a practically irreversible pollution of the lake.

The Gary Works, of course, is not unique. Steel mills are a major source of water pollution in the United States, using one-fifth of all water used in manufacturing. And the pollutants from steelmaking, including cyanide, phenols, ammonia, oil, and particulates are especially damaging to the environment. Moreover, industrial wastewater discharges have been steadily increasing in the period since World War II. From 1959 to 1968 the steel industry increased its discharge of wastewater by a third.[56] And these pollutants are concentrated in the waterways which are already the most polluted.[57] The Gary Works is the worst water polluting steel mill in the nation and the single largest polluter of Lake Michigan.[58]

In addition to this massive routine pollution, intermittent accidents also occur, resulting in "outbreaks" of huge discharges. For instance, in the late 1960s the regular discharge of oil from the Gary Works averaged 20 tons each day. Then on November 12, 1971, the sewer at the coke plant emitted an oil spill which caused a nine-mile slick.[59] The giant fleet of ore ships which the corporation maintains on Lake Michigan also periodically discharge oil into the lake. As the summer shipping season progresses, the beach at Gary manifests more and heavier oil slicks.

In principle, the city, the state of Indiana, and the federal government have all the powers necessary to compel the corporation to stop using the Grand Calumet River as an open sewer. Neither the city nor Indiana have done so; and the federal government's impact has been limited.

While Mayor Hatcher's administration took some initiatives with respect to local air pollution, it has simply not been a factor in water pollution at all. This is in large part because unlike air pollution, where the impact is greatest in the immediate vicinity of its sources, water pollution affects the city far less directly. Even though the total harm to the environment from Gary Works water pollution is probably more severe than its air pollution, and even though the nation's water pollution has been less successfully checked than its air pollution, the absence of popular pressure for wastewater control has meant no municipal action.

When the city's waterworks were constructed between 1906 and 1908, corporation engineers utilized the most advanced techniques and planned for a population of 200,000. So farseeing was their design that not until the mid-60s was there a need to build a supplementary intake tunnel. The original one passes underneath the Gary Works and draws in water three miles out from the shore.

Because the prevailing water flow in southwestern Lake Michigan is from south to north in a westerly direction, the pollutants discharged from the Gary Works do not pass into the city's own water system. Instead, some three to four days after discharge they reach Chicago's water system. By the late 1920s, Chicago's water supply had a noticeably phenol taste due to coke plants of the Calumet region, and threats of lawsuit by Illinois compelled the steel manufacturers to somewhat limit their discharges. The main solution, however, was for the Chicago Sanitary District to shunt discharges from the Indiana Harbor Canal into the Mississippi River to pollute other parts of the country. Gary's own water, though having a high iron particle count which gives it an unpalatable taste, remains relatively safe for human consumption. Thus until Richard Hatcher campaigned for mayor in 1967, the question of water pollution had never been a public issue in local politics. His program called for a local water pollution ordinance to be implemented by a new agency.

After Hatcher's election, however, nothing was done to implement this campaign promise. From my perspective as director of the Office of Program Coordination it seemed that several reasons combined to explain this inactivity. At first, Hatcher did not control either the Board of Health or the city council. Compared with the pressing administrative problems of attempting to maintain coherence in municipal administration in the face of inexperience and deep political opposition from the former officeholders, the issue of water pollution was ranked so low as to drop completely off the agenda: no one even discussed the question. Nor was there any local public concern over the problem; what few environmental reform energies existed in Gary were concentrated on the more acute and visible question of air pollution. Furthermore, City Hall personnel were completely ignorant about what was actually happening to the Grand Calumet. Finally, a tacit fear of creating still another controversy with the corporation prevailed, especially since it was felt that the burdens for any cleanup would be placed on the community through reductions in production and employment.

Given this unfavorable context, the appointment of Dr. Bornstein as health commissioner was as much of an initiative as could be expected. Dr. Bornstein requested the Indiana Stream Pollution Control Board to perform laboratory tests on water samples from the Grand Calumet to determine if pollution constituted a violation of Indiana law. This request was refused on the grounds that this service was only performed for local health departments when drinking water samples were involved. Soon thereafter, in a pattern common to regulatory processes in the United States, one of the key Indiana officials involved in this adverse decision was appointed as director of environmental control by another steel company.[60]

Dr. Bornstein attempted to proceed on his own, obtaining a search warrant from the Gary City Court on June 24, 1971, an action unprecedented in the city's history. Dr. Bornstein arrived at the Gary Works with his warrant, took water samples from the Grand Calumet River, and sent them off for analysis to a private laboratory. Gary Works superintendent J. David Carr angrily referred to the event as a "raid," and charged it was "a carefully organized effort to create an incident." Bornstein then found himself at an impasse, since neither the state nor federal authorities responded to his test results and the mayor took no initiatives to increase his legal powers to permit him to effectively act on his own. Indeed, Hatcher appears to have explicitly decided not to do so: his 1971 campaign platform, published just prior to the "raid," represented a step backward from his earlier stance. The new platform stated he would develop a municipal ordinance only if it seemed advisable. Despite his new city council majority, he has taken no action.

While the city has been moribund, the state of Indiana has been worse. Perhaps not surprisingly for a state government with such an unusual solicitude for giant corporations, it has in effect served as legal shield for corporation water pollution. The Indiana Stream Pollution Control Board has the formal power to curtail industrial water pollution, but, as in the case of air pollution and other regulatory activities, it lacks both the funding and will to effectively enforce its mandate.[61]

Not until the federal government passed the 1965 Water Quality Act did the Indiana Stream Pollution Control Board even begin to go through the motions of obtaining industrial compliance with the Indiana law. After the federal Lake Michigan Water Quality Conference of that year it took almost two years to promulgate specific water quality criteria for the Grand Calumet River; the board beat the federal deadline by two weeks. These criteria were lax: limits were placed on discharges of dissolved solids, ammonia-nitrate, and phenol, but no limits were placed on iron particles or cyanide, and those on suspended solids and oil were completely inadequate.[62]

Nevertheless, the corporation violates even these standards. After three years the Indiana board held a hearing on the matter, resulting in an order that U.S. Steel cease discharging "raw and inadequately treated wastewater" into the Grand Calumet River, and that it "institute at once the necessary procedures for the construction of additional waste treatment facilities needed to eliminate the pollution of waters." The corporation was allowed eighteen months to carry out the construction work.

U.S. Steel's response to the first legal demand since it built the Gary Works that it stop polluting the water was to request a rehearing, at which time the board reaffirmed its order, and U.S. Steel filed a petition for judicial review. At the trial, the corporation pointed out that the board had made numerous vital errors in conduct, including, for instance, failing to take a transcript at the initial hearing! The superior court reversed the Stream Pollution Control Board, and held that it would have to begin its enforcement procedure all over again. However, this decision was due to the board's inadequate case, rather than a proindustry bias. At virtually the same time, the same judge upheld the far stronger order of the Gary Air Pollution Review Board with respect to Gary Works air pollution. Thus, in April 1971 the state began laborious enforcement proceedings against U.S. Steel. The corporation's position at this *de novo* hearing was: "We all pollute."[63]

Soon thereafter, effective control over Gary Works water pollution was transferred to the federal government, as enforcement actions by the city and Indiana authorities were substantially merged into regulatory efforts of the EPA. There followed several years of complex delays, while the corporation took full advantage of legal possibilities under the various water pollution statutes and regulations. Finally, after unsuccessful efforts to reach a negotiated settlement with U.S. Steel, on October 31, 1974, the EPA unilaterally issued a water permit setting forth the limits to discharges and requiring substantial improvements by July 1977.

Over the latter half of the 1960s, such delaying tactics allowed the steel industry to defer most expenditures on water pollution control equipment: total industry capital expenditure for water pollution control between 1965 and 1969 was only $24 million, or less than 0.6 percent of capital investment.[64] At the Gary Works, U.S. Steel finally did undertake some relatively inexpensive measures which significantly reduced its discharge of suspended solids and oils, but from the late 1960s through 1977 there were actual increases in discharges of cyanide, ammonia, and phenol.[65]

Even though the EPA permit allowed the Gary Works to operate initially within discharge limits "selected to allow, in general, the continuation of present plant operations," the corporation contested its terms, requesting, among other amendments, the right to double its discharge of suspended solids. During the period from 1972 to 1977 there have been no significant capital expenditures on water pollution control at the Gary Works.[66]

The corporation took the position that during litigation it is not obliged to make any significant expenditures. It also asserted that if deadlines approach due to these delays, it should be given additional time to install control devices. Ultimately, these arguments did not prevail and after further federal court proceedings, on May 13, 1977, the United States Court of Appeals issued an order requiring the corporation to install pollution control equipment costing $8.6 million in capital expenditures and $2 million annually in operating expenses, as well as institute continuous monitoring of all discharges to make further enforcement possible. In addition, U.S. Steel had to pay a $3.25 million fine and agree to reduce ammonia discharges by 60 percent, cyanide by 95 percent, and phenol by 90 percent over a thirty-month period.[67] Theoretically, there are steep penalties for further failures to meet this deadline, but the actual course of developments will wait on events. While it seems likely that there will be further improvements in water pollution control at the Gary Works, a substantial end to effluents, although technically feasible, does not seem imminent. The entire pollution regulatory process is bounded by considerations of capitalist economic rationality, rendering significant progress unlikely.

Corporation Strategy

Clearly the corporation has pursued a strategy of entirely avoiding or at least deferring for as long as possible major pollution control expenditures. Since these expenditures would be considerable for a major industrial polluter, it is basic to the interests of capital to oppose the needs of the people. In order to continue to do so, therefore, it is essential that the steelmakers proceed to neutralize potential political forces that could require an effective end to their pollution.

Compelled by positive examples of pollution control in other steel industries around the world to give up its claims that ending its effluents is technically impossible, the corporation instead asserts that it is simply not economically feasible; the choice is to accept continuing pollution or drive the industry bankrupt. For instance, Edgar Speer, chairman of the U.S. Steel board of directors, recently asserted that simply to comply with existing air pollution regulations would cost the steel industry $12 billion, adding, "It would be difficult to find a more effective method for bringing economic growth to a halt."[68] In a situation in which the American steel industry has been undergoing a relative decline, this claim sounds plausible. Thus in its October 1977 report on the steel industry, the President's Council on Wage and Price Stability expressed serious concern that environmental standards are creating "a strong disincentive to modernization" of steel mills, and hence substantially contributing to the industry's difficulties.[69]

Apart from the fact that steel industries in other nations are spending at least as large a portion of investment on pollution control, the expenditures actually made by the U.S. steel industry, although significant, are by no means as large as U.S. Steel propaganda would imply. For instance, the industry insists that it will cost $1.3 billion simply to meet OSHA health regulations for the coke ovens, although both the EPA and President's Council on Wage and Price Stability put forth estimates which are one-fifth that amount. The current annual level of pollution control expenditures by U.S. Steel nationwide is no more than $200 million, and the actual increase in the cost of a ton of steel as a result of the pollution control measures undertaken so far is about 2.5 percent. Furthermore, the corporation's rate of net capital investment on pollution control equipment has never been more than 1 percent of the total.[70] Indeed, as we mentioned, the corporation's cost estimates are so dubious that they are under investigation by the Securities and Exchange Commission.

It is of course impossible to predict with certainty the costs of future control measures. But the EPA estimate for bringing the entire steel industry into compliance with even the strict 1983 standards for complete water pollution control is $267 million. It is unlikely, therefore, that complete compliance by the industry with all forms of environmental regulation would reach the 10 percent increase in costs estimated by the President's Council on Wage and Price Stability.

At the local level, however, the corporation is even more effective in its assertions that pollution control will result in economic devastation. In every community with steel plants, U.S. Steel has threatened cutbacks in investments and jobs if strict pollution control measures are enforced,[71] and local residents are unwilling to put this to the test. The experience with control of Gary open hearth emissions demonstrated that U.S. Steel's threats, even if exaggerated, are not idle ones.

To the extent that it must make pollution control expenditures, the corporation has been quite successful in shifting the costs onto the general population by way of the tax structure. In addition to favorable federal tax treatment, U.S. Steel is the beneficiary of an Indiana statute which excludes from all state and local taxation all expenditures on pollution control equipment. The Indiana air and water pollution control boards, notorious for their bias on behalf of industry, determine which equipment qualifies, and the Indiana attorney general has instructed them to interpret this statute with extreme liberality.[72]

Once such a facility has been so certified, the township assessor determines how much value can be deducted from the local tax bill. In Gary, my own estimate is that this legislative generosity to U.S. Steel costs the municipal treasury about $1 million a year in lost revenue. Thus, the working people of Gary wind up sharing the costs of pollution control with those responsible for it. From the standpoint of pluralist ideology, this is only fair, since both workers and capitalists are joint participants in and beneficiaries of the American political economy. But it seems to me to more truly indicate that the working people of Gary remain subordinate to the hegemony of capital, forced to participate in their own continued oppression.

Conclusion

When I went to Gary in 1968 to join the administration of Mayor Richard Hatcher I believed that U.S. Steel exercised hegemony over the city and exemplified the political control held by monopoly capital. Here was a company town, and wherever covert political power did not reside, economic influence would suffice. After immersion in the political life of Gary and a decade of research and reflection upon it, I no longer believe that this model is adequate as explanation.[1]

It now seems to me that political power in the United States is in large measure shared between competitive and monopoly capital,[2] and that it is this sharing of power, articulated through the constitutional system, which is the specific genius of American politics. This close alignment of the petty bourgeoisie with monopoly capital in control of the government and civil society, together with the virtual absence of any autonomous working-class political activity, explains contemporary American political life.[3]

For many years, Marxist theory has tended to underestimate the role of intermediary classes in society. Recently, however, there has been a new effort to put the question of the petty bourgeoisie at the center of debates about the class structure of advanced capitalist nations.[4] The main contribution of this book has been to attempt to address the role of competitive capital in our political life: it argues that it is misleading and reductionist to see this social class either as a marginal vestige of an earlier epoch or as a mere creature of monopoly capital.[5]

If this is indeed a contribution it is because I have tried to follow the cue provided by Gramsci as to how to approach the problem of political power in advanced capitalism: not to attempt to develop a "Marxist theory of the state," but rather to essay an historical inquiry into how popular consent is achieved. In such an investigation, Gramsci suggests, it is necessary to look to how the hegemonic class incorporates the real interests of other classes into the state and public policy.[6]

This historical methodology contrasts sharply with those Marxists who are engaged in elaborating a theoretical framework akin to those of the natural sciences. I would argue that it is not possible to know in advance what the balance of class forces will be by studying the structure of society.[7] The political outcomes in Gary could be determined only by the actual engagement of people in battle over them. And more broadly, at what point the limits of reform within the existing civilization will be reached can be revealed only through political struggles which reach them. And for this to happen, the mass of oppressed working people, whom, as Lenin pointed out, ordinarily remain "completely outside of political life and society," must enter and master their destiny.[8]

Our task is to participate in this process. As Antonio Gramsci put it:

> If one applies one's will to the creation of a new equilibrium among the forces which really exist and are operative—basing oneself on the particular force which one believes to be progressive and strengthening it to help it to victory—one still moves on the terrain of effective reality, but does so in order to dominate and transcend it. . . . What "ought to be" is therefore concrete; indeed it is the only realistic and historicist interpretation of reality, it alone is history in the making and philosophy in the making, it alone is politics.[9]

Notes

Introduction

1. In a self-criticism of the "extremely formalized theoretical systems" constructed by Marxist "structuralists" influenced by Louis Althusser, Manuel Castells now admits them to be of limited usefulness. "The most important task, from the point of view of the present phase of theoretical work, is not therefore to define elements and formalize their structure, but to detect the historical laws at work, in the so-called 'urban' contradictions and practices." *The Urban Question: A Marxist Approach* (Cambridge: MIT Press, 1977), p. 438.
2. For instance, mainstream pluralist Seymour Martin Lipset had concluded that the United States "is the good society itself in operation." *Political Man* (New York: Anchor Books, 1963), p. 439. And critic and poet Delmore Schwartz asserted that

   > when the future of civilization is no longer assured, a criticism of American life in terms of a contrast between avowed ideals and present reality cannot be a primary preoccupation and source of inspiration. For America . . . is now the sanctuary of culture; civilization's very existence depends upon America, upon the actuality of American life, and not the ideals of the American Dream. To criticize the actuality upon which all hope depends thus becomes a criticism of hope itself.

   Quoted in James Atlas, *Delmore Schwartz: The Life of an American Poet* (New York: Avon Books, 1978), p. 323.
3. Examples of this widespread pattern are discussed in Robert S.

Lynd and Helen Merrell Lynd, *Middletown in Transition* (New York: Harcourt, Brace and Co., 1937); Sidney Fine, *Sit-Down: The General Motors Strike of 1936-1937* (Ann Arbor: University of Michigan Press, 1969); Bruce M. Stave, *The New Deal and the Last Hurrah: Pittsburgh Machine Politics* (Pittsburgh: University of Pittsburgh Press, 1970).

4. Edward Greer, "The New Mayors: Black Power in the Big Cities," *The Nation* 219, no.17 (November 23, 1974): 525–28.

5. Examples include Warner Bloomberg, Jr., "The Power Structure of an Industrial Community" (Ph.D., University of Chicago, 1961); Peter H. Rossi and Phillip Cutright, "The Impact of Party Organization in an Industrial Setting," in *Community Political Systems*, ed. Morris Janowitz (Glencoe, N.Y.: The Free Press, 1961); Thomas Francis Thompson, "Public Administration in the Civil City of Gary, Indiana" (Ph.D., Indiana University, 1960).

6. Robert Dahl's *Who Governs?* (New Haven: Yale University Press, 1961), generally regarded as the preeminent pluralist community power study, is critiqued for these tendencies in Chapter 6.

7. In an analysis of decision-making structures of 51 cities including Gary, Terry Clark assigned each an index score of decentralization, which varied from 3.3 to 9.4. The mean score was 6.8, as was Gary's score. "Community Structure, Decision-Making, Budget Expenditures, and Urban Renewal in 51 American Cities," in *Community Politics: A Behavioral Approach*, ed. Charles M. Bonjean et al. (New York: The Free Press, 1971), p. 297, table 3.

8. The public policy issues discussed in this book are commonly chosen as representative ones in community power studies. For instance, Terry Clark picks as the four areas for comparison urban renewal, the election of the mayor, air pollution, and antipoverty programs. Ibid., pp. 293–313. Also see Peter H. Rossi and Robert Crain, "The NORC Permanent Community Sample," *The Public Opinion Quarterly* 32, no. 2 (Summer 1968): 261–72, and Clair W. Gilbert, "Community Power and Decision-making: A Quantitative Examination of Previous Reserch," in *Community Structure and Decision-making: Comparative Analyses*, ed. Terry N. Clark (San Francisco: Chandler, 1968), pp. 139–56.

9. See, for example, the critiques by Marxists Herbert Aptheker and Paul Sweezy reprinted in *C. Wright Mills and The Power Elite*, ed. G. William Domhoff and Hoyt B. Ballard (Boston: Beacon Press, 1968), pp. 115–64; and the incisive comments by Alan Stone in a review in *The American Political Science Review* 72, no. 2 (June 1978): 673–74.

10. As Peter Dreier points out, elite theory also "results in a kind of cynicism and fatalism" about the possibilities of social change. "Power Structures and Power Struggles," *The Insurgent Sociologist* 5, no. 3 (Spring 1975): 233.

11. "It is nonsense to say ... that reform does not 'really' affect the ruling class. ... The squealing is ... more than mere sham: the sense of being adversely affected and constrained is real; and this is often an accurate reflection of the concrete impact of this or that measure and action of the state." Ralph Miliband, *Marxism and Politics* (Oxford: Oxford University Press, 1977), p. 88.

12. Antonio Gramsci, *Selections from the Prison Notebooks*, ed. and trans. Quinton Hoare and G. Nowell-Smith (New York: International Publishers, 1971), p. 182. Cf. Nicos Poulantzas, *State, Power, Socialism* (London: New Left Books, 1978), p. 31.

13. The last serious investigation of competitive capital appears in C. Wright Mills, *White Collar* (New York: Oxford University Press, 1956) and its data largely derives from the 1940s. More recent radical research has largely focused on other intermediary social strata. This absence of empirical investigation is tied to an *a priori* belief that since the economy is dominated by monopoly capital, the polity must be as well.

Chapter 1: The Beginnings of Reform

1. For information on this civil rights struggle see Elizabeth Balanoff, "A History of the Black Community of Gary, Indiana 1906-1940" (Ph.D., University of Chicago, 1976); John Kaplan, "Segregation, Litigation, and the Schools—Part III: The Gary Litigation," *Northwestern University Law Review* 59, no. 1 (May-June 1964): 123–67; Max Wolff, "Segregation in the Schools of Gary, Indiana," *The Journal of Educational Sociology* 36, no. 6 (February 1963): 251–61; and *Bell v. School City of Gary*, 324 F. 2d 209, 7th (1963).

2. For further information on Hatcher's early career, see Philip T. Drotning and Wesley W. South, *Up from the Ghetto* (New York: Washington Square Press, 1971), pp. 73–86; Hal Higdon, "Gary's Next Mayor: White, Pink, or Black?" *The Reporter* 37 (November 2, 1967): 41–42; James Haskins, *A Piece of the Power: Four Black Mayors* (New York: The Dial Press, 1972), pp. 55–62; James B. Kessler, ed., *Empirical Studies of Indiana Politics: Studies of Legislative Behavior* (Bloomington: Indiana University Press, 1970);

Alex Poinsett, *Black Power Gary Style: The Making of Mayor Richard Gordon Hatcher* (Chicago: Johnson, 1970); and Carl B. Stokes, *Promises of Power: A Political Autobiography* (New York: Simon & Schuster, 1973), pp. 270–71.

3. See Edward Greer, "The 'Liberation' of Gary, Indiana," *Transaction* (January 1971): 30–39, and "Richard Hatcher and the Politics of Gary," *Social Policy* 2, no. 4 (November-December 1971): 23–28. Other black mayors have encountered similar problems. For example, as Carl Stokes put it: "Or take the councilman who used to make money on zoning changes. This man has learned to sustain his family's style on additional sources of income. He can't live on $12,500 a year. . . . There is only so long you can hold him. It is sheer economics." *Promises of Power*, p. 246. See also Kenneth R. Greene, "Overt Issue Conflict on the Cleveland City Council, 1970-1971" (paper delivered at the American Political Science Association Convention, 1973). On Newark, see Robert Curvin, "The Persistent Minority: The Black Political Experience in Newark" (Ph.D., Princeton University, 1975).

4. William Edward Nelson, Jr., "Black Political Mobilization: The 1967 Mayoral Election in Gary, Indiana" (Ph.D., University of Illinois at Urbana-Champaign, 1971), p. 289.

5. Ibid., pp. 179, 297; Poinsett, *Black Power Gary Style*, p. 78; interview with Henry Coleman, June 9, 1971; and Warner Bloomberg, Jr., "The Power Structure of an Industrial Community" (Ph.D., University of Chicago, 1961), pp. 208–10.

6. *Electoral Analysis Report*, #1 (typescript in author's possession).

7. In 1932 socialists Norman Thomas and Paul Blanshard argued:

> The power of every urban democratic machine in this country could be traced back to an urban plutocracy if the investigators had the will and understanding to do it. Tammany is an organization for private profit existing in a business system operated for private profit and the two cannot be separated.

The U.S. Communist Party also argued that "to fight corruption, above all to bare its roots in the capitalist system . . . was to fight in the interests of the workers, for it was they who paid most heavily for corrupt and inefficient government." Simon W. Gerson, *Pete: The Story of Peter V. Cacchione, New York's First Communist Councilman* (New York: International Publishers, 1976), pp. 65, 48.

8. A study of restaurants in nine cities by the Food and Drug Administration revealed that only one of these cities "aggressively enforced" sanitation ordinances and that 90 percent of the inspected restaurants were unsanitary. *New York Times*, December 15, 1975.

9. Hatcher's new health commissioner, Dr. Herschel Bornstein, explained that this violation of state law was the reason "he refused to authorize the plans when they were submitted to him . . . before the work was performed. All the other departments with jurisdiction signed it, as the one that handled the layout for the new street at the school site. Despite the lack of Bornstein's approval of the plans, work proceeded anyway on installing the sewers and water main and then paving Park Street on top of the lines." *Post-Tribune*, July 24, 1971, and September 4, 1971.

10. David Graham Nelson, "Black Reform and Federal Resources" (Ph.D., University of Chicago, 1972), p. 39. Robert Dahl reports on a similar phenomenon in New Haven. See *Who Governs?* (New Haven: Yale University Press, 1961), p. 82.

11. Efforts at theoretical rehabilitation of the urban machines can be viewed as ideologically congruent with the overall Cold War celebration of the American political system. Marxist notions of the class character of the state would be discredited if the machines simultaneously served the interests of all social classes. Moreover, pluralist notions that American politics were similar to an economic "free market"—in which the wealth of the rich was counterbalanced by the larger number of votes of the poor—that maximized the public interest, was buttressed by asserting that the machine performed this very mediating task. Cf. Christopher Lasch, "The Cultural Cold War: A Short History of the Congress for Cultural Freedom," in *Towards a New Past: Dissenting Essays in American History*, ed. Barton J. Bernstein (New York: Pantheon, 1968), pp. 322–59, and Jesse Lemisch, *On Active Service in War and Peace: Politics and Ideology in the American Historical Profession* (Toronto: New Hogtown Press, 1975).

12. Robert K. Merton, *Social Theory and Social Structure: Toward the Codification of Theory and Research* (Glencoe: The Free Press, 1949).

13. Oscar Handlin, for example, assimilated Merton's thesis into his study of Boston's immigrant history. According to Handlin, the machine boss benevolently "intervened at the points at which his people encountered the difficulties of the law. Between the rigid, impersonal rulings of the statute and the human failings of those ignorant of its complexities he stood as mediator." Moreover, it was the reformers opposed to machine politics who, in attempting to reduce local expenditures, tried to fire the immigrant municipal employees for whom the machine had provided jobs. Naturally the immigrant workers voted for the machine bosses. See Oscar Handlin,

Boston's Immigrants: A Study in Acculturation (Rev. ed., New York: Atheneum, 1975), pp. 212–21.

14. See Fred I. Greenstein, "The Changing Pattern of Urban Politics," and Elmer E. Cornwall, Jr., "Bosses, Machines, and Ethnic Groups," in *City Bosses and Political Machines,* ed. Lee S. Greene; *The Annals of the American Academy of Political and Social Science* 353 (May, 1964): 1–13 and 27–39; and James Q. Wilson, review of Edward Tufte, "Political Control of the Economy" in *Commentary* 66, no. 6 (December 1978): 82.

15. Thus, this analyst continues, "Mayor Daley is a representative of that class in no uncertain terms." Jack Metzgar, "Mayor Daley and the Working Class," *Socialist Revolution* 7, no. 2 (March-April 1977): 128. An acceptance of the pluralist paradigm is also found in the work of "new left" urbanist Ira Katznelson (*Black Men, White Cities: Race, Politics, and Migration in the United States 1900-30 and Britain 1948-68* [New York: Oxford University Press, 1973], pp. 111–16, and "Urban Counter-revolution," in *1984 Revisited: Prospects for American Politics,* ed. Robert Paul Wolff [New York: Alfred A. Knopf, 1973], pp. 142–44, 155) and that of William E. Nelson, Jr. and Philip J. Meranto (*Electing Black Mayors: Political Action in the Black Community* [Columbus: Ohio State University Press, 1977], p. 22).

16. See Raymond Wolfinger, *The Politics of Progress* (Englewood Cliffs, N.J.: Prentice-Hall, 1974), p. 67.

17. For New Haven, see ibid., pp. 67–79; for Chicago, see Katznelson, *Black Men,* p. 101. Generally, see Allan Rosenbaum, "Machine Politics, Class Interest and the Urban Poor" (paper presented at 1973 American Political Science Association Annual Convention), and Marguerite Ross Barnett and James A. Hefner, eds., *Public Policy for the Black Community: Strategies and Perspectives* (New York: Alfred Knopf, 1976), p. 9.

   Stephan Thernstrom's detailed study of the Boston Irish at the turn of the century reveals that despite their capture of Boston's political machinery, they lagged occupationally behind other ethnic immigrants in that city who began in a comparable position. *The Other Bostonians: Poverty and Progress in the American Metropolis, 1880-1970* (Cambridge: Harvard University Press, 1973), pp. 143, 167. Cf. the review by Edward Greer in *Monthly Review* 26, no. 9 (February 1975): 51–57.

18. Matthew Holden, *The White Man's Burden* (New York: Chandler, 1973), pp. 94–119, and John M. Allswang, *Bosses, Machines, and*

Urban Voters: An American Symbiosis (Port Washington, N.Y.: Kennikat Press, 1977), p. 106. And see Wolfinger, *Politics of Progress*, p. 47. Furthermore, Allan Rosenbaum indicates that the machines played only a marginal role in socially integrating newcomers to the city. "Machine Politics," pp. 12–16.

19. For the definition of the petty bourgeoisie used here see Arno Mayer, "The Lower Middle Class as Historical Problem," *Journal of Modern History* 47, no. 3 (September 1975): 424.

    The Democratic Party affiliation of most urban machines reflects the historic concentraton of non-Protestant, nonmonopoly businesses within its ranks. Richard F. Hamilton, *Class and Politics in the United States* (New York: John Wiley & Sons, 1972). As G. William Domhoff puts it:

    > The machine Democrats are not the creatures of the most important business interests in their region. They are instead ethnic Americans who look out for the interests of Irish, Italian, Jewish, and Polish businessmen in little uptown banks, construction companies, insurance agencies, real-estate firms, and marginal businesses that sell supplies and services to government agencies and large corporations.

    Fat-Cats and Democrats: The Role of the Big Rich in the Party of the Common Man (Englewood Cliffs, N.J.: Prentice-Hall, 1972), p. 98.

20. According to Paul Peterson:

    > Machine politicians, too, have an ideological commitment to the principles and practices of institutionalized bargaining. Indeed, at times even these master politicos will place the preservation of this bargaining structure above any immediate electoral gain. . . . The Chicago machine, though it bargained with diverse groups and interests, responded differently to demands from interests outside the institutionalized bargaining order. With these "illegitimate" interests, pluralist bargaining could not proceed without violating a basic component of the ideology that supported and legitimated the structure of power that the Chicago machine had constructed.

    School Politics, Chicago Style (Chicago: University of Chicago Press, 1976), pp. 50–51.

21. C. Wright Mills, "The Middle Classes in Middle-Sized Cities," in *Power, Politics, and People: The Collected Essays of C. Wright Mills*, ed. Irving Louis Horowitz (New York: Oxford University Press, 1967), p. 282, and Raymond Wolfinger, "Ethnic Political Behavior," in *White Ethnics: Life in Working-Class America*, ed.

Joseph A. Ryan (Englewood Cliffs: Prentice-Hall, 1973), pp. 134–37.

Expressing this relationship from a different standpoint, Sidney Verba and Norman H. Nie make the same point. See *Participation in America: Political Democracy and Social Equality* (New York: Harper and Row, 1972), p. 281.

22. Rosenbaum, "Machine Politics," and J. David Greenstone, *Labor in American Politics* (New York: Alfred A. Knopf, 1969). On the postwar relations between the Gary machine and the Steelworkers' Union see William Kornblum, *Blue Collar Community* (Chicago: University of Chicago Press, 1974), pp. 220–21.

23. Raymond E. Wolfinger, "Why Political Machines Have Not Withered Away and Other Revisionist Thoughts," *The Journal of Politics* 34, no. 4 (May 1972): 377.

As V. I. Lenin put it in *State and Revolution:*

> In particular, it is the petty bourgeoisie who are attracted to the side of the big bourgeoisie and largely subordinated to them through [the state] apparatus, which provides the upper sections of the peasants, small artisans, tradesmen and the like with comparatively comfortable, quiet, and respectable jobs raising their holders *above* the people.

Selected Works in Three Volumes, Vol. II (New York: International Publishers, 1967), p. 228.

24. Wolfinger, *Politics,* pp. 120–21; Virginia B. Ermer, "Housing Inspection in Baltimore: Vermin, Mannequins, and Beer Bottles," in *Blacks and Bureaucracy: Readings in the Problems and Politics of Change,* ed. Virginia B. Ermer and John H. Stranger (New York: Thomas Y. Crowell, 1972), pp. 82–92; and Nelson, "Black Reform," p. 39.

25. Not only did the New Deal reforms fail to undermine the machines, they actually strengthened them by providing them with vast additional "favors" to distribute. Wolfinger, *Politics,* p. 109; Stave, *The New Deal,* pp. 22, 170; and Gene Delon Jones, "The Origins of the Alliance Between the New Deal and the Chicago Machine," *Journal of the Illinois State Historical Society* 67, no. 3 (June 1974): 253–74.

26. As Merton puts it, for workers "participation in revolutionary organizations . . . can be seen . . . as an alternative form of organizational adjustment" to machine politics. *Social Theory and Social Structure,* p. 373, note 105. See Antonio Gramsci on the similar phenomenon of *trasformismo* which accompanied the formation of the Italian state in the nineteenth century. *Selections from the*

Prison Notebooks, ed. and trans. Quinton Hoare and G. Nowell-Smith (New York: International Publishers, 1971), pp. 58–59.

27. The case of trade union accommodation to the machines, which has reduced the class combativeness and served to block the development of autonomous working-class political activity, is the main case of this sort. Greenstone, *Labor in American Politics,* and C. Wright Mills, *The New Men of Power: America's Labor Leaders* (New York: Harcourt, Brace, 1948), p. 184. Also see Karl Klare, "The Judicial Deradicalization of the Wagner Act and the Origins of Modern Legal Consciousness, 1937-1941," *Minnesota Law Review* 62, no. 3 (March 1978): 265–339.

28. In contrast to the white ethnic vote for the New Deal, due largely to the enrollment of previous nonvoters, an actual decision apparently was made by large numbers of previously Republican blacks to shift to the Democratic Party. Norman H. Nie, Sidney Verba, and John R. Petrocik, *The Changing American Voter* (Cambridge: Harvard University Press, 1976), pp. 74–95, 214, note 7.

29. Katznelson, *Black Men,* pp. 62–119, and Charles V. Hamilton, "Racial, Ethnic and Social Class Politics and Administration," *Public Administration Review* 32 (October 1972): 638–48.

30. John H. Fenton, *Midwest Politics* (New York: Holt, Rinehart and Winston, 1966), p. 182, note 15; Richard O. Boyer, *The Legend of John Brown: A Biography and a History* (New York: Alfred A. Knopf, 1973), p. 83; and Emma Lou Thornbrough, *The Negro in Indiana Before 1900* (Indianapolis: Indiana State Historical Society, 1957), and "Segregation in Indiana During the Klan Era of the 1920s," *Mississippi Valley Historical Review* 47 (March 1961): 594–618.

31. Neil Betten and Raymond A. Mohl, "The Evolution of Racism in an Industrial City, 1906–1940: A Case Study of Gary, Indiana," *The Journal of Negro History* 59, no. 1 (January 1974): 64. See also Powell A. Moore, *The Calumet Region: Indiana's Last Frontier* (Indianapolis: Indiana State Historical Society, 1959), pp. 540–50.

32. Balanoff, "Black Community of Gary," pp. 458–61. See also James B. Lane, *City of the Century: A History of Gary, Indiana* (Bloomington: Indiana University Press, 1978), p. 48.

33. The overall vote in Gary in 1932 gave Hoover a slight majority. For a longer discussion of the relationship of blacks to political parties in Gary, see Richard Julius Meister, "A History of Gary, Indiana: 1930-1940" (Ph.D., University of Notre Dame, 1967), p. 272, and John Foster Potts, "A History of the Growth of the Negro Population

of Gary, Indiana" (M.A., Cornell University, 1937), pp. 47–48. Generally, see Paul R. Abramson, *Generational Change in American Politics* (Lexington, Mass.: D. C. Heath, 1975), p. 9, and Harold F. Gosnell, "The Chicago 'Black Belt' as a Political Battleground," *The American Journal of Sociology* 39, no. 3 (November 1933): 338–39.

34. Horace R. Cayton and George S. Mitchell, *Black Workers and the New Unions* (Chapel Hill: University of North Carolina Press, 1939), pp. 379, 389–92. For similar patterns in other northern industrial communities of the period see Larry Cuban, "A Strategy for Racial Peace: Negro Leadership in Cleveland, 1900-1919," *Phylon* 28 (Fall 1967): 299–311. In Steelton, where Bethlehem Steel controlled the local Republican Party, there was also a black city councilman who never criticized company policy. John C. Bodnar, "Peter C. Blackwell and the Negro Community of Steelton, 1860-1920," *The Pennsylvania Magazine of History and Biography* 97, no. 2 (April 1973): 199–209.

35. Nie, *Changing American Voter,* pp. 74–96, and Meister, "History of Gary," p. 274. In Chicago, where blacks were only 9 percent of the population, they constituted almost 20 percent of the Republican voters, and control over this vote was decisive for victory in the primaries and vital for the general election. Gosnell, *Political Battleground,* p. 341.

Regardless of precisely when and how the urban ethnic working-class vote turned decisively Democratic, it is sufficient to realize that at the end of the 1920s and early 1930s a new, majority Democratic Party coalition was emerging. On this historical event see David Burner, *The Politics of Provincialism: The Democratic Party in Transition, 1918-1932* (New York: Alfred A. Knopf, 1968); Jerome M. Club and Howard W. Allen, "The Cities and the Election of 1928: Partisan Realignment," *The American Historical Review* 74, no. 4 (April 1969): 1204–20; Abramson, *Generational Change;* and Bernard Sternsher, "The Emergence of the New Deal Party System: A Problem in Historical Analysis of Voter Behavior," *The Journal of Interdisciplinary History* 6, no. 1 (Summer 1975): 127–49. For Chicago in particular see Humbert S. Nelli, "Ethnic Group Assimilation: The Italian Experience," in *Cities in American History,* ed., Kenneth F. Jackson and Stanley K. Schultz (New York: Alfred A. Knopf, 1972), pp. 199–215; Jones, "New Deal and the Chicago Machine," pp. 253–74; John D. Buenker, "The Dynamics of Chicago Ethnic Politics 1900-1930," *Journal of the Illinois State Historical*

Society 67, no. 2 (April 1974): 175–200; and Nie, *Changing American Voter*, pp. 74–95, 214, note 7.

36. The first black Democrat was elected to Gary's city council in 1934 (Potts, "Growth of the Negro Population," pp. 47–48), and in 1936 Gary went for Roosevelt by two to one. Nationally, in 1938, 85 percent of black voters considered themselves Democrats (Meister, "History of Gary," pp. 284–94, and Abramson, *Generational Change*, p. 9). Two case studies of this shift—in Chicago by John M. Allswang and in Cincinnati by Ernest M. Collins—appear in *The Negro in Depression and War: Prelude to Revolution, 1930-1945*, ed. Bernard Sternsher (Chicago: Quadrangle Books, 1969).

37. Of course, at no time did blacks obtain their fair share of the better paid city jobs; the positions were largely lowly ones.

38. Abramson, *Generational Change*, pp. 9, 24, table 2.3.

39. Bloomberg, "Power Structure," pp. 208–10.

40. Peter H. Rossi and Philips Cutright, "The Impact of Party Organization in an Industrial Setting," in *Community Political Systems*, ed. Morris Janowitz, Vol. 1, *International Yearbook of Political Behavior Research* (Glencoe: The Free Press, 1961), pp. 87–93; Verba and Nie, *Participation in America*, pp. 164–70.

41. See George Crile, "A Tax Assessor Has Many Friends," *Harper's Magazine* 245, no. 1470 (November 1972): 106. For other examples see Richard Balzer, *Street Times: Text Based on Conversations with Fred Harris* (New York: Grossman Publishers, 1972), pp. 16–17, and Peter Schuck and Harrison Wood, "Democracy and the Good Life in a Company Town: The Case of St. Mary's, Georgia," *Harper's Magazine* 224, no. 1464 (May 1972): 57.

42. Cf. M. McMullan, "A Theory of Corruption," The Sociological Review 9, no. 2 (July 1961): 181–201.

43. Quoted in Nelson and Meranto, *Black Mayors*, p. 183.

44. For Gary, see David R. Meyer, "Classification of U.S. Metropolitan Areas by the Characteristics of Their Nonwhite Populations," in *City Classification Handbook: Methods and Applications*, ed. Brian J. L. Berry (New York: John Wiley & Sons, 1972), p. 69. For a detailed discussion of this question with regard to Detroit, see Joel D. Aberbach and Jack L. Walker, *Race in the City: Political Trust and Public Policy in the New Urban System* (Boston: Little, Brown, 1973), pp. 28–30. Generally, see Michael J. Flax, *Blacks and Whites: An Experiment in Social Indicators* (Washington, D.C.: The Urban Institute, 1971), p. 58, table 23. Carl Stokes sums up this transforma-

tion by asserting that "by 1965 it was becoming clear to me that the ethnic machine that had run Cleveland for more than a generation was running out of steam." *Promises of Power*, p. 80. And see Stave, *New Deal*, pp. 175–82.

45. Meister, "History of Gary," pp. 279–89, and Daniel Epstein, *Ray J. Madden: Democratic Representative from Indiana*, Ralph Nader Congress Project (New York: Grossman Publishers, 1972), pp. 1–5.

46. Kornblum, *Blue Collar Community*, pp. 220–21. See also Mills, *New Men*, pp. 62–107; Greenstone, *Labor in American Politics*, pp. 40–65; Bloomberg, *Power Structure*, p. 90; Raymond A. Mohl and Neil Betten, "Gary, Indiana: The Urban Laboratory as a Teaching Tool," *The History Teacher* 4, no. 2 (January 1971): 9; and John Conroy, "Mill Town: Part Three," *Chicago Magazine* 26, no. 1 (January 1977): 114 ff.

47. Thomas Francis Thompson, "Public Administration in the Civil City of Gary, Indiana" (Ph.D., Indiana University, 1960), p. 77. See also Crile, "Tax Assessor," p. 102; Fenton, *Midwest Politics*, pp. 166–67; Victor S. Navasky, *Kennedy Justice* (New York: Atheneum, 1971), pp. 166–67; and Arthur M. Schlesinger, Jr., *Robert Kennedy and His Times* (New York: Houghton Mifflin, 1978), pp. 383–84.

48. Bloomberg, "Power Structure," pp. 173–74.

49. Crile, "Tax Assessor." Generally, see Michael Stone, "The Housing Crisis, Mortgage Lending, and Class Struggle," *Antipode* 7, no. 2 (September 1975): 28.

50. Interview with Professor David Nelson, June 14, 1972. Such had not always been the pattern. When the Republican mayor went to prison in 1925 (later to be pardoned by President Coolidge after serving only a fraction of his sentence) he did so with a public expression of sympathy from superintendent William P. Gleason. In 1929 he was reelected mayor, and again indicted in 1932 for using city money in the construction of a summer cottage. *New York Times*, March 29, 1925; May 9, 1929; and January 21, 1932.

51. See Nelson, "Black Reform," p. 75.

52. According to Paul E. Peterson, "in 1967, after his position [of opposition to] integration became clear, his percentage in these white wards increased to 69 percent, in 1971 it increased again to 72 percent, and in 1975 it reached a peak of 79 percent." *School Politics*, pp. 33–35.

53. Chuck Stone, "Report—Gary, Indiana," *The Atlantic* 220, no. 4 (October 1957): 28–29.

54. *Post-Tribune*, February 8, 1967, and February 28, 1967.

55. "Mass Media and the Black Community," *The Black Scholar* 5, no. 1 (September 1973): 4. Nelson and Meranto characterize the newspaper as extraordinarily harsh in its coverage of the Hatcher administration, "playing up mistakes and underplaying important accomplishments." *Black Mayors*, p. 367.
56. *Post-Tribune*, March 19, 1967; April 17, 1967; and April 18, 1967.
57. For further information on the *Post-Tribune* see Moore, *Calumet Region*, pp. 428–41; Meister, "History of Gary," pp. 67, 118–21; and *Post-Tribune*, January 6, 1967.
58. For a detailed discussion of Hatcher's campaign organizations see Nelson, Jr., "Mobilization," pp. 322–96.
59. Rossi and Cutright, "Party Organization," p. 100; "Electoral Analysis"; *Post-Tribune*, March 21, 1967; March 27, 1967; April 25, 1967; and May 7, 1967; Nelson, Jr., "Mobilization," p. 470; and interviews with confidential informants. Generally, see Katznelson, *Black Men*, p. 99, and Stokes, *Promises of Power*, pp. 82, 91.
60. Nelson and Meranto, *Black Mayors*, pp. 235–36.
61. *Post-Tribune*, May 20, 1967.
62. Ibid., March 21, 1967; May 3, 1967; and May 7, 1967. See also Michael Rogin, "Politics, Emotion, and the Wallace Vote," *British Journal of Sociology* 20, no. 1 (March 1969): 27–49, and Thomas F. Pettigrew, "Ethnicity in American Life: A Social Psychological Perspective," in *Ethnicity in American Life*, ed. John Hope Franklin et al. (New York: Anti-Defamation League of B'nai Brith, 1971), pp. 29–31.
63. Kornblum, *Blue Collar Community*, pp. 202–3.
64. *Post-Tribune*, May 20, 1967.
65. Quoted in Nelson, Jr., "Mobilization," p. 405. Hatcher and other key members of his administration have reiterated this point to me repeatedly.
66. Poinsett, *Black Power Gary Style*, pp. 80–81.
67. *Post-Tribune*, September 30, 1967.
68. On the technical issue of voter registration see Roger K. Oden, "Black Political Power in Gary, Indiana: A Theoretical and Structural Analysis" (Ph.D., University of Chicago, 1977), pp. 37–38; on the general election campaign see Nelson and Meranto, *Black Mayors*, pp. 270–321.
69. Nelson, Jr., "Mobilization," p. 428. As Carl Stokes, who was simultaneously running for mayor of Cleveland, put it: "The national Democratic Party wanted a black Democrat as mayor of a major city to solidify its support from black voters." *Promises of Power*, p. 97.

70. See Chuck Stone, *Black Political Power in America* (Indianapolis: Bobbs-Merrill, 1968), pp. 213–18; Nelson, Jr., "Mobilization," pp. 397–472; and Thomas F. Pettigrew, "When a Black Candidate Runs for Mayor: Race and Voting Behavior," in *People and Politics in Urban Society*, ed. Harlan Hahn, *Urban Affairs Annual Review* 6 (Beverly Hills: Sage Publishers, 1972), pp. 95–118.

Chapter 2: The Origins of an Industrial Center

1. See Harvey O'Connor, *Steel-Dictator* (New York: John Day, 1935), p. 24; Melvin I. Urofsky, *Big Steel and the Wilson Administration: A Study in Business-Government Relations* (Columbus: Ohio State University Press, 1969), p. 8; George E. Mowry, *The Era of Theodore Roosevelt and the Birth of Modern America, 1900-1912* (New York: Harper and Brothers, 1958), pp. 218–19; Gertrude G. Schroeder, *The Growth of Major Steel Companies, 1900-1950*, The Johns Hopkins University Studies in Historical and Political Science, Series 70, no. 2 (Baltimore: The Johns Hopkins Press, 1953), pp. 39, 175, 216; and Henry R. Seager and Charles A. Gulick, Jr., *Trust and Corporation Problems* (New York: Harper and Brothers, 1929), p. 224.

2. Schroeder, *Growth of Major Steel*, pp. 38, 125–26. See also Peter Temin, *Iron and Steel in Nineteenth Century America: An Economic Inquiry* (Cambridge: MIT Press, 1964), 189–93; U.S. Steel, *First Annual Report*, pp. 38–39; Seager and Gulick, *Trust and Corporation*, p. 255; and Kenneth Warren, *The American Steel Industry, 1850-1970: A Geographical Interpretation*, Oxford Researches in Geography (Oxford: Clarendon Press, 1973), p. 132.

3. William T. Hogan, *Economic History of the Iron and Steel Industry in the United States* (Lexington, Mass.: D. C. Heath, 1971), Vol. I, pp. 218–24, Vol. II, pp. 402, 649; Maurice H. Yeates and Barry J. Garner, *The North American City* (New York: Harper and Row, 1971), p. 45; and Allan R. Pred, *The Spatial Dynamics of U.S. Urban-Industrial Growth, 1800-1914: Interpretative and Theoretical Essays* (Cambridge: MIT Press, 1966), pp. 16–17.

4. Pennsylvania Station was designed by the architectural firm of McKim, Mead, and White, the same firm that designed the impressive annex of the New York Life Insurance Company; the head of the latter, George W. Perkins, later became a key member of the board of directors of U.S. Steel. While various illicit relationships between

the two corporations were revealed by the New York State Armstrong Commission, Perkins escaped indictment. Morton Keller, *The Life Insurance Enterprise, 1895-1910: A Study in the Limits of Corporate Power* (Cambridge: Harvard University Press, 1963), pp. 39, 181; John A. Garraty, *Right-Hand Man: The Life of George W. Perkins* (New York: Harper and Brothers, 1960); Temin, *Iron and Steel*, pp. 127–30, 222–23; and Carl W. Condit, *American Building: Materials and Techniques from the First Colonial Settlements to the Present* (Chicago: University of Chicago Press, 1968), pp. 179–83.

5. Hogan, *Economic History*, Vol. I, pp. 211, 303–5, Vol. II, pp. 649–51, 708–9. See also *The Iron Age* 77 (March 22, 1906): 1022, and Condit, *American Building*, pp. 117–18, 125, 256.

6. Prior to World War I, however, the automobile industry was not a significant steel consumer. For instance, in 1909 less steel was used for automobiles than in constructing the Manhattan Bridge. As late as 1917 only 7 percent of steel was produced in the form of sheets. (By 1940 this proportion had risen to 24 percent.) Temin, *Iron and Steel*, p. 230.

7. Pred, *Spatial Dynamics*, pp. 12, 21; Yeates and Garner, *North American City*, p. 30. For more information see John R. Borchert, "American Metropolitan Evolution," *The Geographical Review* 57, no. 3 (July 1967): 319; David Ward, *Cities and Immigrants: A Geography of Change in Nineteenth-Century America* (New York: Oxford University Press, 1971), pp. 13, 41; Gunnar Alexandersson, *The Industrial Structure of American Cities: A Geographic Study of Urban Economy in the United States* (London: George Allen and Unwin, 1956), pp. 38–39; and A. Michael Turner, "Gary, Indiana: The Establishment and Early Development of an Industrial Community, 1906-1930" (B.A., University of Keele, 1971), pp. 4–6.

8. Hogan, *Economic History*, Vol. I, p. 325. The Calumet region consists of the southern industrial section of Chicago and the industrial region of northern Lake County, Indiana. See John B. Appleton, *The Iron and Steel Industry of the Calumet Region: A Study in Economic Geography* (Urbana: University of Illinois, 1927), pp. 10–11, and Powell A. Moore, *The Calumet Region: Indiana's Last Frontier* (Indianapolis: Indiana Historical Bureau, 1959), p. 1.

9. Stanley Buder, *Pullman: An Experiment in Industrial Order and Community Planning, 1880-1930* (New York: Oxford University Press, 1967), pp. 17–26, 49; Sam Bass Warner, Jr., *The Urban Wilderness: A History of the American City* (New York: Harper and

Row, 1972), p. 105; and Harold M. Mayer and Richard C. Wade, *Chicago: Growth of a Metropolis* (Chicago: University of Chicago Press, 1969), p. 186. Also see Graham Romeyn Taylor, *Satellite Cities: A Study of Industrial Suburbs* (New York: D. Appleton, 1915).

10. Pred, *Spatial Dynamics*, p. 66; Appleton, *Iron and Steel Industry*, p. 31; Isaac James Quillen, "Industrial City: A History of Gary, Indiana to 1929" (Ph.D., Yale University, 1942), pp. 52–53; and Raymond A. Mohl and Neil Betten, "The Failure of Industrial City Planning: Gary, Indiana, 1906-1910," *Journal of the American Institute of Planners* (July 1972): 204.

11. On the one hand, locating closer to the market would gain as additional profit what would otherwise have to be paid on railroads in freight charges, but on the other hand, monopoly conditions made it rational to protect existing capital by sheltering older plants for longer periods than would be the case under competitive conditions. Thus, U.S. Steel did maintain the bulk of its production facilities in Pittsburgh for decades after the market had shifted westward. See Alan Rodgers, "Industrial Inertia—A Major Factor in the Location of the Steel Industry in the United States," *The Geographical Review* (January 1952): 61.

12. Speech of Judge Elbert Gary in Duluth, Minnesota, June 12, 1918, as quoted in Turner, "Gary, Indiana," p. 7. Also see Stephen Becker, *Marshall Field III: A Biography* (New York: Simon & Schuster, 1964), p. 52; Graham Romeyn Taylor, "Creating the Newest Steel City," *The Survey* 22 (April 3, 1909): 21–22; and Mayer and Wade, *Chicago*, pp. 234–48.

13. Paul R. Hanna, I. James Quillen, and Gladys L. Patter, *Ten Communities* (Chicago: Scott, Foresman, 1940), pp. 428–30.

14. "County Population, 1810-1960," *Indiana History Bulletin* 45, no. 6 (June 1968): 74. As in the large majority of such cases, the promoters were unsuccessful. John W. Reps, *The Making of Urban America: A History of City Planning in the United States* (Princeton, N.J.: Princeton University Press, 1965), ch. 14.

15. See Moore, *Calumet Region*, pp. 130–256.

16. H. S. Norton, "Gary, Indiana," *The Coupon*, 1, no. 9 (August 1922): 2.

17. Moore, *Calumet Region*, p. 259.

18. See O'Connor, *Steel-Dictator*, p. 14; Quillen, "Industrial City," pp. 52–59, 84–85; Mohl and Betten, "Industrial City Planning," p. 204; "U.S. Steel—I," *Fortune* (March 1936): 195; and Robert Murray

Hague, "The Unearned Increment in Gary," *Political Science Quarterly* 32 (March 1917): 81–82.

19. U.S. Steel, *Fourth Annual Report* (1905), p. 25. See also Reps, *Making of Urban America*, p. 427; Mohl and Betten, "Industrial City Planning," p. 206; and *The Iron Age* 77: 1417.

20. It was not until the *Fifth Annual Report* that mention was made the decision to also build a city.

21. Taylor, "Creating the Newest Steel City," p. 24. Similarly, the two most important new additions to the steelmaking capacity of the Pittsburgh district, Clairton and Donora, each has its own town. *The Iron Age* 77: 1022. See also Horace Davis, "Company Towns," *Encyclopedia of the Social Sciences* (New York: Macmillan, 1931), Vol. 4, p. 119.

22. Turner, "Gary, Indiana," p. 14. See also Harold M. Mayer, "Politics and Land Use: The Indiana Shoreline of Lake Michigan," *Annals of the Association of American Geographers* 54, no. 4 (December 1964): 508–23, and Henry P. Fuller, "An Industrial Utopia: Building Gary, Indiana to Order," *Harper's Weekly* 51, no. 2651 (October 12, 1907): 1482.

   Currently, "the filled area extends about 1,800 to 2,000 feet into the lake and roughly parallels the original shore. Using Gary Harbor as a reference, the fill extends along the shore about 9,700 feet to the east and about 21,400 feet to the west." Letter to the author from James P. Jones, Chief, Operations Division, U.S. Army Corps of Engineers, Chicago District (November 13, 1973).

23. See the article by land agent A. K. Knotts in the Gary *Post-Tribune*, June 3, 1931, and *Journal of the Indiana State Senate during the Sixty-Fifth Session of the General Assembly* (Indianapolis: Wm. B. Burford, 1907), pp. 168, 210, 1884, 1948.

24. Nevertheless, the line was in constant economic troubles; despite an agreement with the Elgin to carry overflow war order freight of the Gary Works, it went into receivership by the end of World War I. See George W. Hilton and John F. Due, *The Electric Interurban Railways in America* (Stanford: Stanford University Press, 1960); William D. Middleton, *South Shore: The Last Interurban* (San Marino, Cal.: Golden West Books, 1970); and Glen E. Holt, "The Changing Perception of Urban Pathology: An Essay on the Development of Mass Transit in the United States," in *Cities in American History*, ed. Kenneth E. Jackson and Stanley K. Schultz (New York: Alfred A. Knopf, 1972), p. 331.

25. From 1901 to 1910 the corporation expended $290 million on all

capital improvements, and its total steel capacity rose from 15 million tons in 1906 to 20 million tons in 1910. This vigorous expansion policy enabled it to maintain its hegemony over the industry. See U.S. Steel, *Annual Reports*, 1906 through 1911.

26. Taylor, *Satellite Cities*, p. 180.

27. U.S. Steel, *Sixth Annual Report* (1907), p. 31. The company made substantial profits by selling these utilities at high prices (30 percent above those prevailing in Chicago). And company officials who owned the stock (such as board chairman E. J. Buffington) made immense profits. Ultimately this became so scandalous that the corporation in 1930 divested itself of ownership. See Quillen, "Industrial City," p. 287, and Richard Julius Meister, "A History of Gary, Indiana: 1930-1940" (Ph.D., University of Notre Dame, 1967), pp. 144–46.

28. See Graham Romeyn Taylor, "Satellite Cities—V. Gary," *The Survey* 29 (March 1913): 796.

29. See Hogan, *Economic History*, Vol. II, pp. 363, 376, 427; Appleton, *Iron and Steel Industry*, pp. 70–72; and U.S. Steel, *Ninth Annual Report* (1910), p. 28. Also new was the choice of the open hearth over the Bessemer steelmaking process. Whereas in 1901 one-third of American steel was produced in open hearths, in 1910, after the massive Gary installations, the proportion was two-thirds. Temin, *Iron and Steel*, pp. 272–73.

30. See Moore, *Calumet Region*, pp. 301, 327–30; U.S. Steel, *Eighth Annual Report* (1909), pp. 29–30, and *Ninth Annual Report* (1910), p. 28; Seager and Gulick, *Trust and Corporation*, p. 250; Appleton, *Iron and Steel Industry*, pp. 33–34; and Schroeder, *Growth of Major Steel*, p. 114, table 4.

31. See Leifur Magnusson, *Housing by Employers in the United States* (Washington: Government Printing Office, 1920), p. 12; Pierre Merlin, *New Towns: Regional Planning and Development* (London: Methuen, 1971), p. 243; and Rex A. Lucas, *Minetown, Milltown, Railtown: Life of Canadian Communities of Single Industry* (Toronto: University of Toronto Press, 1971), pp. 17–20.

32. See Davis, "Company Towns," pp. 119–21; James B. Allen, *The Company Town of the American West* (Norman: University of Oklahoma Press, 1966), pp. 4–5; Philip L. Cook, "Tom M. Girdler and the Labor Policies of Republic Steel Corporation," *Social Science* 42, no. 1 (January 1967): 22–23; and William L. Patterson, *The Man Who Cried Genocide: An Autobiography* (New York: International Publishers, 1971), p. 127.

33. See Magnusson, *Housing by Employers*, pp. 10–13, 170; Davis, "Company Towns," pp. 119–20; Allen, *The Company Town*, pp. 82, 102; and David Brody, *Steelworkers in America: The Nonunion Era* (Cambridge: Harvard University Press, 1960), p. 88.

34. Quoted in Brody, *Steelworkers in America*, p. 87. See also Reps, *Making of Urban America*, pp. 424–26, and Turner, "Gary, Indiana," p. 31.

35. Becker, *Marshall Field*, p. 52.

36. See O'Connor, *Steel-Dictator*, p. 15, and Buder, *Pullman*, pp. 16, 30–31, 208–12.

37. Buffington had first met Judge Gary in 1898, when Gary was conducting negotiations to set up the American Steel and Wire Company through the purchase of various independent steel producers. Buffington sold his firm to Gary and in the course of negotiations the two men developed a high mutual esteem. Buffington was made the president of both the new operating division, the Indiana Steel Corporation, and the Gary Land Company, which built the city. Ultimately he became a director of the corporation. Ida M. Tarbell, *The Life of Elbert H. Gary: A Story of Steel* (rep.ed., New York: Greenwood Press, 1969), pp. 85–86.

38. Eugene J. Buffington, "Making Cities for Workmen," *Harper's Weekly* 53, no. 2733 (May 8, 1909): 15–16. See also Charles A. Gulick, *Labor Policy of the United States Steel Corporation* (New York: AMS Press, 1924).

39. Quoted in Quillen, "Industrial City," pp. 89–90. See also Mayer and Wade, *Chicago*, pp. 234–38.

40. Taylor, *Satellite Cities*, p. 180, and Brody, *Steelworkers in America*, pp. 80–95.

41. As Graham Romeyn Taylor summarized the content of his interviews with leading corporation executives: "they say frankly that the building of the town was incidental, that their main concern was to construct a steel plant, and that city-making was a side issue into which necessity alone drove them." "Creating the Newest Steel City," p. 24. Such a devolution of power is now the norm where companies initiate towns. See Lucas, *Minetown, Milltown, Railtown*, p. 60.

42. Quillen, "Industrial City," p. 191. As Brody puts it, "The more substantial merchants and professionals recognized a kinship with the plant officialdom. They lived in the same sections, frequented the same clubs and churches, and shared its outlook on industrial and business matters." *Steelworkers in America*, p. 118.

43. U.S. Steel, *Sixth Annual Report* (1907), p. 31; Quillen, "Industrial City," pp. 181, 224; and Moore, *Calumet Region*, pp. 265–66, 432–35, 540.
44. Gary Planning Commission, *Master Plan Report Number One: Physical Data* (Evanston, Ill.: Tech-Search, Inc., 1963), p. 35. In this Gary was like most American cities. See John L. Hancock, "Planners in the Changing American City, 1900-1940," *American Urban History*, ed. Alexander B. Callow (New York: Oxford University Press, 1969), p. 551.
45. Warner, Jr., *The Urban Wilderness*, p. 21.
46. Taylor, "Creating the Newest Steel City," p. 26. See also Michael T. Klare, "The Architecture of Imperial America," *Science and Society* 33, no. 3 (Summer-Fall 1969): 276–77.
47. Fewer than one-tenth of the 43,000 lots which now constitute Gary ever belonged to U.S. Steel. Mohl and Betten, "Industrial City Planning," pp. 206, 210; Moore, *Calumet Region*, 287; and U.S. Steel, *Sixth Annual Report* (1907), p. 31.
48. Gary Planning Commission, *Master Plan*, pp. 25–27, 41. See also Charles Abrams, "The Uses of Land in Cities," in *Cities* (New York: Alfred A. Knopf, 1966), p. 124.
49. Robert R. R. Brooks, *As Steel Goes . . . , Unionism in a Basic Industry* (New Haven: Yale University Press, 1940), p. 31.
50. See Quillen, "Industrial City," pp. 172, 281–89, 453–59, and Moore, *Calumet Region*, pp. 264–65, 334–35.
51. Taylor, *Satellite Cities*, p. 166.
52. U.S. Senate, *Report on Conditions of Employment in the Iron and Steel Industry in the United States*, Vol. III, *Labor Conditions* (Washington, D.C.: Government Printing Office, 1931), p. 438.
53. See Moore, *Calumet Region*, p. 284, note 60; Buder, *Pullman*, pp. 86–90; Taylor, *Satellite Cities*, p. 187; and Taylor, "Satellite Cities—V. Gary," p. 788.
54. U.S. Steel Corporation, Bureau of Safety, Sanitation, and Welfare, *Bulletin*, no. 5, p. 56, quoted in Brody, *Steelworkers in America*, p. 110. See also Taylor, *Satellite Cities*, p. 189, and Roy Lubove, *The Progressive and the Slums: Tenement House Reform in New York City, 1890-1917* (Pittsburgh: University of Pittsburgh Press, 1962).
55. Mohl and Betten, "Industrial City Planning," p. 212. See also Forest McDonald, "Street Cars and Politics in Milwaukee, 1896-1901," *Wisconsin Magazine of History* 39, no. 3 (Spring 1956): 166 ff., and no. 4 (Summer 1956): 253 ff.

Chapter 3: Early History, 1906-1928

1. John Foster Potts, "A History of the Growth of the Negro Population of Gary, Indiana" (M.A., Cornell University, 1937), p. 4, and
A. Michael Turner, "Gary, Indiana: The Establishment and Early
Development of an Industrial Community, 1906-1930" (B.A., University of Keele, 1971), p. 57.
2. See Paul S. Taylor, *Mexican Labor in the United States: Chicago
and the Calumet Region* (Berkeley: University of California Press,
1932), pp. 42–43, and Herbert G. Gutman, "Work, Culture, and
Society in Industrializing America," *The American Historical
Review* 78, no. 3 (June 1973): 546.
3. Edna Hatfield Edmondson, *Juvenile Delinquency and Adult Crime*
(Bloomington: Indiana University Press, 1921), p. 82.
4. Carl Sandburg, "The Mayor of Gary," in *Smoke and Steel* (New
York: Harcourt, Brace and Co., 1920).
5. "Field Notes," *Foreign-Born* 1, no. 2 (December, 1919): 31.
6. N. N. Bolkhovitinov, "The Study of United States History in the
Soviet Union," *The American Historical Review* 74, no. 4 (April
1969): 1224.
7. Charles A. Gulick, *Labor Policy of the United States Steel Corpora-
tion* (New York: AMS Press, 1924), p. 86. See also Turner, "Gary,
Indiana," pp. 55–56; U.S. Senate, *Report on Conditions of Employ-
ment in the Iron and Steel Industry in the United States*, Vol. II,
Wages and Hours of Labor (Washington, D.C.: Government Printing
Office, 1912), pp. 96–98.
8. Gutman, "Work, Culture, and Society," p. 540. For examples of
Lenin's and Gramsci's views, see V. I. Lenin, "Capitalism and
Workers' Immigration," *On the United States of America* (Moscow:
Progress Publishers, 1967), pp. 82–85, and Antonio Gramsci, *Selec-
tions from the Prison Notebooks*, ed. and trans. Quinton Hoare and
G. Howell-Smith (New York: International Publishers, 1971), p. 272.
9. Quoted in Richard Julius Meister, "A History of Gary, Indiana:
1930-1940" (Ph.D., University of Notre Dame, 1967), p. 81. See also
Isaac James Quillen, "Industrial City: A History of Gary, Indiana
to 1929" (Ph.D., Yale University, 1942), p. 162, table I; Stanley
Aronowitz, *False Promises: The Shaping of American Working
Class Consciousness* (New York: McGraw-Hill, 1973), p. 166; and
David Brody, *Steelworkers in America: The Nonunion Era* (Cambridge: Harvard University Press, 1960), p. 109. Such heterogeneous

workforces were typical of large manufacturing plants. Cf. Jonathan Schwartz, "Henry Ford's Melting Pot," in *Ethnic Groups in the City: Culture, Institutions, and Power*, ed. Otto Feinstein (Lexington, Mass.: D. C. Heath, 1971), p. 195.

10. When the Gary Land Company in 1908 took its own private census, in enumerating the various nationalities it significantly lumped together both the native-born workers and "old immigrants" from English-speaking countries. See Brody, *Steelworkers in America*; John A. Garraty, "The United States Steel Corporation Versus Labor: The Early Years," *Labor History* 1, no. 1 (Winter 1960): 3–38; and Paul F. McGouldrick and Michael B. Tannen, "Did American Manufacturers Discriminate Against Immigrants Before 1914?" *Journal of Economic History* 37, no. 3 (September 1977): 723–46. Cf. Stephan Thernstrom, "Immigrants and WASPS: Ethnic Differences in Occupational Mobility in Boston, 1890-1940," *Nineteenth-Century Cities: Essays in the New Urban History*, ed. Stephan Thernstrom and Richard Sennett (New Haven: Yale University Press, 1969), p. 155.

11. Brody, *Steelworkers in America*, p. 91. See also *Report on Conditions*, Vols. I-IV; Garraty, "The United States Steel Corporation"; Horace B. Davis, *Labor and Steel* (New York: International Publishers, 1933); Charles Rumford Walker, *Steel: The Diary of a Furnace Worker* (Boston: The Atlantic Monthly Press, 1922), p. 44; and U.S. Bureau of Labor Statistics Bulletin No. 234, *The Safety Movement in the Iron and Steel Industry 1907 to 1917* (Washington, D.C.: Government Printing Office, 1918), pp. 144–46.

12. "Field Notes," p. 31. "The case of a young Spanish girl who married and soon had a household of twenty-four boarders is the rule rather than the exception." Cf. Claudia Goldin, "Female Labor Force Participation: The Origin of Black and White Differences, 1870-1880," *The Journal of Economic History* 37, no. 1 (March 1977): 87–112. See also Gutman, "Work, Culture and Society," p. 553; Edmondson, *Juvenile Delinquency and Adult Crime*, p. 62; and *Report on Conditions*, Vol. III, pp. 22, 147–49.

13. "Educational Events—Undernourished Children," *School and Society* 18, no 460 (October 20, 1923): 460–61.

14. Survey by Dr. E. R. Hayhurst, September 23, 1911, as quoted in Peter Roberts, *The New Immigration: A Study of the Industrial and Social Life of the Southeastern Europeans in America* (New York: Macmillan, 1912), p. 167, note 3.

15. See, for example, Richard S. Sorrell, "Life, Work, and Acculturation

Patterns of Eastern European Immigrants in Lackawanna, New York: 1900-1922," *The Polish Review* 14, no. 4 (Autumn 1969): 65–91; Niles Carpenter, *Nationality, Color and Economic Opportunity in the City of Buffalo* (Buffalo, N.Y.: University of Buffalo, 1927); John Bodnar, "Immigration and Modernization: The Case of Slavic Peasants in Industrial America," *Social History* 10, no. 1 (Fall 1976): 44–71; and Joseph Schacter, "Net Immigration of Gainful Workers into the United States, 1870-1930," *Demography* 19, no. 1 (February 1972): 92–93.

16. Elizabeth Balanoff, "A History of the Black Community of Gary, Indiana 1906-1940" (Ph.D., University of Chicago, 1976).

17. A great deal of confusion has developed about housing practices because of the claim by some historians that there was a "permanent ghetto" among blacks, and because of all the attention paid to the Irish in Boston and the Jews in New York. Actually these cases were atypical. See Roberts, *The New Immigration*, p. 160, and David Ward, *Cities and Immigrants: A Geography of Change in Nineteenth Century America* (New York: Oxford University Press, 1971), pp. 120–21.

18. This was certainly the case for blacks. As W. E. B. DuBois reported with respect to Philadelphia's blacks in the 1890s (when that city had the biggest black population of any northern city), the most densely black ward was three-fourths white. In Cleveland in 1910, 138 of 155 census tracts had some black residents; in none of them were they even close to a majority. Similar patterns held for the various "new immigrant" neighborhoods: in prewar Chicago "no set, rigid and unchanging Italian colony existed. Italian areas of settlement expanded and shifted their location over the passage of years." W. E. B. DuBois, *The Philadelphia Negro: A Social Study* (New York: Schocken Books, 1967), p. 58. See also Kenneth L. Kusmer, *A Ghetto Takes Shape: Black Cleveland, 1870-1930* (Urbana: University of Illinois Press, 1976), p. 42, and Humbert S. Nelli, *Italians in Chicago, 1880-1930: A Study in Ethnic Mobility* (New York: Oxford University Press, 1970), p. 53.

19. See H. S. Norton, "Gary, Indiana," *The Coupon* 1, no. 9 (August 1922): 3; Meister, "History of Gary," pp. 49–54; and Raymond A. Mohl and Neil Betten, "Gary, Indiana: The Urban Laboratory as a Teaching Tool," *The History Teacher* 4, no. 2 (January 1971): 6.

20. Powell A. Moore, *The Calumet Region: Indiana's Last Frontier* (Indianapolis: Indiana Historical Bureau, 1959), p. 399. See also Turner, "Gary, Indiana," p. 63, and Graham Romeyn Taylor, *Satel-*

lite Cities: A Study of Industrial Suburbs (New York: D. Appleton, 1951), p. 207.

21. See Brody, *Steelworkers in America,* p. 194; St. Sava Orthodox Church, *Fiftieth Anniversary: Our Religious Heritage in America, 1914-1964* (Chicago: Palendach Press, n.d.), pp. 82, 109; and Dolly Millender, *Yesterday in Gary: History of the Negro in Gary* (Gary: privately printed, 1967), p. 28.

22. See Lorenzo J. Greene and Carter G. Woodson, *The Negro Wage Earner* (Washington, D.C.: Association for the Study of Negro Life and History, 1930), p. 247; Emma Lou Thornbrough, *The Negro in Indiana: A Study of a Minority* (Indianapolis: Indiana Historical Bureau, 1957), pp. 349–51; Marion Hayes, "A Century of Change: Negroes in the U.S. Economy, 1860-1960," *Monthly Labor Review* 85, no. 12 (November 1962): 1360; and Herbert R. Northrup, "The Negro and the United Mine Workers of America," *The Southern Economic Journal* 9, no. 4 (April 1943): 313–26.

23. Sam Bass Warner, Jr. and Colin B. Burke, "Cultural Change and the Ghetto," *The Journal of Contemporary History* 4, no. 4 (1969). See also T. Lynn Smith, "The Redistribution of the Negro Population of the United States 1910-1960," *The Journal of Negro History* 51, no. 3 (July 1966): 160–61; and Martin Meyerson, "Some Changing Patterns of American Urbanism," in *Education for Urban Administration,* ed. Frederick M. Cleveland (Philadelphia: American Academy of Political and Social Science, 1973), p. 24.

24. See Paul Taylor, *Mexican Labor,* p. 157, table 22; Potts, "Growth of the Negro Population," p. 7, table I; and Brody, *Steelworkers in America,* p. 186. See also Alma Herbst, *The Negro in the Slaughtering and Meat Packing Industry in Chicago* (Boston: Houghton Mifflin, 1932); William M. Tuttle, Jr., "Labor Conflict and Racial Violence: The Black Workers of Chicago, 1894-1919," *Labor History* 10, no. 3 (Summer 1969): 418–21; and Allan H. Spear, *Black Chicago: The Making of a Black Ghetto, 1890-1920* (Chicago: University of Chicago Press, 1967), p. 29.

25. Gutman, "Work, Culture and Society," p. 554.

26. Brody, *Steelworkers in America,* p. 261.

27. Richard O. Boyer and Herbert Morais, *Labor's Untold Story* (New York: Cameron Press, 1955), p. 205.

28. William Z. Foster, *The Great Steel Strike and Its Lessons* (New York: B. W. Huebsch, 1920), and David Brody, *Labor in Crisis: The Steel Strike of 1919* (Philadelphia: J. B. Lippincott, 1965).

29. Randolph Bourne, *The Gary Schools* (Boston: Houghton Mifflin, 1916), pp. 4–5.
30. See Meister, "History of Gary," pp. 40–46; Quillen, "Industrial City," pp. 396–410; and Moore, *Calumet Region*, p. 339.
31. U.S. Bureau of the Census, 1930 Census of Distribution, *Retail Trade in Gary, Indiana* (Preliminary Report); E. C. Rightor, "The Bonded Debt of 207 Cities as of January 1, 1925," *National Municipal Review* 14, no. 6 (June 1925): 372; and E. C. Rightor, "The Comparative Tax Rates for 215 Cities," *National Municipal Review* 14, no. 12 (December 1925): 759.
32. Gary August, *God's Gentleman* (New York: Alfred A. Knopf, 1932), p. 77.
33. Meister, "History of Gary," pp. 62–63. See also E. L. Thorndike, *Your City* (New York: Harcourt Brace and Co., 1939), and U.S. Department of Commerce, Bureau of Foreign and Domestic Commerce, *Consumer Market Data Handbook, 1939*, Domestic Commerce Series No. 102 (Washington, D.C.: Government Printing Office, 1939).
34. Norton, "Gary, Indiana," p. 3; Gary Planning Commission, *Comprehensive Plan* (Evanston, Ill.: Tech-Search, Inc., 1964); and Neil Betten and Raymond A. Mohl, "The Evolution of Racism in an Industrial City, 1906-1940: A Case Study of Gary, Indiana," *The Journal of Negro History* 59, no. 1 (1974): 58.
35. Information on housing compiled from Moore, *Calumet Region*, p. 341; Albert E. Dickens, *Economic Factors for Planning Gary* (Chicago: Evert Kincaid & Associates, 1955); Quillen, *Industrial City*, pp. 403–10; U.S. Works Progress Administration, *Real Property Survey and Low Income Housing Area Survey of Gary, Indiana* (Gary: Gary Housing Authority, 1940); and *Indiana Business Review* 13, no. 1 (January 28, 1938): 5, and 17, no. 1 (January 20, 1942): 11.
36. See Moore, *Calumet Region*, pp. 326, 340, and Betten and Mohl, "The Evolution of Racism," pp. 51–64. Cf. Sam Bass Warner, Jr., *The Urban Wilderness: A History of the American City* (New York: Harper and Row, 1972), p. 169.
37. Donald O. Cowgill, "Trends in Residential Segregation of Nonwhites in American Cities, 1940-1950," *American Sociological Review* 21, no. 1 (February 1956): 45, table I.
38. See James B. Lane, *City of the Century: A History of Gary, Indiana* (Bloomington: Indiana University Press, 1978), p. 146, and Emma Lou Thornbrough, "Segregation in Indiana During the Klan Era of

the 1920s," *Mississippi Valley Historical Review* 47 (March 1961): 594–618. Cf. Paul L. Murphy, "Sources and Nature of Intolerance in the 1920s," *Journal of American History* 51 (June 1964): 61, and Blaine A. Brownell, "Birmingham, Alabama: New South City in the 1920s," *The Journal of Southern History* 38, no. 1 (February 1972): 21–48.

39. See Paul Taylor, *Mexican Labor*, p. 48; Moore, *Calumet Region*, p. 305; Spear, *Black Chicago*, p. 151; Green and Woodson, *Negro Wage Earner*, pp. 247–49; Arvah E. Strickland, *History of the Chicago Urban League* (Urbana: University of Illinois Press, 1966), p. 58; Lloyd Ulman, "The Union and Wages in Basic Steel: A Comment," *The American Economic Review* 48, no. 3 (June 1958): 420; and Harold Baron, "The Demand for Black Labor: Historical Notes on the Political Economy of Racism," *Radical America* 5, no. 2 (March-April 1971): 1–46.

40. As the superintendent of the nation's largest steel mill had written in 1875: "My experience has shown that Germans and Irish, Swedes and . . . young American country boys, judiciously mixed, make the most attractive and tractable force you can find." Quoted in Davis, *Labor and Steel*, p. 28.

41. John W. DuBose, quoted in Horace Mann Bond, *Social and Economic Influences on the Public Education of Negroes in Alabama, 1865-1930* (Washington, D.C.: The Associated Publishers, 1939), pp. 144–45. See also Virginia Van der Veer Hamilton, *Hugo Black: The Alabama Years* (Baton Rouge: Louisiana State University Press, 1972), pp. 34–35, and Justin Fuller, "History of the Tennessee Coal, Iron & Railroad Company" (Ph.D., University of North Carolina at Chapel Hill, 1966). Generally see James C. Green, "The Brotherhood of Timber Workers, 1910-1913," *Past and Present*, no. 60 (August 1973): 161–200.

42. Calculated from Potts, "Growth of the Negro Population," p. 7, table I, and p. 36, table VII, and Paul Taylor, *Mexican Labor*, p. 157, table 22. (This data is contradictory to Brody's implication to the effect that blacks as well as "new immigrants" were experiencing upward occupational mobility in the steel mills during the 1920s. Cf. Brody, *Steelworkers in America*, pp. 107–8, 267.)

43. Potts, "Growth of the Negro Population," pp. 6–8.

44. Quotes in Paul Taylor, *Mexican Labor*, pp. 93–94. See also Herbst, *Meat Packing Industry*, pp. xvii–xxii, 103–8; B. J. Widick, *Detroit: City of Class and Race Violence* (Chicago: Quadrangle Books, 1972), p. ix; Robert Ozanne, *A Century of Labor-Management Rela-*

tions at McCormick and International Harvester (Madison: University of Wisconsin Press, 1967), pp. 184–85; and Philip S. Foner, *Organized Labor and the Black Worker, 1619-1973* (New York: Praeger, 1974), pp. 133–34.

45. In addition to sources already cited see Paul B. Worthman, "Working Class Mobility in Birmingham, Alabama, 1880-1914," in *Anonymous Americans: Explorations in Nineteenth-Century Social History,* ed. Tamara K. Hareven (Englewood Cliffs, N.J.: Prentice-Hall, 1971), pp. 172–213; Richard J. Hopkins, "Status, Mobility and the Dimensions of Change in a Southern City: Atlanta, 1870-1910," in *Cities in American History,* ed. Kenneth K. Schultz (New York: Alfred A. Knopf, 1972), pp. 216–31; and Stephan Thernstrom, *The Other Bostonians: Poverty and Progress in the American Metropolis, 1880-1970* (Cambridge: Harvard University Press, 1973).

46. Quoted in St. Clair Drake and Horace R. Cayton, *Black Metropolis: A Study of Negro Life in a Northern City* (New York: Harcourt, Brace and Co., 1945), p. 336.

47. Quillen, "Industrial City," p. 416; Balanoff, "Black Community of Gary," pp. 311–12; Schacter, "Net Immigration," p. 97; *Report on Conditions,* Vol. I, p. xii, Vol. III, p. 101; Seymour E. Harris, *A Statistical Portrait of Higher Education* (New York: McGraw-Hill, 1974), p. 942; Timothy L. Smith, "Native Blacks and Foreign Whites: Varying Responses to Educational Opportunity in America, 1880-1950," *Perspectives in American History* 6 (1972): 328–29; and Herman Feldman, *Racial Factors in American Industry* (New York: Harper and Brothers, 1931), p. 51.

   The notion that black labor was less qualified is commonly held by both radical and mainstream economic historians. See, for instance, Paul A. Baran and Paul M. Sweezy, *Monopoly Capital* (New York: Monthly Review Press, 1966), p. 257, and Robert Higgs, "Race, Skill, and Earnings: American Immigrants in 1909," *The Journal of Economic History* 31, no. 2 (June 1971): 420–28.

48. The effect on the consciousness of white workers of the arbitrary relative advantage is discussed in detail in Arnold Birenbaum and Edward Greer, "Toward a Structural Theory of Contemporary Working Class Culture," *Ethnicity* 3, no. 1 (March 1976): 4–18. A more detailed discussion of employment discrimination and comparisons to other capitalist nations appears in Edward Greer, "Racial Employment Discrimination in the Gary Works, 1906-1974," in *Social Class in the Contemporary United States,* ed. Gerald Erick-

son and Harold L. Schwartz (Minneapolis, Minn.: Marxist Educational Press, 1977), pp. 29–74.

Chapter 4: Later History, 1929-1966

1. Gary August, *God's Gentleman* (New York: Alfred A. Knopf, 1932), p. 221. For documentation of consumer purchasing see U.S. Bureau of the Census, *1930 Census of Distribution, Retail Trade in Gary, Indiana* (Preliminary Report), and U.S. Department of Commerce, Bureau of Foreign and Domestic Commerce, *Consumer Market Data Handbook, 1939 Edition*, Domestic Commerce Series No. 102 (Washington, D.C.: Government Printing Office, 1939), p. 211.

2. For further information see Leo Grebler et al., *Capital Formation in Residential Real Estate* (Princeton, N.J.: Princeton University Press, 1956), pp. 39, 59, 100; Marion Clawson and Peter Hall, *Planning and Urban Growth* (Baltimore: The Johns Hopkins Press, 1973), pp. 12–13; U.S. Works Progress Administration, *Real Property Survey and Low Income Housing Area Survey of Gary, Indiana* (Gary: Gary Housing Authority, 1940); Albert E. Dickens, *Economic Factors for Planning Gary* (Chicago: n.p., 1955), p. 7; and J. Harvey Kerns, *A Study of the Social and Economic Conditions of the Negro Population of Gary, Indiana* (New York: National Urban League, 1944), pp. 17–19.

3. For the effect of the Depression on the steel industry see Irving Bernstein, *The Lean Years: A History of the American Worker, 1920-1933* (Boston: Houghton Mifflin, 1966); *New York Times*, March 9, 1941; Albert Rees, "Postwar Wage Determinations in the Basic Steel Industry," *The American Economic Review* 41, no. 3 (June 1951): 389–404; Leonard C. Weiss, *Case Studies in American Industry* (New York: John Wiley & Sons, 1967), pp. 189–91; and Gardiner C. Means, *Pricing Power and the Public Interest* (New York: Harper and Brothers, 1962).

4. For the effect of the Depression on blacks in Gary, see Elizabeth Balanoff, "A History of the Black Community of Gary, Indiana 1906-1940" (Ph.D., University of Chicago, 1976), pp. 198–99, and E. Franklin Frazier, "Some Effects of the Depression on the Negro in Northern Cities," *Science and Society* 2, no. 4 (Fall 1938): 492. On black family structure, see Herbert G. Gutman, *The Black Family in Slavery and Freedom, 1750-1925* (New York: Pantheon, 1976);

Stanley L. Engerman, "Black Fertility and Family Structure in the U.S., 1880-1940," *Journal of Family History* 2, no. 2 (Summer 1977): 117–38.

5. See Charles F. Peake, "Negro Occupation-Employment Participation in American Industry," *The American Journal of Economics and Sociology* 34, no. 1 (January 1975): 67–86; Herbert R. Northrup, "The Negro and Unionism in the Birmingham, Alabama Iron and Steel Industry," *The Southern Economic Journal* 10, no. 1 (July 1943): 28–30; and Neil Betten and Raymond A. Mohl, "From Discrimination to Repatriation: Mexican Life in Gary, Indiana During the Great Depression," *Pacific Historical Review* 57, no. 3 (August 1973): 377.

6. Richard L. Rowan, "The Negro in the Steel Industry," in *Negro Employment in Basic Industry,* ed. Herbert R. Northrup (Philadelphia: University of Pennsylvania, 1970), pp. 28–29.

7. Kerns, *Negro Population,* p. 8, and Jack Stieber, *The Steel Industry Wage Structure* (Cambridge: Harvard University Press, 1959), p. 236.
   In the auto industry, too, blacks were consigned largely to "undesirable jobs." "A small minority performed semiskilled and even skilled operations, but the latter were almost invariably hot, noisy, dirty, dusty, hazardous, or required exceptional physical exertion." Lloyd H. Bailer, "The Negro Automobile Worker," *Journal of Political Economy* 51 (1943): 417. Also see Robert Ozanne, *The Negro in the Farm Equipment and Construction Machinery Industries* (Philadelphia: University of Pennsylvania, 1972), p. 62.

8. For further information on Mexican workers see Paul S. Taylor, *Mexican Labor in the United States: Chicago and the Calumet Region* (Berkeley: University of California Press, 1932); Mark Reisler, "The Mexican Immigrant in the Chicago Area During the 1920s," *Journal of the Illinois State Historical Society* 66, no. 2 (Summer 1973): 144–58; Julian Samora and Richard J. Lamanna, *Mexican-Americans in a Midwest Metropolis* (Los Angeles: University of California, 1967); and Powell A. Moore, *The Calumet Region: Indiana's Last Frontier* (Indianapolis: Indiana Historical Bureau, 1959).

9. Quoted in Betten and Mohl, "Mexican Life," p. 379.

10. Ciro Sepulveda, "La Colonia del Harbor: Mexicanos in East Chicago 1919-1932" (paper at American Historical Association Convention, 1974), p. 21. See also Richard Julius Meister, "A History of Gary, Indiana: 1930-1940" (Ph.D., University of Notre Dame, 1967), p. 73, and Isaac James Quillen, "Industrial City: A History of Gary, Indiana to 1929" (Ph.D., Yale University, 1942), pp. 413–15.

More generally see Arthur F. Corwin, "Causes of Mexican Emigration to the United States: A Summary View," *Perspectives in American History* 7 (1973): 557–635; John Womack, Jr., "The Chicanos," *The New York Review of Books* 19, no. 3 (August 31, 1972); Emory S. Bogardus, *The Mexicans in the United States* (Los Angeles: University of Southern California Press, 1934); and Abraham Hoffman, *Unwanted Mexican Americans in the Great Depression* (Tucson: University of Arizona Press, 1974).

11. *Steel & Metal Notes* 6, no. 7 (May 1938): 3; Barbara Wayne Newell, *The Labor Movement* (Urbana: University of Illinois Press, 1961), p. 117, note 4. Richard F. Hamilton points out that "in the course of the twentieth century the working class has been transformed from a rank made up largely of ex-farmers to one that is increasingly drawn from the children of manual workers." *Class and Politics in the United States* (New York: John Wiley & Sons, 1972), p. 327.

12. See Balanoff, "Black Community of Gary," pp. 221–32; Len DeCaux, *Labor Radical* (Boston: Beacon Press, 1970); and Robert R. R. Brooks, *As Steel Goes* (New Haven: Yale University Press, 1940).

13. Quoted in Russell E. Porter, "When Night Skies Glow Above Steel's Big Towns," *New York Times Magazine*, March 14, 1937, p. 19.
    Twenty years later, Roosevelt was still a "magic word" to Gary steelworkers. Interview with Very Reverend Msgr. Stephen Sedor, April 7, 1976.

14. Karl Klare, "The Judicial Deradicalization of the Wagner Act and the Origins of Modern Legal Consciousness, 1937-1941," *Minnesota Law Review* 62, no. 3 (March 1978): 265–339; Staughton Lynd, "The United Front in America: A Note," *Radical America* 8, no. 4 (July-August 1974): 34; E. J. Hobsbawm, "Labor History and Ideology," *Journal of Social History* 7, no. 4 (Summer 1974): 337; and Sidney Fine, *Sit-Down* (Ann Arbor: University of Michigan Press, 1969).

15. For further information see *New York Times*, March 9, 1941; Victor Perlo and Witt Bowden, "Labor Unit Cost in 20 Manufacturing Industries, 1919-1939," *Monthly Labor Review* 51, no. 1 (July 1940): 36, table 2; "Injury Experience in the Iron and Steel Industry, 1938 and 1939," *Monthly Labor Review* 51, no. 2 (August 1940): 322–33; and *Steel & Metal Notes* 5, no. 12 (October 1937).

16. *New York Times*, November 6, 1937; *Steel & Metal Notes* 5, no. 5 (March 1937). For an analysis of the effects on minority workers in the steel industry see Rowan, "Steel Industry," pp. 260–310; Stieber, *Wage Structure*, p. 237, table 15; William Kornblum, *Blue Collar Community* (Chicago: University of Chicago Press, 1974), pp. 100–1;

and Philip Foner, *Organized Labor and the Black Workers 1619-1973* (New York: Praeger, 1974), pp. 218–37.

17. Orley C. Ashenfelter and Lamond I. Godwin, "Some Evidence on the Effects of Unionism on the Average Wage of Black Workers Relative to White Workers, 1900-1967," *Proceedings of the 24th Annual Meeting of the Industrial Relations Research Association*, pp. 217–24. Generally see Orley Ashenfelter, "Racial Discrimination and Trade Unionism," *Journal of Political Economy* 80, no. 3, part I (May-June 1972): 435–64; Richard Child Hill, "Unionization and Racial Income Inequality in the Metropolis," *American Sociological Review* 39, no. 4 (August 1974): 520; Michael Reich, "Economic Theories of Racism," in *Schooling in a Corporate Society*, ed. Martin Carnoy (New York: David McKay, 1972), pp. 67–79; and Sylvia Small, "Black Workers in Labor Unions—A Little Less Separate, a Little More Equal," *Ethnicity* 3 (1976): 174–96.

18. David Montgomery and Ronald Schatz, "Facing Layoff," *Radical America* 10, no. 2 (March-April 1976): 15–28; Ozanne, *Construction Machinery Industries*, p. 102; and *New York Times*, April 17, 1976. For a related study, see Elaine Glovka Spencer, "Between Capital and Labor: Supervisory Personnel in Ruhr Heavy Industry Before 1914," *Journal of Social History* 9, no. 2 (Winter 1975): 178–92.

19. St. Clair Drake and Horace R. Cayton, *Black Metropolis* (New York: Harcourt, Brace and Co., 1945), p. 340, and Horace R. Cayton and George Mitchell, *Black Workers and the New Unions* (Chapel Hill: University of North Carolina Press, 1939).

20. *Steel & Metal Notes* 6, no. 6 (April 1938); Montgomery and Schatz, "Facing Layoff"; Bailer, "Automobile Worker," p. 423; and Foner, *Organized Labor*, p. 233.

21. Stieber, *Wage Structure*, pp. 236–72; Ashenfelter and Godwin, "Effects of Unionism," p. 221; and Victor Perlo, *Economics of Racism U.S.A.* (New York: International Publishers, 1975), p. 207.

22. Frank Emspak, "The Break-Up of the CIO, 1945-1950" (Ph.D., University of Wisconsin, 1972), and D. Donati, "Some Observations on the Labor Scene," *Political Affairs* 55, no. 4 (April 1976): 15–25.

23. Hal Baron, "The Demand for Black Labor: Historical Notes on the Political Economy of Racism," *Radical America* 5, no. 2 (March-April 1971): 28, and Meister, "History of Gary," p. 322.

24. For further information see Hugh M. Ayer, "Hoosier Labor in the Second World War," *Indiana Magazine of History* 59, no. 2 (June 1963): 96, table I; Neil A. Wynn, "The Impact of the Second World War on the American Negro," *Journal of Contemporary History* 6,

no. 2 (1971); U.S. Department of Labor, Bureau of Labor Statistics, Bulletin No. 826, *Impact of the War on 181 Centers of War Activity* (Washington, D.C.: Government Printing Office, 1945), p. 7; Kenneth Warren, *The American Steel Industry, 1850-1970* (London: Oxford University Press, 1973), p. 240; Lynn W. Turner, "Indiana in World War II—A Progress Report," *Indiana Magazine of History* 52, no. 1 (March 1955): 8; Corwin, "Mexican Emigration," pp. 594–95; and Warren M. Banner, *A Study of the Social and Economic Conditions in Three Minority Groups: Gary, Indiana* (New York: National Urban League, 1955), p. 3.

25. Kerns, *Negro Population*, p. 11; Banner, *Three Minority Groups*, p. 19; Kornblum, *Blue Collar*, p. 55; Drake and Cayton, *Black Metropolis*, p. 55; Perlo, *Economics*; Montgomery and Schatz, "Facing Layoff"; and U.S. Department of Labor, Bureau of Labor Statistics, Bulletin No. 1119, *Negroes in the United States: Their Employment and Economic Status* (Washington, D.C.: Government Printing Office, 1952), p. 42, table 16.

26. Rowan, "Steel Industry," p. 271. See also Ayer, "Hoosier Labor," 97; Banner, *Three Minority Groups*, p. 19; Therese D'Agostino, "Women as Steelworkers," *Political Affairs* 55, no. 5 (May 1976): 12; Ruth Milkman, "Women's Work and the Economic Crisis: Some Lessons from the Great Depression," *The Review of Radical Political Economics* 8, no. 1 (Spring 1976): 87, table 2; Howard Dratch, "The Politics of Child Care in the 1940s," *Science & Society* 38, no. 2 (Summer 1974); U.S. Department of Labor, Women's Bureau, Ethel Erickson, *Women's Employment in the Making of Steel, 1943*, Bulletin No. 192–5 (Washington, D.C.: Government Printing Office, 1944); and United Steelworkers of America, Research Department, *The Braddock Steelworkers* (1945).

27. For further information on postwar suburbanization, see Martin W. Reinemann, "The Pattern and Distribution of Manufacturing in the Chicago Area," *Economic Geography* 36, no. 2 (April 1960): 139–44; John F. Kain, "The Distribution and Movement of Jobs and Industry," in *The Metropolitan Enigma*, ed. James Q. Wilson (Cambridge: Harvard University Press, 1967), pp. 1–43; Brian J. L. Berry and Jehosua S. Cohen, "Decentralizing Commerce and Industry: The Restructuring of Metropolitan America," in *The Urbanization of the Suburbs*, ed. Louis H. Masotti and Jeffrey K. Hadden (Beverly Hills: Sage Publications, 1973), p. 441; and Brian J. L. Berry et al., *Chicago: Transformation of an Urban System* (Cambridge, Mass.: Ballinger, 1976).

28. For Gary's demographic shifts, see *Calumet Area Report* (1962), p. 28; Wes Scharlach, *Population Characteristics and Trends in the Gary-Hammond-East Chicago Standard Metropolitan Statistical Area* (Lake County Community Development Committee, 1968), p. 6; Edwin S. Mills, *Studies in the Structure of the Urban Economy* (Baltimore: The Johns Hopkins Press, 1972), p. 28; and Brian J. L. Berry, *Growth Centers in the American Urban System* (Cambridge, Mass.: Ballinger, 1973), p. 36.

29. Gary Redevelopment Commission, *Community Renewal Program* (Mishawaka: Community Planning Associates, 1968), and *Post-Tribune*, January 25, 1970. Also see Esther Pesonen Niemi, "A Study of Commercial Banking in Two Economically Depressed Cities: Youngstown, Ohio and Wheeling, West Virginia, 1951-1967" (Ph.D., Case Western Reserve University, 1969), pp. 69–73.

30. U.S. Department of Health, Education and Welfare, Public Health Service, Bureau of Community Environmental Management, Region V, *An Assessment of Rat Problems and Associated Environmental Conditions in the City of Gary, Indiana* (1971), p. 3. See also U.S. Bureau of the Census, Census of Population and Housing: 1970; *Census Tracts*, Final Report PHC (1)–79, table H-2; and Michael A. Stegman, *Housing Investment in the Inner City* (Cambridge: MIT Press, 1972), p. 7, note 1.

   In Detroit between 1960 and 1970 there was "an overall loss of 4 percent of the housing units in the city." Lynda Ann Ewen, *Corporate Power and Urban Crisis in Detroit* (Princeton, N.J.: Princeton University Press, 1978), p. 19.

31. Steven J. Eagle, "Shopping Center Control: The Developer Beseiged," *Journal of Urban Law* 51, no. 4 (May 1974): 585–86, and Judith J. Friedman, "Variations in the Level of Central Business District Retail Activity Among Large U.S. Cities: 1954 and 1967," *Land Economics* 49, no. 3 (August 1973): 326.

32. See, for instance, John H. Allan, "East St. Louis: Urban Bankruptcy," *New York Times*, May 14, 1972.

33. Albert E. Dickens, *Economic Factors for Planning Gary* (Chicago: Evert Kincaid & Associates, 1955), pp. 1–5.

34. Gary Downtown Improvement Association, *Gary, Indiana: Downtown Development Plan and Program* (Gary: Marcou, O'Leary and Associates, 1969), and *Census Tracts*, table P-3.

35. Information based on ibid., as well as an interview with an anonymous Gary accountant, June 15, 1972, and Marguerite Ross Barnett and James A. Hefner, eds., *Public Policy for the Black Com-*

munity (New York: Alfred, 1976), pp. 62–64. Cf. George Sternlieb, *The Tenement Landlord* (New Brunswick, N.J.: Rutgers University Press, 1966).

36. *Downtown Development Plan*, p. 23, and interview with anonymous Gary attorney, June 14, 1972. Only one-fifth of suburban residents of Detroit now enter the city more often than once a month. Ewen, *Urban Crisis*, p. 33, note 34.

37. Cf. John D. Borchert, "American Metropolitan Evolution," *The Geographical Review* 57, no. 3 (July 1967): 328–29.

38. Allen R. Pred, *The Spatial Dynamics of U.S. Urban-Industrial Growth* (Cambridge: MIT Press, 1966), p. 21, and David Ward, *Cities and Immigrants* (New York: Oxford University Press, 1971), p. 13.

39. Edward Greer, "The Political Economy of U.S. Steel Prices in the Postwar Period," in *Research in Political Economy: An Annual Compilation of Research*, ed., Paul Zarembka (Greenwich, Conn.: JAI Press, 1977), pp. 59–86, and Edward Greer, "Placebos for a Sick Industry," *The Nation* 226, no. 8 (March 4, 1978): 235–38.

40. "Local Area Personal Income," *Survey of Current Business* 54, no. 5, pt. II (May 1974): 14, table I, and Philip R. Swenson, "Per Capita Personal Income Trends in Indiana: A Look at Standard Metropolitan Statistical Areas," *Indiana Business Review* 46 (October-November 1971): 26.

41. See Gil Green, *What's Happening to Labor* (New York: International Publishers, 1976).

42. U.S. Bureau of the Census, *City Employment in 1949*, G-GE49-No. 6 (1950), p. 12; Oden, *Political Power*, p. 181; and James O'Connor, *The Fiscal Crisis of the State* (New York: St. Martin's Press, 1973).

43. Eli Ginzberg, "The Job Problem," *Scientific American* 237, no. 5 (November 1977): 43–51, and Harry Braverman, *Labor and Monopoly Capital* (New York: Monthly Review Press, 1974).

44. See, for instance, Stephan Thernstrom, *The Other Bostonians* (Cambridge: Harvard University Press, 1973), and the review by Edward Greer in *Monthly Review* 26, no. 9 (February 1975): 51–57.

45. Perlo, *Economics*, pp. 52–53, 84.

46. Paul Baran and Paul Sweezy, *Monopoly Capital* (New York: Monthly Review Press, 1966), p. 269; Baron, "Black Labor," p. 37; Rowan, "Steel Industry," p. 296; Perlo, *Economics*, pp. 74–76; Foner, *Organized Labor*, p. 270; and Edward Greer and Michael Tanzer, "AT&T: Sexism, Racism and Consumer Gouging" (paper at Institute for Policy Studies Conference on Alternative Political Economy, 1973).

47. On the problem of "inflation" of census job categories, see Braverman, *Labor*, pp. 424–49.
48. Edward Greer, "Racial Employment Discrimination in the Gary Works, 1906-1974," in *Social Class in the Contemporary United States*, ed. Gerald Erickson and Harold L. Schwartz (Minneapolis, Minn.: Marxist Educational Press, 1977), pp. 29–73.
49. *Job Patterns*, Vol. I, p. 314; Rowan, "Steel Industry," p. 297; Kerns, *Negro Population*, p. 8; City of Gary, Indiana, Human Relations Commission, "Gary Human Relations Commission vs. U.S. Steel, Gary Works" (typescript, 1968); interview with William Todd, vice president, Local 1065, June 13, 1972; Joseph Hill, "Steel: Changing Workplace," *Dissent* (Winter 1972): 44; and Steve Packard, "Steelmill Blues," *Liberation* 19, no. 3 (May 1975): 10. For European parallels, see Stephen Castles and Godula Kosack, *Immigrant Workers and Class Structure in Western Europe* (New York: Oxford University Press, 1973), and Jacques Fremontier, *La forteresse ouvrière: Renault* (Paris: Atheme Fayard, 1971).
50. *United States v. Bethlehem Steel*, 312 F. Supp. 977 (1970), p. 981.
51. J. William Lloyd et al., "Long-Term Mortality Study of Steelworkers," *Journal of Occupational Medicine* 11, no. 6 (June 1969): 304–5 and "Respiratory Cancer in Coke Plant Workers," 13, no. 2 (February 1971): 67.
52. For a more detailed discussion of the steel industry seniority system see Benjamin W. Wolkinson, *Blacks, Unions and the EEOC: A Study of Administrative Futility* (Lexington, Mass.: D. C. Heath, 1973), pp. 20–23; "Notes: Title VII, Seniority Discrimination, and the Incumbent Negro," *Harvard Law Review* 80, no. 6 (April 1967): 1260–83; William B. Gould, "Black Power in the Unions: The Impact Upon Collective Bargaining Relationships," *The Yale Law Journal* 79, no. 1 (November 1969): 46–85; and "Last Hired, First Fired: Layoffs and Title VII," *Harvard Law Review* 88, no. 7 (May 1975): 1544–70. Also see Peter B. Doeringer and Michael J. Piore, *Internal Labor Markets and Manpower Analysis* (Lexington, Mass.: D. C. Heath, 1971), ch. 7.
53. To give a typical example, the Justice Department's suit against U.S. Steel's Fairfield Works showed that in 1970 the average white pay was $10,000 and the average black pay was $8,100 for production workers; the average black "made $1,739.64 less than did whites of comparable years of plant seniority." U.S. Department of Justice, *United States of America v. United States Steel Corporation et al.*, Civil Action No. 70-906, "Request No. 1," pp. 1–8. Also see "Resis-

tance Mounts to Steel Pact," *The Guardian*, May 15, 1974, and Henry Winston, *Black and White—One Class, One Fight* (New York: New Outlook, 1972), p. 39. For a description of the comparable situation in General Electric's Philadelphia Switchgear Plant—where the black-white wage differential is $1,600—see *Wall Street Journal*, December 10, 1974.

54. *Wall Street Journal*, August 8, 1973, and *New York Times*, May 13, 1976. Generally see Wolkinson, *Blacks*, pp. 81–138, and Mike Bayer, "The Seniority Principle in Steel," *Political Affairs* 53, no. 5 (May 1974): 4–9.

55. See Samora and Lamman, *Mexican-Americans*, pp. 73–80.

56. See Niles Carpenter, *Nationality, Color and Economic Opportunity in the City of Buffalo* (Buffalo, N.Y.: University of Buffalo, 1927), pp. 190–91, and Castles and Kosack, *Immigrant Workers*, p. 7.

    The effect of the arbitrary advantage on white workers' consciousness is outlined in Arnold Birenbaum and Edward Greer, "Toward a Structural Theory of Contemporary Working Class Culture," *Ethnicity* 3, no. 1 (March 1976): 4–18.

57. One form of this confusion is to rewrite history to make it appear that the white ethnic workers shared with the ruling class responsibility for the development of institutional racism in the north. See, for instance, Ira Katznelson, *Black Men, White Cities* (New York: Oxford University Press, 1973), p. 115, and Richard Sennett, in *New York Times*, May 10, 1976. Another is to assert that racism is no longer in the direct interest of capital but is instead the result of a diffuse social consensus among all classes of white Americans. For instance, Christopher Lasch asserts that "racism . . . though it once furnished a rationale for slavery and other forms of exploitation, no longer has a clear basis in economic self interest." Christopher Lasch, "Populism, Socialism, and McGovernism," *The New York Review of Books* 19, no. 1 (July 20, 1972). Also see Eugene Genovese, *In Red and Black* (New York: Pantheon, 1971), pp. 59–60.

58. Baran and Sweezy, *Monopoly Capital*, pp. 263–71. This approach is followed by many radical commentators, such as Michael Tanzer, *The Sick Society* (New York: Holt, Rinehart and Winston, 1971), p. 96; William K. Tabb, *The Political Economy of the Black Ghetto* (New York: W. W. Norton, 1970); and Al Syzmanski, "Trends in Economic Discrimination Against Blacks in the U.S. Working Class," *The Review of Radical Political Economics* 7, no. 3 (Fall 1975): 1–21. It is ably critiqued by Donald J. Harris, "The Black Ghetto as Colony: A Theoretical Critique and Alternative Formula-

tion," *The Review of Black Political Economy* 2, no. 4 (Summer 1972): 3–33.

59. Joseph Wilson, "Cold Steel: The Political Economy of Black Workers and the Reform Movement in the United Steelworkers of America, 1977" (Ph.D., Columbia University, 1979).

60. David M. Gordon et al., "Economic Consequences on Steel Workers of Strikes and the Right to Strike in the Basic Steel Industry (1949-1960)," Appendix A to Plaintiff's Trial Memorandum on Hearing for a Preliminary Injunction. The suit is described in *New York Times,* January 8, 1973.

61. See United Steelworkers of America, District No. 31, *District Conference Report* (October 1977).

62. John Kaplan, "Segregation, Litigation and the Schools—Part III: The Gary Litigation," *Northwestern University Law Review* 59, no. 1 (May-June 1964): 123–67, and Max Wolff, "Segregation in the Schools of Gary, Indiana," *The Journal of Educational Sociology* 36, no. 6 (February 1963): 251–61.

Chapter 5: The Police Department

1. See, for instance, James Q. Wilson, *Varieties of Police Behavior* (Cambridge: Harvard University Press, 1968).

2. *Report of the National Advisory Commission on Civil Disorders* (New York: Bantam Books, 1968), and Roscoe Pound, "Criminal Justice and the American City," in *Criminal Justice in Cleveland,* ed. Roscoe Pound and Felix Frankfurter (Cleveland: Cleveland Foundation, 1922), p. 576.

3. Police brutality encompasses three types of illegal use of force: 1) force against an individual for whom there is no legal basis for an arrest, as in the dispersion of lawful demonstrators; 2) summary physical punishment after an arrest; 3) substantially more force than necessary to effectuate a lawful arrest. (These cases are often complex, such as for instance, whether it is "lawful" to kill a fleeing felon.) See Barry C. Feld, "Police Violence and Protest," *Minnesota Law Review* 55, no. 4 (March 1971): 759; Paul Chevigny, *Police Power* (New York: Vintage, 1969); Hubert G. Locke, "Police Brutality and Civilian Review Boards," *Journal of Urban Law* 44 (Summer 1967): 626; Nicolas John DeRoma, "Justifiable Use of Deadly Force by the Police," *William and Mary Law Review* 12, no. 1 (Fall 1970):

67–76; Van R. Mayhall, Jr., "Use of Deadly Force in the Arrest Process," *Louisiana Law Review* 31, no. 1 (December 1970): 131–49; and *New York Times*, December 6, 1976.

4. Rodney Stark, *Police Riots* (Belmont, Cal.: Wadsworth, 1972), p. 77.

5. This has been stated so often that leading scholars do not even bother to cite evidence to support it. See Seymour Martin Lipset, "Why Cops Hate Liberals—and Vice Versa," *The Atlantic* 223, no. 3 (March 1969); Gary T. Marx, "Civil Disorder and the Agents of Social Control," *Journal of Social Issues* 26, no. 1 (Winter 1970): 19–58; and Andrew Hacker, "Safety Last," *The New York Review of Books* 24, no. 14 (September 15, 1977): 4.

6. Seymour Martin Lipset, *Political Man* (New York: Doubleday, 1960), p. 114. Cf. Christopher Lasch, "The Cultural Cold War," in *Towards a New Past*, ed. Barton J. Bernstein (New York: Pantheon, 1968), pp. 332–59, and Jesse Lemisch, *On Active Service in War and Peace* (Toronto: New Hogtown Press, 1975).

7. Richard K. Hamilton, *Class and Politics in the United States* (New York: John Wiley and Sons, 1972), ch. 11.

8. This is a main aspect of the second transition of political power in Gary, one which closely parallels the shift in the department that occurred during the New Deal, when U.S. Steel was compelled to give up direct political control of city government. A realistic summary of the use of police power in advanced capitalist societies under varying political circumstances appears in Ralph Miliband, *Marxism and Politics* (New York: Oxford University Press, 1977), pp. 91–92.

9. "Field Notes," *Foreign-Born* 1 (December 1919): 31; Mrs. Harry Sternberger, "Are Our Foreign-Born Emigrating?" *The Survey* 43, no. 15 (February 7, 1920): 539; and David Brody, *Steelworkers in America: The Nonunion Era* (Cambridge: Harvard University Press, 1960), p. 104.

10. Brody, *Steelworkers in America*, p. 105; Powell A. Moore, *The Calumet Region: Indiana's Last Frontier* (Indianapolis: Indiana Historical Bureau, 1959), pp. 291–92; Richard Julius Meister, "A History of Gary, Indiana, 1930-1940" (Ph.D., University of Notre Dame, 1967), p. 24; and Isaac James Quillen, "Industrial City: A History of Gary, Indiana to 1929" (Ph.D., Yale University, 1942). For direct linkages between the police and the leading manufacturers in industrial centers before the New Deal, see Sidney L. Harring and Lorraine M. McMullan, "The Buffalo Police 1872-1900: Labor Unrest, Political Power and the Creation of the Police Institution,"

Crime and Social Justice (Fall-Winter 1975): 5–14, and Sidney Fine, *Sit-Down: The General Motors Strike of 1936-1937* (Ann Arbor: University of Michigan Press, 1969), p. 108.

11. Quillen, "History of Gary," pp. 166–67; Neil Betten and Raymond A. Mohl, "The Evolution of Racism in an Industrial City, 1906-1940: A Case Study of Gary, Indiana," *The Journal of Negro History* 59, no. 1 (January 1974): 51–64; Edna Hatfield Edmondson, *Juvenile Delinquency and Adult Crime*, Indiana University Studies, 8, no. 49 (Bloomington: Indiana University, 1921), pp. 74–88; and John Foster Potts, "A History of the Growth of the Negro Population of Gary, Indiana" (M.A., Cornell University, 1937), p. 50.

12. Emerson Hough, "Round Our Town," *The Saturday Evening Post* (February 21, 1920): 102; Meister, "A History of Gary," p. 252; Robert K. Murray, *Red Scare: A Study of National Hysteria, 1919-1920* (Minneapolis: University of Minnesota Press, 1955), pp. 135–52; and Stephen Spitzer and Andrew F. Scull, "Privatization and Capitalist Development," *Social Problems* 25, no. 1 (October 1977): 18–29.

13. William A. Westley, *Violence and the Police* (Cambridge: MIT Press, 1970), pp. xiii–xiv. On the sharp improvement of police status between 1947 and 1961 during an ebb of class conflict, see John H. McNamara, "Uncertainties in Police Work: The Relevance of Police Recruits' Background and Training," in *The Police: Six Sociological Studies*, ed. David J. Bordua (New York: John Wiley & Sons, 1967), p. 167.

14. Quillen, "History of Gary," pp. 178–79, 191.

15. Brody, *Steelworkers in America*, p. 118.

16. Meister, "History of Gary," pp. 27–28; Clark Douglas Kimball, "Patriotism and the Suppression of Dissent in Indiana During the First World War" (Ph.D., Indiana University, 1971), pp. 141–50; and Quillen, "History of Gary," pp. 330–32.

17. Hough, "Round Our Town," p. 102.

18. As a member of the Loyalty League explained:

> Every one of us has a deputy's star in his pocket, a heavy gun under his left shoulder and a blackjack in his right hand. . . . Our method of work was to grab a man's right arm with the operator's own left hand, then bring down the blackjack across the hand bones and wrist of the man thus caught.

Moore, *Calumet Region*, pp. 505–20; Hough, "Round Our Town," p. 102; and David Brody, *Labor in Crisis: The Steel Strike of 1919* (Philadelphia: J. B. Lippincott, 1965), p. 111.

19. Brody, *Steelworkers in America*, p. 110, and Moore, *Calumet Region*, p. 289. At this time the foremen were recruited "almost entirely from the ranks of the skilled craftsmen" and were largely native born. U.S. Senate, *Report on Conditions of Employment in the Iron and Steel Industry in the United States*, Vol. III, *Labor Conditions* (Washington, D.C.: Government Printing Office, 1913), p. 82, and Irving Bernstein, *The Lean Years* (Boston: Houghton Mifflin, 1966), p. 48.

20. Edmondson, *Juvenile Delinquency*, p. 105; Moore, *Calumet Region*, pp. 289, 365; and Mary Field Parton, ed., *The Autobiography of Mother Jones* (Chicago: Charles H. Kerr, 1972), pp. 213–14.

21. Elizabeth Balanoff, "A History of the Black Community of Gary, Indiana, 1906-1940" (Ph.D., University of Chicago, 1974); Moore, *Calumet Region*, pp. 539–51; and *New York Times*, March 29, 1925; May 9, 1929; and January 21, 1932.

22. Moore, *Calumet Region*, pp. 365–66, 502, 543; Horace B. Davis, *Labor and Steel* (New York: International Publishers, 1933), p. 96; and *The Daily Worker*, September 1, 1925.

23. Peter Roberts, *The New Immigrants* (New York: Macmillan, 1912), pp. 142–43.

24. Moore, *Calumet Region*, pp. 369–70; Edmondson, *Juvenile Delinquency*, pp. 62–88; Paul Taylor, *Mexican Labor in the United States: Chicago and the Calumet Region* (Berkeley: University of California Press, 1932), p. 79; and Daniel J. Elazar, *Cities of the Prairie* (New York: Basic Books, 1970), pp. 223–25.

25. Hugh M. Ayer, "Hoosier Labor in the Second World War" (Ph.D., Indiana University, 1957), pp. 126–27. See also Meister, "History of Gary," p. 252, and Balanoff, "Black Community," p. 206.

26. James B. Lane, *City of the Century: A History of Gary, Indiana* (Bloomington: Indiana University Press, 1978), p. 182. See also Virgil W. Peterson, *Barbarians in Our Midst: A History of Chicago Crime and Politics* (Boston: Little, Brown, 1952), pp. 180–81, and William L. Patterson, *The Man Who Cried Genocide: An Autobiography* (New York: International Publishers, 1971), p. 141.

27. Lane, *City*, pp. 212, 247; Westley, *Violence*, pp. 39, 53; and confidential informants. Also see Julian B. Roebuck, "The Negro Numbers Man as a Criminal Type: The Construction and Application of a Typology," *The Journal of Criminal Law, Criminology, and Police Science* 54, no. 1 (March 1953): 48–60.

28. William E. Nelson, Jr., *Black Politics in Gary: Problems and Prospects* (Washington, D.C.: Joint Center for Political Studies,

1972), and Peter H. Rossi and Philip Cutwright, "The Impact of Party Organization in an Industrial Setting," in *Community Political Systems*, ed. Morris Janowitz (Glencoe: The Free Press, 1961), pp. 81–116.

29. See Edward Greer, "The New Mayors: Black Power in the Big Cities," *The Nation* 219, no. 17 (November 23, 1974): 525–29.

30. This police intervention was hardly unique. The historic use of the police and vigilante forces to prevent blacks from voting in the South is well known. But it has a recent northern component as well. For example, when Mayor Carl Stokes of Cleveland ran for reelection in 1969, 400 off-duty police appeared at the polls in black neighborhoods to challenge voters' registration. See Cyril D. Robinson, "The Mayor and the Police," in *Police Forces in History*, ed. George L. Mosse (Beverly Hills: Sage Publications, 1975), p. 306.

31. Interview with Police Chief Charles Boone, June 19, 1972; interview with Director of Public Safety William T. Johnson, June 3, 1971; Richard G. Hatcher, *Gary, 1968: The Mayor's Report to the People* (1969), p. 5; *The Daily World*, May 20, 1972; and *Post-Tribune*, March 27, 1967; April 1, 1967; January 2, 1970; and February 2, 1970.

32. David H. Bayley, "The Police and Political Development in Europe," in *The Formation of National States in Europe*, ed. Charles Tilly (Princeton, N.J.: Princeton University Press, 1975), pp. 388–99, and Douglas Hay, "Property, Authority and the Criminal Law," in *Albion's Fatal Tree: Crime and Society in Eighteenth-Century England*, ed. Douglas Hay et al. (New York: Pantheon, 1975), p. 18.

33. James Q. Wilson, "The Dilemma of the Urban Police," in *American Urban History*, ed. A. B. Callow Jr. (New York: Oxford University Press, 1973), p. 589.

34. Robert Reinders, "Militia and Public Order in Nineteenth-Century America," *American Studies* 11, no. 1: 81–101. See also Richard Quinney, *Criminology: Analysis and Critique of Crime in America* (Boston: Little, Brown, 1975), pp. 165–66, and Alan Silver, "The Demand for Order in Civil Society: A Review of Some Themes in the History of Urban Crime, Police and Riot," in *Police*, ed. Bordua.

35. Harring and McMullan, "Buffalo Police," pp. 5–14; Robert S. Lynd and Helen Merrell Lynd, *Middletown in Transition* (New York: Harcourt Brace and Co., 1937), pp. 38–39, 351; and Donald J. Curran, *Metropolitan Financing* (Madison: University of Wisconsin Press, 1973), pp. 88–89.

36. See, for example, E. Terrance Jones, "Evaluating Everyday Policies: Police Activity and Crime Incidence," *Urban Affairs Quarterly* 8, no. 3 (March 1973): 267–80; James P. Levine, "The Ineffectiveness of Adding Police to Control Crime," *Public Policy* 23, no. 4 (Fall 1975): 523–45; and Center for Research on Criminal Justice, *The Iron Fist and the Velvet Glove* (Berkeley: Center for Research on Criminal Justice, 1975), pp. 32–52.

37. Reinders, "Public Order," p. 95.

38. Richard Hofstadter, "Reflections on Violence in the United States," in *American Violence,* ed. Richard Hofstadter and Michael Wallace (New York: Alfred A. Knopf, 1970), p. 11. See also Richard Maxwell, *Strain of Violence* (New York: Oxford University Press, 1975). For this pattern in Indiana, see Emma Lou Thornbrough, *The Negro in Indiana* (Indianapolis: Indiana Historical Bureau, 1957), pp. 274–87.

39. Westley, *Violence*, p. 205, and John R. Snibbe and Homa M. Snibbe, *The Urban Policeman in Transition* (Springfield, Ill.: Charles C. Thomas, 1973), pp. 366–67.

40. John H. Maniha, "The Mobility of Elites in a Bureaucratic Organization: The St. Louis Police Department, 1861-1961" (Ph.D., University of Michigan, 1970), pp. 155, 219. The same is true in England, as Westergaard and Resler report:

> Police recruitment within the manual working class . . . draws almost entirely on the skilled layers. Very few policemen come from semi- and unskilled workers' families; a very large minority at least—perhaps even a majority—are from white-collar homes . . . [T]heir links—in styles of life, friendships and social outlook—are closest with the petty bourgeoisie and the most secure, respectable and aspiring ranks of manual workers.

John Westergaard and Henrietta Resler, *Class in a Capitalist Society* (New York: Basic Books, 1975), p. 187.

41. Harry Braverman, *Labor and Monopoly Capital* (New York: Monthly Review Press, 1974), pp. 297, 367–69, and Anthony Giddens, *The Class Structure of the Advanced Countries* (New York: Harper and Row, 1975), p. 180.

42. *The Knapp Commission Report on Police Corruption* (New York: George Braziller, 1973), and John A. Gardiner, *The Politics of Corruption* (New York: Russell Sage Foundation, 1970). This symbiotic relationship between police and small businesses operating on the margin of, or beyond, juridical legitimacy has long been a

theme in American literature and film. And it reflects a deep-rooted historical reality.

43. See Raymond E. Wolfinger, *The Politics of Progress* (Englewood Cliffs, N.J.: Prentice-Hall, 1974), and Carl B. Stokes, *Promises of Power* (New York: Simon & Schuster, 1973), p. 134. See also Matthew Holden, Jr., *The White Man's Burden* (New York: Chandler, 1973), p. 111, and James F. Richardson, *Urban Police in the United States* (Port Washington, N.Y.: Kennikat Press, 1973), p. 46.

44. Robert W. Balch, "The Police Personality," *The Journal of Criminal Law, Criminology, and Police Science* 63, no. 1 (March 1972): 106–19; David H. Bayley and Harold Mendelsohn, *Minorities and the Police* (New York: The Free Press, 1969), pp. 16–30; and Francis J. Ianni, *A Family Business: Kinship and Social Control in Organized Crime* (New York: New American Library, 1973), p. 95. Generally, see Arno Mayer, "The Lower Middle Class as Historical Problem," *Journal of Modern History* 47, no. 3 (September 1975), and Palmiro Togliatti, *Lectures on Fascism* (New York: International Publishers, 1976).

45. See Michael Rogin, "Politics, Emotion and the Wallace Vote," in *Black Liberation Politics: A Reader*, ed. Edward Greer (Boston: Allyn & Bacon, 1971), pp. 194–95. Similarly, a study of police in two midwestern cities in 1968 showed a large minority actually voting for Wallace. For example, Stark, *Police Riots*, p. 161.

46. *Post-Tribune*, March 29, 1967.

47. Harry Higdon, "Gary's Next Mayor: White, Pink, or Black?" *The Reporter* (November 2, 1967), and anonymous scurrilous circulars in possession of author.

48. City of Gary, *Community Renewal Program Report No. 5, A Study of Social Disorganization* (1969), pp. 40–42. This pattern is congruent with the national one. See Marvin Wolfgang and Bernard Cohen, "The Convergence of Crime and Race," in *Race, Crime and Justice*, ed. Charles E. Reasons and Jack L. Kuykensall (Santa Monica, Cal.: Goodyear, 1972), pp. 70–77; Morris E. Ferslund, "A Comparison of Negro and White Crime Rates," *The Journal of Criminal Law, Criminology, and Police Science* 61, no. 2 (June 1970): 214–17; and Michael Lalli and Stanley H. Turner, "Suicide and Homicide: A Comparative Analysis by Race and Occupational Levels," *The Journal of Criminal Law, Criminology, and Police Science* 59, no. 2 (March 1968): 191–200.

49. Frank F. Furstenberg, Jr., "Public Reaction to Crime in the Streets," *The American Scholar* 40, no. 4 (Autumn 1971): 601–10.

50. *Initial Findings on the Gary Mayoralty Election, 1971* (confidential poll, typescript copy in author's possession), p. 49; Sheldon Stryker, "The Urban Scene: Observations from Research," *The Review*, Indiana University (Summer 1969): 13–14; and Thomas Francis Thompson, "Public Administration in the Civil City of Gary, Indiana" (Ph.D., Indiana University, 1970), p. 85.
51. *New York Times*, July 28, 1975. See also Elliot Currie, "Crime: The Pervasive American Syndrome," *In These Times* 1, no. 7 (January 5–11, 1977): 15, and Lynda Ann Ewen, *Corporate Power and Urban Crisis in Detroit* (Princeton, N.J.: Princeton University Press, 1978), p. 33.
52. As Robert F. Wintersmith puts it: "The Black Community is unanimously incensed over the nonenforcement and underenforcement of criminal laws in their community." *Police and the Black Community* (Lexington, Mass.: D. C. Heath, 1974), p. 110. And see Walt Thompson, "What's Left of the Black Left," *Ramparts* (August 1972): 57–58.
53. Edmond J. Keller, "The Impact of Black Mayors on Urban Policy" (paper at 1977 Annual Meeting of American Political Science Association), pp. 6–7.
54. *Post-Tribune*, various dates; *New York Times*, September 26, 1972; November 22, 1972; January 7, 1973; March 28, 1973; April 27, 1973; April 29, 1973; January 27, 1974; April 22, 1974; and July 16, 1974; Joel D. Aberbach and Jack L. Walker, *Race in the City* (Boston: Little, Brown, 1973), pp. 18–20; Leroy C. Gould, "The Changing Structure of Property Crime in an Affluent Society," *Social Forces* 48, no. 1 (September 1969): 51, note 5; and interview with William Johnson.
55. Harvey Juris and Peter Feuille, *Police Unionism* (Lexington, Mass.: D. C. Heath, 1973), p. 27; Harlan Hahn, "A Profile of Urban Police," *Law and Contemporary Problems* 36, no. 4 (Autumn 1971): 446; John H. McNamara, "Uncertainties in Police Work: The Relevance of Police Recruits' Backgrounds and Training," in *Police*, ed. Bordua, p. 193, table 2; Nicholas Alex, *New York Cops Talk Back: A Study of a Beleaguered Minority* (New York: John Wiley & Sons, 1976), pp. 7–53; and Nicholas Alex, *Black in Blue: A Study of the Negro Policeman* (New York: Appleton-Century-Crofts, 1969), p. 4.
56. *New York Times*, December 10, 1974; December 27, 1974; January 4, 1976; and January 6, 1976. Generally see Center for Research on Criminal Justice, *The Iron Fist*, p. 60, and David H. Rafky, "Racial

Discrimination in Urban Police Departments," *Crime and Delin-quency* 21, no. 3 (July 1975): 233–42.

57. *New York Times*, January 11, 1976. Recently, policies of the U.S. armed forces also have resulted in reducing the proportion of black personnel. Such ethnic manipulations take place in many parts of the world. A recent analysis put it this way:

> [Such policies] are often reflections of the current govern-ment's security officials' notions of which groups are politi-cally dependable, which most suspect. State regimes often design police forces with an eye to their own security, not to the security of the public at large.

Cynthia H. Enloe, "Police and Military in the Resolution of Ethnic Conflict," *Annals of the American Academy of Political and Social Science*, no. 433 (September 1977): 141. See also Jay Stone, "Plan for Military Racism," *The Daily World*, March 26, 1977.

58. Warren M. Banner, *A Study of the Social and Economic Conditions of Three Minority Groups: Gary, Indiana* (New York: National Urban League, 1955).

59. Interview with Charles Boone, and Chuck Stone, "Report: Gary, Indiana," *The Atlantic* 220, no. 4 (October 1967): 28–29.

60. Juris and Feuille report that "every one of our black officer inter-viewees from several different cities related incidents of racial abuse by white colleagues." *Police Unionism*, p. 171. See also *Post-Tribune*, January 11, 1967.

61. This pattern of civil service discrimination is national in scope. Bernard Cohen and Jan M. Chaiken, *Police Background Charac-teristics and Performance: A Summary* (New York: Rand Corpora-tion, 1972), p. 14; *New York Times*, August 15, 1973; and Bennett Harrison, *Employment and Urban Poverty* (Washington, D. C.: The Urban Institute, n.d.), p. 54.

62. Interview with William T. Johnson, public safety director. Other black mayors have had similar successes in blackening their police departments. In Detroit, for example, as late as 1965 out of 4,500 police only 131 were black and 4 percent of new recruits were black. Currently, two-thirds of new recruits are black and the force achieved a composition of 40 percent black in 1978. *New York Times*, July 3, 1976, and March 1, 1978. In Newark under Mayor Gibson, between 1971 and 1973 the proportion of black police rose from 11 percent to 25 percent. Robert Curvin, "The Persistent Minority: The Black

Political Experience in Newark" (Ph.D., Princeton University, 1975), p. 182, table 8.

63. Interview with William T. Johnson, and Ellwyn R. Stoddard, "Blue Coat Crimes," in *Crime and Justice*, Vol. II, *The Criminal in the Arms of the Law*, ed. Leon Radzinowicz and Marvin E. Wolfgang (New York: Basic Books, 1971), p. 197.

64. Interviews with Police Chief Charles Boone, and Public Safety Director William T. Johnson; interview with Charlotte Johnson, administrative assistant to Mayor Hatcher, June 18, 1972; *The Daily World*, May 20, 1972; and *Municipal Code of the City of Gary, Indiana (1960)* (Indianapolis: Bobbs-Merrill, 1960), Title 2, ch. 2.

65. *The Daily World*, August 7, 1972; Curvin, "Persistent Minority," p. 192; *New York Times*, October 8, 1974; and Michael Preston, "Limitations of Black Urban Power: The Case of Black Mayors," in *The New Urban Politics*, ed. Louis H. Masotti and Robert L. Lineberry (Cambridge, Mass.: Ballinger, 1976), p. 125.

66. Westley, *Violence*, pp. viii.

67. Ibid., p. 68. See also Aberbach and Walker, *Race*, pp. 50–53.

68. Interview with Burton Wechsler (counsel to Gary Civil Liberties Union), June 12, 1971; *New York Times*, September 19, 1973; and Robert N. Bellah, *The Broken Covenant: American Civil Religion in Time of Trial* (New York: The Seabury Press, 1975), p. 103.

69. Under Gary's civil service law, the maximum penalty the chief can administer on his own authority is one week's suspension (and its exercise precludes any further disciplinary action). Interviews with William T. Johnson, and Charlotte Johnson. See Curvin, "Persistent Minority," pp. 177–78.

70. *Screws v. United States*, 325 U.S. 91 (1945); Sasha Harmon, "Cops in the Courts: Police Misconduct Litigation," *Yale Review of Law and Social Action* 2, no. 4 (Summer 1972): 334–41; Alfred Avins, "Equal Protection Against Unnecessary Police Violence and the Original Understanding of the Fourteenth Amendment," *Buffalo Law Review* 19 (1970), and "Civilians Against the Police," *Harvard Law Review* 77, no. 3 (January 1964): 500; James R. Hudson, "Police Review Boards and Police Accountability," *Law and Contemporary Problems* 36, no. 4 (Autumn 1971): 518; and Bernard Cohen, *The Police Internal Administration of Justice in New York City* (New York: Rand Corporation, 1970), pp. 54–67.

71. Raymond E. Wolfinger, "Why Political Machines Have Not Withered Away and Other Revisionist Thoughts," *The Journal of Politics* 34, no. 2 (May 1972): 371; Mike Royko, *Boss: Richard J. Daley of*

Chicago (New York: E. P. Dutton, 1971); Samuel P. Hays, "The Politics of Reform in Municipal Government in the Progressive Era," *Pacific Northwest Quarterly* 55 (1964): 157–69; James P. Weinstein, *The Corporate Ideal in the Liberal State, 1900-1918* (Boston: Beacon Press, 1968); and Daniel N. Gordon, "Immigrants and Municipal Voting Turnout: Implications for the Changing Ethnic Impact on Urban Politics," *American Sociological Review* 35 (1970): 665–81.

72. Quoted in *Washington Post*, March 4, 1973.

73. Schaible, an intimate of the U.S. Steel executives who had traditionally exercised political hegemony over the community, had recaptured the mayoralty from the Democrats in 1938 as a result of a split in their ranks, and it was clear that he would be Gary's last Republican mayor.

74. The commission consists of a three-member board chosen for three-year terms: one each chosen by the mayor, the city council, and the police. See Westley, *Violence*, p. 20; Meister, "History of Gary," pp. 92, 300–24; *Municipal Code*, ch. 19; and *Burns' Ind. Stat. Anno.*, Secs. 48-6241 to 48-6249. See also Robert R. R. Brooks, *As Steel Goes* (New Haven: Yale University Press, 1940).

75. Interviews with Charles Boone and Charlotte Johnson. See also *New York Times*, July 4, 1974, and *The Daily World*, August 7, 1974, and September 3, 1974.

76. This is the conclusion of one radical analysis of the court system's response to ghetto riots: "Under crisis conditions the impact of local political structure variations on policy outcomes is virtually nil." Issac D. Balbus, *The Dialectics of Legal Repression: Black Rebels Before the American Criminal Courts* (New York: Russell Sage Foundation, 1972), p. 249.

77. James Haskins, *A Piece of the Power: Four Black Mayors* (New York: The Dial Press, 1972), p. 76. See also Holden, Jr., *Burden*, p. 115, and *Annual Reports and Official Opinions of the Attorney General of Indiana 1968*, Official Opinions Nos. 30, 48, pp. 193–205, 298–300.

78. See *Gary Citizen* 2, no. 3 (April 27, 1971): 3, and *Post-Tribune*, May 14, 1971. A review of the fate of civilian review boards around the nation appears in *New York Times*, February 10, 1975.

79. Quoted in *Post-Tribune*, April 3, 1971.

80. Cohen and Chaiken, *Police*, p. 13; Alex, *Black in Blue*; and Victor Perlo, *The Economics of Racism, USA* (New York: International Publishers, 1976).

81. Peter H. Rossi, Richard A. Berk, and Bettye E. Eidson, *The Roots of Ghetto Discontent: Public Policy, Municipal Institutions and the Ghetto* (New York: John Wiley & Sons, 1974), pp. 192–93.

82. *New York Times*, July 7, 1974; December 9, 1974; and May 11, 1976. "It is worth noting in this regard that in Southern cities . . . the rise of civil rights demonstrations coincided with a marked short run decline in violent crimes among blacks." Ted Robert Garr, Peter N. Brabosky, and Richard C. Hula, *The Politics of Crime and Conflict: A Comparative History of Four Cities* (Beverly Hills: Sage Publications, 1977), p. 11.

83. Alex, *New York Cops*; Alex, *Black in Blue*; Edward Palmer, "Black Police in America," *The Black Scholar* 5, no. 2 (October 1973); James Boggs, "Blacks in the Cities: Agenda for the 70s," *The Black Scholar* 4, no. 3 (November-December 1972); Juris and Feuille, *Police Unionism*; and Harold F. Gosnell, *Negro Politicians: The Rise of Negro Politics in Chicago* (Chicago: University of Chicago Press, 1976).

84. See the interchange on this conclusion between myself and Gerda Ray in "Debate," *Crime and Social Justice*, no. 9 (Spring-Summer 1978): 53–71.

Chapter 6: The Limits of Housing Reform

1. *New York Times*, October 5, 1975; Matthew Edel, "Rent Theory and Working Class Strategy: Marx, George and the Urban Crisis," *The Review of Radical Political Economics* 9, no. 4 (Winter 1977): 9; and U.S. Department of Housing and Urban Development (HUD), *Housing in the Seventies: A Report of the National Housing Policy Review* (Washington, D.C.: HUD, 1974), p. 237, table 16.

2. Melvin and Anne White, "Horizontal Inequality in the Federal Income Tax Treatment of Homeowners and Tenants," *National Tax Journal* 18, no. 3 (September 1965): 225–239. See also Henry J. Aaron, *Shelter and Subsidies* (Washington, D.C.: The Brookings Institution, 1972).

3. *Search: A Report from the Urban Institute* 7, no. 1 (Spring 1977): 6–7, and Helen F. Ladd, "The Role of the Property Tax: A Reassessment," in *Broad-Based Taxes*, ed. Richard A. Musgrave (Baltimore: The Johns Hopkins Press, 1973), p. 64.

4. Works Progress Administration, *Real Property Survey and Low Income Housing Area Survey of Gary, Indiana* (Gary, n.p., 1940),

and U.S. Bureau of the Census, Census of Population and Housing: 1970, *Census Tracts* Final Report PHC (1)-79 (Washington, D.C.: Government Printing Office, 1972).

5. See, for instance, Edward Banfield, *The Unheavenly City Revisited* (Boston: Little, Brown, 1974).

6. HUD, *Housing*, pp. 169–76, 235–37.

7. Field Market Analysis Service, Department of Housing and Urban Development, *Analysis of the Gary-Hammond-East Chicago, Indiana Housing Market* as of June 1, 1966. Percentage calculated from HUD, *Housing*, p. 170, table 2.

8. Although there is considerable overlap (e.g., one-sixth of families earning over $25,000 are renters), the two groups have become more divergent.

9. *Chicago Sun-Times*, May 23, 1971.

10. Thomas Vietoriscz and Bennett Harrison, *The Economic Development of Harlem* (New York: Praeger, 1970), p. 11. See also Gilbert Osofsky, *Harlem: The Making of a Ghetto*, 2d ed. (New York: Harper and Row, 1971), and Herrington J. Bryce, "Problems of Governing Large Cities: The Case of Medium and Large Cities with Black Mayors," *Focus* 2, no. 10 (August 1974): A4.

11. HUD, *Housing*, p. 167, table I. George Sternlieb and James W. Hughes conclude after a detailed study of New York City's housing stock that "there is strong evidence of a deterioration in the physical structures which provide housing for the great bulk of the city's residents." Over half of the rental housing was built prior to the Depression. *Housing and Economic Reality: New York City 1976* (New Brunswick, N.J.: Rutgers University Center for Urban Policy Research, 1976), pp. 1, 22.

12. Gary Redevelopment Commission, *Community Renewal Program: Housing in Gary* (Washington, D.C.: City Planning Associates, 1966), p. A-17.

13. Lawrence M. Freidman, "Public Housing and the Poor," in *Housing Urban America*, ed. John Pynoos et al. (Chicago: Aldine, 1973), p. 450.

14. Between 1937 and 1949 fewer than one-third of cities with populations over 25,000 built public housing. Those which did so had generally more dilapidated housing and powerful local interests encouraging local governments to act. Michael Aiken and Robert R. Alford, "Community Structure and Innovation: The Case of Public Housing," *The American Political Science Review* 64, no. 3 (September 1970): 843–64.

15. Quoted in Gary Housing Authority, *The First Twenty Years, 1939-1959*. The corporation's support for public housing in Gary con-

tinued thereafter. As late as 1968 when Mayor Hatcher took office, two of the five members of the Housing Authority Board were executives of U.S. Steel.

16. The corporation was perfectly willing to go against the preferences of the local petty bourgeoisie to further its own ends. In this sense its policy partook of the same rationale Karl Marx pointed to in explaining why nineteenth-century English manufacturers supported the reduction of food tariffs against the interests of the rural landlords. The workers' movement naturally took advantage of this internal split in the ruling class to advance its own interests within the system. See David Harvey, "Labor, Capital, and Class Struggle around the Built Environment in Advanced Capitalist Societies," *Politics & Society* 6, no. 3 (1976): 274.

17. Hugh M. Ayer, "Hoosier Labor in the Second World War" (Ph.D., Indiana University, 1957), pp. 67–73.

18. Aaron, *Shelter*, p. 109.

19. The main bank in Gary has maintained a "policy of heavy investment in government securities at the expense of the person seeking mortgage credit." Gary Redevelopment Commission, *Community Renewal Program* (Mishawaka, Ind.: Community Planning Associates, 1968). See also *Post-Tribune*, January 25, 1970, and Esther Pesonen Niemi, "A Study of Commercial Banking in Two Economically Depressed Cities: Youngstown, Ohio and Wheeling, West Virginia" (Ph.D., Case Western Reserve University, 1969), pp. 69–73.

20. Richard G. Hatcher, "Report on Gary Housing," speech, December 3, 1968, prepared by author.

21. Gary Housing Authority, *Annual Report: 1976-77.* The authority has also leased 1,000 units of private housing which it subsidizes rents on with federal funds. Edmond J. Keller, "The Inpact of Black Mayors on Public Policy" (paper at 1977 American Political Science Association Convention), p. 14. Thus, Mayor Hatcher's statement to the *New York Times* (March 20, 1978) that by 1973 "our administration had overseen the building of 3,000 federally subsidized housing units" is in error. It should be seen as part of his efforts to obtain more federal assistance from the Carter administration and, perhaps, President Carter's effort to hire Hatcher to serve on the White House staff as chief liaison with the black community. *New York Times*, April 24, 1978.

22. Pynoos et al., *Housing*, pp. 5–8, and *New York Times*, December 12, 1973 and July 8, 1977.

23. See Hugh O. Nourse, "Redistribution of Income from Public Housing," in *The Effect of Public Policy on Housing Markets,* ed. Hugh O. Nourse (Lexington, Mass.: D. C. Heath, 1973), p. 41.
24. Aaron, *Shelter,* p. 108.
25. See Joseph A. Pechman and Benjamin A. Okner, *Who Bears the Tax Burden?* (Washington, D.C.: The Brookings Institution, 1974); Robert M. Brandon et al., *Tax Politics* (New York: Pantheon, 1976); and Michael H. Best and William E. Connolly, *The Politicized Economy* (Lexington, Mass.: D. C. Heath, 1976), ch. 3.
26. League of Women Voters (Frederica W. Wechsler), *Know Your Local Government* (Gary: League of Women Voters, n.d.), p. 26.
27. Gary Redevelopment District Trustee Board "Annual Report: 1977," mimeo, p. 4.
28. Michael Aiken and Robert R. Alford, "Community Structure and Innovation," p. 650–64.
29. HUD, *Housing,* p. 157, and U.S. Advisory Committee on Intergovernmental Relations, *Relocation: Unequal Treatment of People and Businesses Displaced by Governments,* Report A-26 (January 1965), p. 34. Another example is provided by Oakland, California:

> The overriding pressure for urban renewal was the exodus of the white middle-class homeowners . . . and their replacement by low-income, largely black and Chicano renters. . . . Between 1959 and 1965 vacancies in the downtown area rose to a phenomenal 21 percent. . . . [The] city's first plan for redevelopment was introduced . . . largely to save the remaining downtown merchants from total economic collapse.

Edward C. Hayes, *Power Structure and Urban Policy: Who Rules in Oakland?* (New York: McGraw-Hill, 1972), p. 108.
30. Matthew Edel, "Planning, Market or Warfare?—Recent Land Use Conflict in American Cities," in *Readings in Urban Economics,* ed. Matthew Edel and Jerome Rothenberg (New York: Macmillan, 1972), p. 146.

As Chester Hartman points out:

> The urban renewal program through 1967 demolished 404,000 dwelling units with another 356,000 scheduled for demolition in presently approved projects, while only 107,000 units have been constructed on renewal sites, and only 196,000 are planned—a net loss of nearly a half million units, even under the unlikely assumption that all planned units will eventually be built.

"Relocation: Illusory Promises and No Relief," *Virginia Law Review* 57, no. 5 (June 1971): 804–5.

31. Jerome Rothenberg, "The Nature of Redevelopment Benefits," in *Readings*, ed. Edel and Rothenberg, p. 215.

32. Raymond E. Wolfinger, "Nondecisions and the Study of Local Politics," *The American Political Science Review* (December 1971): 1067, note 25, and Aiken and Alford, "Community Structure and Innovation," pp. 651–52.

33. Rober A. Dahl, *Who Governs? Democracy and Power in an American City* (New Haven: Yale University Press, 1961). On Dahl's prestige, see Walter B. Roettger, "Strata and Stability: Reputations of American Political Scientists," *PS* 11, no. 1 (Winter 1978): 6–12.

34. Ibid., pp. 75, 84. Dahl concedes that urban renewal in New Haven would have been impossible if the local banks opposed it; and leaves open the possibility that overt opposition by the chamber of commerce might have blocked it; see pp. 125, 137–38.

35. Ibid., pp. 115–40. The diverse class strata of the coalition is described on p. 129. Dahl also avers, on p. 60: "Yet in its appeal redevelopment—far from taking on a class aspect—cuts across class or socioeconomic differences more than any other issue has done in decades."

36. G. William Domhoff, *Who Really Rules? New Haven and Community Power Reexamined* (Santa Monica, Cal.: Goodyear, 1978), pp. 39–120.

37. Edel, "Planning, Market or Warfare?" p. 146.

38. Vincent Scully, *American Architecture and Urbanism* (New York: Praeger, 1969), p. 246. Such outcomes are typical. For instance, the impact of redevelopment in Boston is described in Joe R. Feagin et al., *Subsidizing the Poor: A Boston Housing Experiment* (Lexington, Mass.: D. C. Heath, 1972).

39. See Harris Stone, *Workbook of an Unsuccessful Architect* (New York: Monthly Review Press, 1973).

40. Gary Redevelopment Commission, *Community Renewal Program*, p. 5.

41. See, for instance, Hayes, *Power Structure*, p. 83, and Domhoff, *Who Really Rules?* p. 60.

42. League of Women Voters, *Know Your Local*, p. 27, and *Municipal Code of Gary, Indiana 1960*, ch. 10, sec. 2-1003.

43. Interview with Charlotte Johnson, administrative assistant to Mayor Hatcher (June 7, 1971), and interview with Professor David Nelson (June 14, 1972).

44. Inner City Research Corporation, *Middle Income Housing: Gary, Indiana* (1968), and Richard G. Hatcher, *Gary, 1968: The Mayor's Report to the People* (1969), p. 6.

45. Gary Redevelopment Commission, *Annual Report: 1963*, pp. 19–20.

46. Ibid., pp. 23–38. Nationally, relocated businesses obtained an average payment of only $1,400 and consequently "35.3 percent discontinue operations." Advisory Committee, *Relocation*, p. 53. And see Domhoff, *Who Really Rules?* p. 112.

47. U.S. Senate, Committee on Government Operations, Subcommittee on Intergovernmental Relations, *Hearings on Impact and Administration of the Property Tax* (Washington, D.C.: June 26, 1972), testimony of Tom Fadell, pp. 34–35.

48. Gary Redevelopment Commission, *Annual Report: 1963*, p. 24. Nationally, a fifth of those displaced by urban renewal are relocated into public housing. Advisory Committee, *Relocation*, p. 27.

49. David Graham Nelson, "Black Reform and Federal Resources" (Ph.D., University of Chicago, 1972), p. 122. All studies of urban renewal show the displacees compelled on the average to pay "substantial increases" in their rent. Hartman, "Relocation: Illusory Promises," p. 791.

50. Interview with David Nelson, June 14, 1972. For the similar effect in New Haven see Stone, *Workbook*, and Scully, *Architecture*, pp. 247–48; for Baltimore see Michael A. Stegman, *Housing Investment in the Inner City* (Cambridge: MIT Press, 1972), p. 183, table 6.2. Hartman sums up the "relocation effect" as follows: "It appears beyond doubt that forced residential relocation produces net damage to the universe of displacees, as measured by both objective and subjective indices." Hartman, "Relocation: Illusory Promises," p. 802.

51. Gary Redevelopment Commission, *Organization of Urban Renewal Programs in Gary* (1968), p. 2.

52. *Post-Tribune*, June 22, 1972.

53. Nelson, "Black Reform," p. 71.

54. While the downtown plan called for an addition of 1,300 parking spaces to the 2,000 already in existence, so far a 300-car garage is all that has been built. Gary Downtown Improvement Association, *Gary, Indiana: Downtown Development Plan and Program* (1969).

55. While redevelopment in Gary was supported by the large commercial capitalists, it had "only limited participation of smaller businessmen or representatives of the Negro subcommunity." Nelson, "Black Reform," p. 186.

56. Gary Redevelopment Commission, *Annual Report: 1977*, p. 4.
57. Gary Redevelopment Commission, *The Linear Park* (1974), p. 13.
58. Gary Redevelopment Commission, *Community Renewal Program*, pp. 5, 7–72. The latter proviso explains why part of the petty bourgeoisie takes a "conservative" position in opposition to urban renewal. See Sam Bass Warner, Jr., *The Urban Wilderness* (New York: Harper and Row, 1972), p. 133.
59. See Nelson, "Black Reform," p. 122, who details this process, and Hartman, "Relocation: Illusory Promises," pp. 809–13.
60. A similar process occurred in Oakland, the major capitalists finally agreeing to new public housing as the prerequisite of continuing urban renewal. See Hayes, *Power Structure*, p. 83.
61. Personal knowledge of author and Gary Redevelopment Commission, *Annual Report: 1976*.
62. Cf. Edward R. Tufte, *Political Control of the Economy* (Princeton, N.J.: Princeton University Press, 1978) for a discussion of how federal expenditures are manipulated by presidents to effect short-term visible expansion of the economy immediately prior to elections.
63. Stegman makes a similar estimate for black renters in Baltimore. *Housing Investment*, pp. 8–11.
64. Philip Thigpen, "Blacks in the Housing Market: The Politics of Exclusion," in *The Politics of Housing in Older Urban Areas*, ed. Robert E. Mendelson and Michael A. Quinn (New York: Praeger, 1976), p. 156; A. Thomas King and Peter Miekzkowski, "Racial Discrimination, Segregation, and the Price of Housing," *Journal of Political Economy* 81, no. 3 (May–June 1973): 590–606; and Sternlieb and Hughes, *Economic Reality*, p. 17.
65. See U.S. Senate, *Hearings on Impact*, p. 54. Generally see Mortgage Bankers Association of America, *Redlining: Solution Requires Unified Approach* (1977).
66. HUD, *Housing*, pp. 18–86, and Stegman, *Housing Investment*, p. 163. See also Jane Jacobs, *The Death and Life of the Great American Cities* (New York: Random House, 1961).
67. See "Shaping and Misshaping the Metropolis," *Search* 7, no. 1 (Spring 1977): 4–8; Rothenberg, "Redevelopment Benefits," p. 220; Edward Greer, "Racial Biases in the Property Tax System," *The Review of Radical Political Economics* 7, no. 3 (Fall 1975): 22–32; and Dick Netzer, *Impact of the Property Tax: Its Economic Implications for Urban Problems*, Joint Economic Committee, Congress of the United States (Washington, D.C.: Government Printing Office, 1968).

68. *Municipal Code of Gary, Indiana: 1960,* Title 2, Secs. 1501-24, and Title 5.
69. HUD, *Housing,* p. 160; Warner, Jr., *Urban Wilderness,* pp. 26–27; 219–20; and cf. Stephen A. Kersten, "Housing Regulation and Reform in Boston, 1822-1924," Working Paper No. 7, Boston Studies in Urban Political Economy.
70. See Bruce Ackerman, "Regulating Slum Housing Markets on Behalf of the Poor: Of Housing Codes, Housing Subsidies and Income Redistribution Policy," *The Yale Law Journal* 80, no. 6 (May 1971): 1160–61.
71. See Roger S. Ahlbrandt, Jr., *Flexible Code Enforcement* (Washington, D.C.: National Association of Housing and Redevelopment Officials, 1976), p. 68.
72. *New York Times,* June 26, 1972, June 27, 1972, and John A. Gardiner, *The Politics of Corruption: Organized Crime in an American City* (New York: Russell Sage Foundation 1970), pp. 29–30, 83–84.
73. Thomas Francis Thompson, "Public Administration in the Civil City of Gary, Indiana" (Ph.D., Indiana University, 1960), p. 72; Chuck Stone, "Report: Gary, Indiana," *The Atlantic* 220, no. 4 (October 1967): 28–38; and League of Women Voters, *Know Your Local,* p. 24.
74. Gary Redevelopment Commission, *Community Renewal Program,* pp. 106–7. Such understaffing is commonplace. For Oakland, see Hayes, *Power Structure,* p. 94; for Baltimore, see Virginia B. Ermer, "Housing Inspection in Baltimore: Vermin, Mannequins, and Beer Bottles," in *Blacks and Bureaucracy: Readings in the Problems and Politics of Change,* ed. Virginia B. Ermer and John H. Strange (New York: Thomas Y. Crowell, 1972), pp. 84–87.
75. See Thompson, "Public Administration," p. 66. Gary's pattern was not exceptional. For instance, some months after Mayor Kenneth Gibson took office in Newark, the New Jersey State Task Force on Urban Problems cited a tradition of "lack of supervision and clear assignments" in building code enforcement as the basis for refusing additional state aid. *New York Times,* November 13, 1971.
76. Gary Redevelopment Commission, *Community Renewal Program,* pp. 105–7. It is well recognized in the field that serious enforcement efforts require the permanent assignment of city attorneys. Ahlbrandt, Jr., *Code Enforcement,* p. 27.
77. Warren M. Banner, *A Study of the Social and Economic Conditions in Three Minority Groups: Gary, Indiana* (New York: National Urban League, 1955), p. 28.

78. This information is detailed in Edward Greer, "Memorandum to Mayor Hatcher," July 24, 1968 (typescript in author's possession); Thompson, "Public Administration," p. 66; and Nelson, "Black Reform," p. 172.

79. *Municipal Code*, Title 5, Secs. 1614 (d) (1), 1614 (a) (3). Generally, see Daniel R. Mandelker, "Housing Codes, Building Demolition and Just Compensation: A Rationale for the Exercise of Public Powers over Slum Housing," *Michigan Law Review* 67 (February 1969): 635–78.

80. Interview with Morris Kaufman, director, Code Enforcement Program of Gary Building Department, June 15, 1972, and League of Women Voters, *Know Your Local*, p. 24. The annual number of demolitions in Gary has been: 1966: 15; 1967: 51; 1968: 37; 1969: 15; 1970: 0; 1971: 61; 1972: 50; 1973: 234; 1974: 222; 1975: 113; and 1976: 105. Gary Building Department, *Annual Reports: 1966-1976*.

81. "The current vacancy rate [in 1969] for sale housing in the city is estimated at 0.3 percent . . . [and] for rental housing is estimated at 3.7 percent." City of Gary, *Model Cities Program: Second Year Action Plan* (1970), p. II-61. Gary is not unique in this: "The vacate order, though inherently the most effective remedy, is tied to the existence of an adequate vacancy ratio; particularly in the low-rent housing. Thus the vacate order is likely to remain an extraordinary sanction for quite some time." Judah Gribetz and Frank P. Grad, "Housing Code Enforcement: Sections and Remedies," *Columbia Law Review* 66, no. 7 (November 1966): 1275.

82. Gribetz and Grad, "Housing Code Enforcement," pp. 1255–56. A detailed critique of the failure of Chicago's housing court appears in Legal Assistance Foundation of Chicago et al., *Judgment Landlord: A Study of Eviction Court in Chicago* (Chicago: Legal Assistance Foundation, 1968). On the failure of New York City's housing court, see *New York Times*, February 4, 1979.

83. This is typical. In New York City in 1967 only one out of thirty cases brought to court resulted in a fine—and the fines averaged $14. Gribetz and Grad, "Housing Code Enforcement," p. 1276. In Baltimore, the average conviction rate was 15 percent and the average fine $10—in comparison in that city of $1,000 per unit to bring the unit up to code standards. Ermer, "Housing Inspection," pp. 84–85, and Stegman, *Housing Investment*, pp. 262–63.

84. Gary Building Department, *Annual Report: 1976*, pp. 2, 5.

85. Cf. National Commission on Urban Problems, *Building the American City* (1968), in *Housing Urban America*, ed. Pynoos et al., p. 499.

86. U.S. Senate, *Hearings on Impact*, p. 54. On the decline in New York
    City's housing stock from 1965 to 1975 see Sternlieb and Hughes,
    Economic Reality, p. 10.
87. "The best housing available to black Americans is generally found
    in . . . relatively high-quality transitional neighborhoods on the
    periphery of the central-city ghetto." John F. Kain, "Housing Segre-
    gation, Black Employment, and Metropolitan Decentralization: A
    Retrospective View," in *Patterns of Racial Discrimination*, Vol. I,
    ed. George M. Furstenberg et al. (Lexington, Mass.: D. C. Heath,
    1974), p. 13. Osofsky describes this phenomenon in Harlem during
    the 1920s, when rapid racial turnover led to black access to improved
    housing stock.

Chapter 7: Tax Politics as Class Politics

1. See David Graham Nelson, "Black Reform and Federal Resources"
   (Ph.D., University of Chicago, 1972), p. 39.
2. Details as to the affluence of the corporation are set forth in Edward
   Greer, "The Political Economy of U.S. Steel Prices in the Postwar
   Period," in *Research in Political Economy: An Annual Compila-
   tion of Research*, Vol. I, ed. Paul Zarembka (Greenwich, Conn.: JAI
   Press, 1977), pp. 59–86. Also see Edward Greer, "Placebos for a Sick
   Industry," *The Nation* 226, no. 8 (March 4, 1978): 235–39.
3. Joseph A. Pechman and Benjamin A. Okner, *Who Bears the Tax
   Burden?* (Washington, D.C.: The Brookings Institution, 1974), and
   Robert M. Brandon et al., *Tax Politics* (New York: Pantheon, 1976).
   See also Marc Linder, *Anti-Samuelson*, Vol. II (New York: Urizen
   Books, 1977), p. 250.
4. In every advanced capitalist nation, redistribution from the rich as a
   consequence of taxation is most modest—generally their share of
   post-taxation income is reduced by no more than a tenth of the share
   obtained on the market. Edward Tufte, *The Political Control of the
   Economy* (Princeton, N.J.: Princeton University Press, 1978), p. 95,
   table 4.6.

   Furthermore, despite efforts to put the best possible face on the
   data, it appears that government macroeconomic policies in advanced capitalist nations, whether under conservative or social
   democratic regimes, result in relatively modest differences in unemployment rates. (For the U.S. the variance between Democratic

and Republican administrations had been 2 percent.) Douglas A. Hibbs, Jr. *Economic Interest and the Politics of Macroeconomic Policy* (Cambridge: MIT Center for International Studies, 1976).

5. Lester C. Thurow, *Generating Inequality: Mechanisms of Distribution in the U.S. Economy* (New York: Basic Books, 1975), ch. 8.

6. The Indiana constitution mandates a flat rate of taxation on all property. Troy J. Cauley, "The Indiana Tax System: A Critical Survey," *Indiana Business Review* 47 (February-March 1972): 1.

7. U.S. Senate, Committee on Government Operations, Subcommittee on Intergovernmental Relations, *Hearing on Impact and Administration of the Property Tax* (June 26, 1972), p. 31, and "Cities: Gary Presses a Claim," *Business Week* 2086 (August 23, 1969): 40.

8. Municipal disbursements in Gary have a progressive character, even after taking account of the caveats suggested by Donald M. Pappard, Jr., "Toward a Radical Theory of Fiscal Incidence," *The Review of Radical Political Economics* 8, no. 4 (Winter 1976): 1–16. And while there is some question as to the ultimate burden of corporation taxes, it seems that capitalists "bear a large share" of it, and certainly resist it as if they do. George F. Break and Joseph A. Pechman, *Federal Tax Reform* (Washington, D.C.: The Brookings Institution, 1975), p. 94.

9. State disbursements to municipalities have risen between 1954 and 1974 from 44 percent to 56 percent of all state revenues and there is little scope for further expansion. During this period in Indiana, state taxes rose at annual rates of 10 percent to 16 percent—far faster than the state economy. (Nationally, in contrast to federal spending which grew apace with the economy, combined state-local expenditures rose from 5.9 percent of GNP during 1946-1950 to 11.5 percent during 1966-1970.) Donald H. Haider, "Fiscal Scarcity: A New Urban Perspective," in *The New Urban Politics*, ed. Louis H. Masotti and Robert L. Linberry (Cambridge, Mass.: Ballinger, 1976), pp. 180–82; Charles F. Bonsen, "The Indiana Business Tax Roadblock," *Indiana Law Journal* 45, no. 3 (Spring 1970): 363–64; William H. Andrews, *Indiana's Economic Resources and Potential.* Section XII: Public Finance (Bloomington: Indiana University Press, 1955); L. E. Kust, "How Should State and Local Governments Tax Business?: The Impact of Institutional Failure," in Tax Institute of America, *Business Taxes in State and Local Governments* (Lexington, Mass.: D. C. Heath, 1972), p. 167; and James O'Connor, *The Fiscal Crisis of the State* (New York: St. Martins Press, 1973), chs. 8–9.

10. However, there is a major class bias in commercial assessments in Gary, with properties worth over $20,000 assessed at an average of 27 percent of market value and those worth less assessed at an average of 37 percent. U.S. Senate, *Hearing*, pp. 6, 35–37, and Albert E. Dickens, *Economic Factors for Planning Gary* (Chicago: Evert Kincaid & Associates, 1955).

11. They also paid about $500 in Indiana state taxes. U.S. Bureau of Census, Census of Population and Housing 1970, *Census Tracts Final Report FHC* (1)-79 Gary-Hammond-East Chicago, Ind. SMSA (Washington, D.C.: Government Printing Office, 1972); *Indiana Department of Revenue Annual Report* (1970); and *New York Times*, September 15, 1972. For more information see Thomas A. DeCoster and Donald W. Kiefer, "The Property Tax in Indiana: An Overview," *Indiana Business Review* 47 (April-May 1972): 12–16.

12. These biases are detailed in Edward Greer, "Racial Biases in the Property Tax System," *The Review of Radical Political Economics* 7, no. 3 (Fall 1975): 22–32.

13. U.S. Steel, *Annual Report: 1971.*

14. Stanley S. Surrey, *Pathways to Tax Reform* (Cambridge: Harvard University Press, 1973), pp. 77–81, 306, note 63. Between 1963 and 1973 federal corporation income taxes fell from 4.3 percent to 3.7 percent of Gross National Product. A detailed analysis appears in Greer, "The Political Economy of U.S. Steel Prices."

15. U.S. Steel, *Annual Report: 1971.*

16. James B. Kessler, ed., *Current Studies of Indiana Tax Policy* (Indianapolis: Indiana Commission on State Tax and Financing Policy, 1961), pp. 12–13; Thomas A. DeCoster, "Business Tax Topics," *Indiana Business Review* 46, (August-September 1971): 25–28; Richard I. Hofferbert, "Socioeconomic Dimensions of the American States: 1890-1960," *Midwest Journal of Political Science* 12, no. 3 (August 1968): 410, table 3; and Brandon, *Tax Politics*, p. 24.

17. U.S. Senate, *Hearing*, p. 59. In general, see Chuck Kleinhans, "Taxes and Tuition" (Bloomington: Jeff Sharlet Chapter, New University Conference, n.d.), mimeo, p. 7; James G. Coke, "The Development of Urban Policies in Ohio State Government," in *Political Behavior and Public Issues in Ohio*, ed. John H. Gargan et al. (Kent, Ohio: Kent State University Press, 1972), p. 311, table II; and Carolyn E. Johnson, "The Future of Local Government Financing in Indiana," *Indiana Law Journal* 45, no. 3 (Spring 1970): 354.

18. Walker also asserted: "By contrast, in Pennsylvania, also a major area, total [state-local] taxes per $100 of payroll in 1971 were only

about half as much." U.S. Senate, *Hearing*, pp. 59, 75. See also Edward C. Logelin, "In Defense of Business," *Chicago Tribune*, May 16, 1972.

19. Dickens, *Economic Factors*, p. 96, table 35.

20. Walter J. Riley, *Comparative Tax Valuation Report Calumet Region Industries: Lake County, Indiana* (East Chicago, 1926), p. 14; E. E. Rightor, "The Comparative Tax Rate for 215 Cities, 1925," *National Municipal Review* 14, no. 2 (December 1925): 759; and Richard Julius Meister, "A History of Gary, Indiana: 1930-1940" (Ph.D., University of Notre Dame, 1967), pp. 154–58.

21. The newspaper whose editorial policy was "resented by the steel company's officials and also by the conservative segment of Gary's citizens" was driven into bankruptcy in 1909 by an advertising boycott by the large businesses of the community, a boycott apparently encouraged by the corporation. Powell A. Moore, *The Calumet Region: Indiana's Last Frontier* (Indianapolis: Indiana Historical Bureau, 1959), pp. 433–34. Cf. Herbert Gutman, "Class, Status and Community Power in Nineteenth Century Industrial Cities: Paterson, New Jersey: A Case Study," in *Work, Culture and Society in Industrializing America*, ed. Herbert G. Gutman (New York: Vintage, 1977), p. 347.

22. *The Northern Indianian* 3, no. 23 (September 25, 1908). Professor Balanoff kindly brought this source to my attention.

23. Randolph S. Bourne, *The Gary Schools* (Boston: Houghton Mifflin, 1916), p. 7.

24. *Wall Street Journal*, April 5, 1971.

25. U.S. Senate, *Hearing*, pp. 44–49.

26. George Crile, "A Tax Assessor Has Many Friends," *Harper's Magazine* 245, no. 1470 (November 1972): 103.

27. Observed by a local reporter in the Senate hearing room, Chacharis blandly remarked "that he was in Washington on 'personal' business and decided to drop by." *Post-Tribune*, June 27, 1972.

28. Warner Bloomberg, Jr., "The Power Structure of an Industrial City" (Ph.D., University of Chicago, 1961), pp. 173–74.

29. As Michael Stone points out:

> The property tax has been essential for local political and economic power. In most cities real estate ownership is an important basis of power. Large property owners finance the election campaigns of local politicians, and in return local officials grant tax concessions to their supporters.

"The Housing Crisis, Mortgage Lending, and Class Struggle,"

Antipode 7, no. 2 (September 1975): 28. For an example of this phenomenon for Los Angeles, see *The Daily World*, July 2, 1977.
30. *Burn's Indiana Statutes*, 48–1602 (12).
31. Cf. Memorandum of B. K. Delph, city attorney, July 11, 1968, and letter to Maurice Baptiste, city controller, July 9, 1968.
32. *Chicago Sun-Times*, July 11, 1968, and July 12, 1968.
33. *Post-Tribune*, July 14, 1968.
34. A typical example was the letter to the city controller of December 18, 1968:

> Enclosed find check in the amount of Five Thousand Four Hundred and 50/100 Dollars ($5,400.50) for full settlement of building permits and fees for the construction, alteration, and remodeling of buildings and structures and the performance of plumbing and electrical work at Gary Steel Works, Gary Sheet and Tin Works, and Gary Tube Works, for the period January 1 through March 31, 1969. This constitutes construction contemplated in our 1969 annual construction budget adjusted to care for added or deleted work made during the year 1968 and specifically includes the building being constructed by USS for the National Can Company. We make the adjustment involving added or deleted work in January of the succeeding year and pro-rate payments for the current year on a quarterly basis.
> We will consider your acceptance of this check as our receipt for the purpose above stated.

35. Memorandum of author to Mayor Richard G. Hatcher, August 27, 1968.
36. *Burns' Indiana Statutes*, 64–0757. Similar provisions exist elsewhere. Cf. Theodore Reynolds Smith, "Effects of Real Estate Taxes on Investment Yields in the Urban Center," in National Tax Association, *Proceedings of the Sixty-Fourth Annual Conference on Taxation* (Columbus, Ohio: National Tax Association, 1972), p. 399.
37. As Mayor Hatcher testified in 1972:

> The substantive importance of full compliance with the building ordinance lies in the fact that individual building permits would provide the township assessor with a documented total as the basis for year-to-year assessment increases on real property. In the absence of individual building permits reflecting the real estimated costs of new construction, the Township Assessor has no documented basis for arriving at an increase in the following year's assessment.

U.S. Senate, *Hearing*, p. 10.

38. Ibid., p. 54.
39. Letter to City Controller Maurice Baptiste, September 9, 1968.
40. Letter of Maurice Baptiste, September 26, 1968. While the Chicago press found this event worthy of major coverage, Gary's newspaper managed to wait several days before running a brief notice about it. *Chicago Sun-Times*, September 28, 1968, and *Post-Tribune*, September 30, 1968.
41. Transcript of Hearing, *U.S. Steel vs. City of Gary, Indiana*, Lake County Circuit Court (Indiana), October 10, 1968, p. 12.
42. Ibid., pp. 22–24.
43. U.S. Senate, *Hearing*, p. 22.
44. Interview with Clarence Greenwald, June 14, 1972.
45. Mayor Hatcher testified at the subsequent Senate hearing about that part of the meeting as follows:

   > I recall in 1968 there was some extended discussion of this with the previous superintendent of the Gary Works of United States Steel. Mr. George Jedenoff, along with other officials of the company, suggested that as a result of an old city ordinance relating to something called a fire line (and as I understand it, what that simply means was that a line was drawn along the northern end of the city and it was just south of the United States Steel Gary Works and beyond that line the city did not provide fire protection for some reason). This law was cited as a rationale for saying that in effect United States Steel did not come under the regular ordinances of Gary. . . . And for that reason the city in effect had no jurisdiction for laws such as the building permit law to apply.

   U.S. Senate, *Hearing*, p. 20.
46. Moore, *Calumet Region*, pp. 288, 326, 540–41.
47. A clue as to this process of mutual accommodation is provided by a letter sent by U.S. Steel in 1962 to the building commissioner on the question of inspections and permit fees:

   > This matter has been discussed with Mayor George Chacharis, and he has advised that the inspections requested in your letter are not necessary, and that the permit fees are acceptable to the City of Gary. . . . If there are any further questions regarding this matter, may I suggest that they be taken up directly with Mayor Chacharis, as he is conversant with the entire matter.

48. *Post-Tribune*, October 26, 1970.
49. U.S. Senate, *Hearing*, pp. 61–63.

50. Nader's estimate apparently originated with Professor Leslie Singer, who added estimated market prices for each new piece of equipment the corporation announced that it installed in the Gary Works. Ralph Nader, "A Citizen's Guide to the American Economy," *The New York Review of Books* (September 2, 1971): 16, and interview with Leslie Singer (chairman, Economic Department, Indiana University Northwest), June 1972. Reingold's estimate is documented in U.S. Senate, *Hearing*, p. 30. My own is based on the fact that the corporation admits one-fifth of its investment is in the Gary Works, and the cost of rebuilding all their facilities "would require more than $5-billion." *New York Times*, January 10, 1971. Other replacement cost estimates run considerably higher. For example, the Burns Harbor mill (whose size is considerably less than the Gary Works) cost about $900 million. *Wall Street Journal*, December 19, 1978; Allen T. Demaree, "Steel: Recasting an Industry," *Fortune* (March 1971): 141; and Paul Booth and Bob Creamer, "Campaign Against Pollution: U.S. Steel's $16.4 Million Property Tax Steal" (1971), mimeo, p. 3.

51. Gerald J. Karaska and David Bramhill, eds., *Locational Analysis for Manufacturing: A Selection of Readings* (Cambridge: MIT Press, 1960); George F. Break, "Thrust of New Developments in Local Taxation as It Affects Business," in *Tax Institute of America, Business Taxes*, pp. 95–104; Thomas A. DeCoster, "Business Tax Topics," *Indiana Business Review* 46 (August-September 1971): 25; and James W. Wightman, *The Impact of State and Local Fiscal Policies on Redevelopment Areas in the Northeast*, Research Report to the Federal Reserve Bank of Boston, No. 40 (March 1968).

52. When Baltimore doubled industrial property taxes in 1956, new investment fell off to 20 percent of the previous rate until the tax was repealed. Interviews with local industrialists revealed that large expansion plans had been scrapped, and such expansion that did take place was at other plants, in spite of Baltimore's locational advantages. John D. Strasma, *State and Local Taxation of Industry: Some Comparisons*, Research Report to Federal Reserve Bank of Boston, No. 4 (1959), pp. 17–19.

53. U.S. Senate, *Hearing*, pp. 17–18. Columnist Jack Anderson quotes the Muskie subcommittee's background staff report as asserting that U.S. Steel "has used economic threats to retain its tax breaks. If its property taxes go up, the company allegedly warned it will slash the number of jobs at the Gary plant." Quoted in *Post-Tribune*, June 20, 1972. And see, for example, the careful phrasing of U.S. Steel

Vice President Edward Logelin's article in the *Chicago Tribune*, May 16, 1972.
54. Quoted in David Brody, *Steelworkers in America* (Cambridge: Harvard University Press, 1960), p. 114.

Chapter 8: Environmental Regulation

1. James S. Cannon and Frederick S. Armentrout, *Environmental Steel Update: Pollution in the Iron and Steel Industry* (New York: Council on Economic Priorities, 1977), p. 200; "Currents," *Environmental Science and Technology* 7, no. 6 (June 1973): 483; Matthew A. Crenson, *The Un-Politics of Air Pollution* (Baltimore: The Johns Hopkins Press, 1971), p. 36; J. Clarence Davies, III, *The Politics of Pollution* (New York: Western Publishing Company, 1970), p. 85, table 4.4; and Gary, Indiana, *Community Renewal Program* (1968), p. 38.
2. Letter to author from David Kee, Acting Chief, Air Enforcement Branch Enforcement Division, Environmental Protection Agency, Region V (September 24, 1975).
3. Cannon and Armentrout, *Environmental Steel*, pp. 6, 40–41, and *New York Times*, December 22, 1977.
4. Julian Szekely, *The Steel Industry and the Environment* (New York: Marcel Dekker, 1973), and *The Daily World*, January 15, 1976.
5. Cannon and Armentrout, *Environmental Steel*, p. 40. U.S. Steel denies the accuracy of these figures. *Wall Street Journal*, September 26, 1977.
6. In Gary the sulphur dioxide count is sometimes ten times the permissible federal standard. U.S. Environmental Protection Agency, *Our Urban Environment* (Washington, D.C.: Government Printing Office, 1971), p. 42. Council on Economic Priorities, *Environmental Steel* (draft), p. 428; *New York Times*, January 12, 1975; and *Washington Post*, March 3, 1973.
7. For general reading on air pollution and health see Lester B. Lave and Eugene P. Seskin, *Air Pollution and Human Health* (Baltimore: The Johns Hopkins Press, 1977); Walsh McDermott, "Air Pollution and Public Health," *Scientific American* (October 1961): 3; Rajinder K. Koshal and Manjulika Koshal, "Environments and Urban Mortality," *Environmental Pollution* 4, no. 4 (June 1973): 247–60; Thomas A. Hodgson, Jr., "Acute Health Effects Induced by Com-

monly Occurring Nonepisodic Levels of Urban Air Pollution,"
Journal of Urban Law 48, no. 3 (January 1971): 657–87; and Eric J.
Cassell, "The Health Effects of Air Pollution and Their Implications
for Control," *Law and Contemporary Problems* 33, no. 2 (Spring
1968). For citations to the technical literature, see the bibliographies
of U.S. Environmental Protection Agency, Office of Air Programs,
Air Pollution Technical Information Center, *Air Pollution Aspects
of Emission Sources: Iron and Steel Mills, A Bibliography with
Abstracts* (Washington, D.C.: Government Printing Office, 1972);
Virginia Brodine, "Point of Damage," *Environment* 14, no. 4 (May
1972): 13–14; and John R. Goldsmith and Ruth Hartman, "Meetings—
Air Pollution Medical Research," *Science* 163, no. 3868 (February 14,
1969): 706–8.

8. *Post-Tribune*, March 7, 1967.
9. See *National Guardian* (October 23, 1974); J. William Lloyd et al.,
"Long Term Mortality Study for Steelworkers, Part I: Methodology,"
Journal of Occupational Medicine 2, no. 6 (June 1969): 304–5, and
"Part V: Respiratory Cancer in Coke Plant Workers," 13, no. 2
(February 1971): 67; New York Academy of Sciences, *Cancer and
the Worker* (New York: New York Academy of Sciences, 1977);
"Outlook—Controlling Emissions from Coke Ovens," *Environmental
Science and Technology* 6, no. 2 (February 1972): 118; *New York
Times*, August 27, 1972; *The Daily World*, May 14, 1978; and Frank
Goldsmith, "Coke Ovens," *New Engineer* (January 1977): 26–31.
10. Gary, Indiana, *Community Renewal Program: Final Report*
(Mishawaka, Ind.: City Planning Associates, 1968), p. 39. See also
New York Times, October 13, 1975; Philip A. Leighton, "Geographi-
cal Aspects of Air Pollution," *The Geographical Review* 56, no. 2
(April 1966): 152–63; Barry Commoner, *The Closing Circle* (New
York: Alfred A. Knopf, 1971), p. 209; and Virginia Brodine, *Air
Pollution* (New York: Harcourt Brace Jovanovich, 1973), p. 129.
11. Matthew Edel, *Economies and the Environment* (Englewood Cliffs,
N.J.: Prentice-Hall, 1973), p. 82. Generally see Manufacturers Han-
over Trust, "Social Priorities and the Economy," *Economic Report*
(February 1973); Vincent Labeyrie, "Crisis of Environment or Crisis
of Capitalist Economy," *Marxism Today* 17, no. 4 (April 1973): 109;
Gus Hall, *Ecology: Can We Survive Under Capitalism?* (New York:
International Publishers, 1972), pp. 10–11, 46; and Richard England
and Barry Bluestone, "Ecology and Class Conflict," *The Review of
Radical Political Economics* 3, no. 4 (Fall-Winter 1971): 32–34.
12. U.S. Environmental Protection Agency, *Environment Midwest*

(December 1977): 2. See also "Environmental Steel," *Economic Priorities Report* 4, no. 2 (May 1973): 32. On the general opposition of working-class people to pollution see Dale E. Johnson, "Air Pollution: Public Attitudes and Public Action," *American Behavioral Scientist* 15, no. 4 (March-April 1972): 533–62.

13. Quoted in *Post-Tribune*, March 25, 1956. Crenson asserts it would take 35,000 home furnaces (more than Gary had) to produce one-fourth the pollution of the open-hearth furnaces alone; the corporation claims that in 1960 its open-hearth furnaces were responsible for one-third of Gary Works pollution (exclusive of the coke ovens). Thus the noncoke section alone (which was only about half of the total) was responsible for more than twelve times as much pollution as the homeowners. Crenson, *Un-Politics*, p. 65, and Exhibit "A," *Program of U.S. Steel to Control Gary Works Air Pollution* (June 4, 1965).

14. *Post-Tribune*, March 15, 1967.

15. Quoted in *New York Times*, May 4, 1971. See U.S. Steel, *Putting Our Record in Perspective: A Special Report for U.S. Steel People in the Chicago-Gary Area* (July 1970).

16. *New York Times*, June 1, 1978. For a similar pattern of resistance from the electric power industry see Samuel A. Bleicher, "Economic and Technical Feasibility in Clean Air Act Enforcement Against Stationary Sources," *Harvard Law Review* 89, no. 2 (December 1975): 316–54.

17. *Indiana Air Pollution Control Law*, ch. 171, Acts of 1961, as amended. For more information on water pollution see Edward Greer, "Obstacles to Taming Corporate Polluters: Water Pollution Politics in Gary, Indiana," *Environmental Affairs* 3, no. 2 (Spring 1974): 199–220; Edward Greer, "Filthy Flows the Calumet," *The Progressive* 40, no. 6 (June 1976): 27–31; and Lettie Maire Wenner, "Enforcement of Water Pollution Control Laws in the United States" (Ph.D., University of Wisconsin, 1972). On occupational health in the Calumet steel mills see Staughton Lynd, "Blue Collar Organizing: A Report on CEOHC," *Working Papers for a New Society* 1, no. 1 (Spring 1973): 28–34.

18. U.S. Environmental Protection Agency, Air Pollution Control Office, Division of Control Agency Development, *An Evaluation of Air Pollution Control Capacity in Indiana* (February 1971). For Indiana's funding record, see Indiana Air Pollution Control Board, *Annual Report 1970-1971* (Indianapolis, 1971), pp. 2, 8, and U.S. Bureau of the Census, *Environmental Quality Control Expenditure and Em-*

ployment for Selected Large Governmental Units: Fiscal 1969-70
(Washington, D.C.: Government Printing Office, 1972), pp. 16–17,
42. Cf. Davies III, *Politics,* pp. 126–27, table 6.2. Generally, see Peter
Nelson, "Dimensions of Air Pollution Policies Among the American
States" (paper at American Political Science Association Conven-
tion, 1972), p. 10, and Robert G. Vaughn, "State Air Pollution
Control Boards: The Interest Group Model and the Lawyer's Role,"
Oklahoma Law Review 24, no. 1 (February 1971): 30.

19. Anita L. Morse and Julian C. Juergensmeyer, "Air Pollution Control
    in Indiana in 1968," *Valparaiso Law Review* 2:306–12. This problem
    is scarcely unique to Indiana. As Geoffrey J. Lanning points out:
    "Michigan statutes frequently lack the effective sanctions and the
    efficient enforcement procedures which are essential to effective
    environmental administration." "State Management of the Environ-
    ment Part I: An Evaluation of the Michigan Experience," *University
    of Michigan Journal of Law Reform* 8, no. 2 (Winter 1975): 322.

20. See U.S. Environmental Protection Agency, *An Evaluation of Air
    Pollution,* and Indiana Air Pollution Control Board, *Annual Report,
    1970-1971,* pp. 13–15.

21. *Post-Tribune,* March 15, 1967, and *New York Times,* December 13,
    1972. On the ubiquity of such relationships see *New York Times,*
    December 3, 1972; *Wall Street Journal,* June 6, 1974; G. Todd
    Norvell and Alexander W. Bell, "Air Pollution Control in Texas,"
    Texas Law Review 47, no. 6 (June 1969): 1086–1123; and Lanning,
    "State Management," p. 310, note 105. Not surprisingly, Indiana's
    air pollution board attempted to block EPA efforts to control auto
    emissions by contesting the accuracy of its models for calculating
    auto emissions. *New York Times,* April 15, 1973, and Noel de
    Nevers, "Enforcing The Clean Air Act of 1970," *Scientific American*
    228, no. 6 (June 1973): 18–20.

22. Letter from J. F. Keppler, Director, Division of Industrial Hygiene,
    Indiana State Board of Health, to Dr. Herschel Bornstein, February
    5, 1971.

23. Crenson, *Un-Politics,* pp. 61–66. During this period Youngstown's
    mayor asserted at a federal hearing on water pollution: "What do we
    care about the river as long as it brings the barges down, the iron
    and coal into the steel mills." Council on Economic Priorities,
    "Environmental Steel," p. 30.

24. See Thomas Francis Thompson, "Public Administration in the
    Civil City of Gary, Indiana" (Ph.D., Indiana University, 1960),
    pp. 132, 151, note 15, and Warner Bloomberg, Jr., "The Power

Structure of an Industrial Community" (Ph.D., University of Chicago, 1961), pp. 173–64.

25. Crenson, *Un-Politics*, p. 68. Crenson is in error in asserting that the Indiana statute "empowered state officials to initiate legal proceedings against any municipality that failed to take appropriate action against a local air pollution problem." Actually section 8(e) provides that if there is a local ordinance and it is not enforced, then the state reserves the right to proceed directly on its own initiative against the *polluter*. (And section 8(a) specifies that municipalities, while permitted to pass local ordinances consistent with or stronger than the state statute, are not required to do so.) Thus, Crenson's hypothesis that Mayor Chacharis acted under compulsion of Indiana law must be rejected; and the possibility of covert intervention by U.S. Steel (rather than a "nondecision" on its part) seems more plausible. Cf. Peter Bachrach and Morton S. Baratz, "Two Faces of Power," *The American Political Science Review* 56, no. 4 (December 1962): 947–52.

26. Crenson, *Un-Politics*, pp. 69–73. On the total inadequacy of the Pittsburgh ordinance see Joy Flowers Conti and Janice I. Gambino, "Local Regulation of Air Pollution: The Alleghany County Experience," *Duquesne Law Review* 11, no. 4 (Summer 1973): 612–52.

27. Crenson, *Un-Politics*, pp. 73–74.

28. Paul Booth and Edward Greer, "Pollution and Community Organization in Two Cities," *Social Policy* 4, no. 1 (July-August 1973): 42–49, and John C. Esposito, *Vanishing Air* (New York: Grossman Publishers, 1970), pp. 82–84.

29. Crenson seems unaware of the character of the agreement and accepts as true the assertion that particulate discharges in Gary dropped off considerably between 1964 and 1965. *Un-Politics*, p. 75. See the *Air Pollution Control Agreement of June 4, 1965* between the city of Gary and U.S. Steel and the annual letters of compliance from U.S. Steel to the City of Gary of June 27, 1966 (xerox copies in author's possession).

30. David Graham Nelson, "Black Reform and Federal Resources" (Ph.D., University of Chicago, 1972), p. 39. For a typical example of the ineffectiveness of municipal agencies, see Esther Roditti Schacter, *Enforcing Air Pollution Controls: Case Study of New York City* (New York: Praeger, 1974).

31. Gary, Indiana, Office of Program Coordination, "A Report on the Gary Health Department" (confidential typescript prepared for

Mayor Hatcher), September, 1968, and Gary Health Department, *Annual Report, 1971,* p. 78.

32. The same sequence took place with respect to Mayor Kenneth Gibson of Newark and his health department, except that their report—which met a similar fate—was prepared by an outside consultant. *New York Times,* October 31, 1971.

33. Gary Health Department, *Annual Report,* 1971, p. 70.

34. As Charles Jones puts it:

> It is possible to observe a shift in the locus of authority with the initial efforts of the federal government to develop a national air pollution control policy. In Allegheny County, for example, there occurred a gradual erosion of local autonomy as both a condition for and a correlate of federal entry. Thus by 1967 the local control agency had become quite dependent on the federal government, both for resources and for the determination of its policy options.

Charles O. Jones, *Clean Air: The Policies and Politics of Pollution Control* (Pittsburgh: University of Pittsburgh Press, 1975), p. 86.

35. Ibid., p. 153, table 11, and letter of J. David Carr, General Superintendent, Gary Works, to members of the Air Pollution Control Advisory Board, December 3, 1970.

    Board Chairman Edwin H. Gott asserted that "there are no instant cures for coke oven pollution" and that "a great deal of new technology must be accomplished." *New York Times,* August 27, 1972. To the extent that this was true, it was because of a failure of the industry to allocate funds for research in this area. *The Iron Age* 210, no. 12 (September 12, 1972): 60; "Outlook—Controlling Emissions from Coke Ovens," p. 118–19; and *New York Times,* September 25, 1972. Currently, coke oven emissions are fully controllable. See Council on Economic Priorities, "Environmental Steel," p. 16, and S. Andonyev and O. Filipyev, *Dust and Fume Generation in the Iron and Steel Industry* (Moscow: Mir Publishers, 1977).

36. The background to this repeal is detailed in Cannon and Armentrout, *Environmental Steel,* pp. 430–31. See also Richard J. Kirkus, "Organizing Neighborhoods: Gary and Newark," in *The World of the Blue-Collar Worker,* ed. Irving Howe (New York: Quadrangle Books, 1972), pp. 72–90.

37. The corporation took this same position with respect to its Clairton Works. See County of Allegheny, Department of Health, Board of

Air Pollution Appeals and Variance Review, *United States Steel, Clairton Coke Works Decision*, Docket #143, November 11, 1971. (Professor Charles O. Jones kindly referred me to this decision.) A similar stance has also been adopted by the copper industry. *New York Times*, November 11, 1972.

38. See Air Pollution Appeal Board, *Hearing Transcript*, March 9-19, 1971. A vivid description of the corporation's coke oven emissions appears in John Quarles, *Cleaning Up America* (Boston: Houghton Mifflin, 1976), pp. 230–31.

39. In a parallel proceeding in Allegheny County, the chairman of the local air pollution board characterized U.S. Steel's behavior as follows: "They have not been committing perjury. But they have not been exactly straightforward either." *Business Week*, March 13, 1971. See Air Pollution Appeal Board, *Hearing Transcript*, pp. 208, 411–12, 549 and compare with *United States Steel Corporation v. Air Pollution Appeal Board, Transcript*, Lake County Superior Court, Case No. 571-585 (November 8, 1971), pp. 57–60, 75.

40. *United States Steel Corporation v. Air Pollution Appeal Board of the City of Gary, Indiana and the City of Gary, Indiana, Findings, Decision, and Order*, Lake County Superior Court, Case No. 471-485 (May 22, 1972); Council on Economic Priorities, "Environmental Steel," p. 31; and letter by Donald D. Horton, U.S. Steel staff attorney, to Donald Dreyfus, health department attorney, May 30, 1972. *New York Times*, July 1, 1972.

41. Cannon and Armentrout, *Environmental Steel*, p. 432. Letter to author from David Kee, Enforcement Division, EPA Region V, September 24, 1975. For a similar sequence in Pittsburgh see Jones, *Clean Air*, pp. 87–92.

42. U.S. Environmental Protection Agency, *Region V Public Report* (June 1973), pp. 3–5; "Currents," *Environmental Science and Technology 7*, no. 6 (June 1973): 483; and Council on Economic Priorities, "Environmental Steel," pp. 33–34.

43. *United States Steel Corporation v. Russell Train et al.*, Civil No. 73H183 (N.D., Indiana, November 21, 1974).

44. It did so although the fine was less than the cost to the corporation of unemployment benefits for the laid-off workers. *Times Magazine*, January 20, 1975. See *New York Times*, December 28, 1974; January 2, 1975; Cannon and Armentrout, *Environmental Steel*, pp. 200–3; and Citizens for a Better Environment, *One* (March 1976): 4–5.

45. *New York Times*, January 5, 1975, and Staughton Lynd and Bill

Walden, "Pollution Law Tested in Steel," *National Guardian,* January 22, 1975.

46. *New York Times,* July 13, 1975.

47. Ibid., April 24, 1975; May 9, 1975; May 31, 1975; and June 1, 1975.

48. Interview with David Ullrich, Attorney, Enforcement Division EPA, Region V, June 12, 1978. For a parallel process of delays with respect to the U.S. Steel Clairton Works see *New York Times,* July 13, 1975.

49. Quoted in *Wall Street Journal,* February 6, 1976. As he explained the process in his excellent study on EPA enforcement procedures:

> This lack of progress was doubtless due in part to confusion and inexperience among the government personnel. But a large part of the explanation was that litigation is almost never simple or quick. . . . And after all this, there may be further delays caused by appeals. The result is that the life cycle of big court cases is measured not in months but in years. Moreover, once any pollution suit was brought, the wave of publicity quickly receded, and the corporate lawyers took over with no pressure from their side to hurry the case along, since expenditures for pollution control were postponed so long as the case dragged on in the courts.

Quarles, *Cleaning Up America,* p. 51.

50. See Powell A. Moore, *The Calumet Region: Indiana's Last Frontier* (Indianapolis: Indiana Historical Bureau, 1959), pp. 104–9, 265, and Stephen Becker, *Marshall Field III: A Biography* (New York: Simon & Schuster, 1964), p. 64.

51. Moore, *Calumet Region,* p. 102, and Isaac James Quillen, "Industrial City: A History of Gary, Indiana to 1929" (Ph.D., Yale University, 1942), pp. 52–53. Quote from letter to author from James P. Jones, Chief, Operations Division, Army Corps of Engineers, Chicago District, November 13, 1973.

52. For information on this history see *United States v. United States Steel Corporation,* 70 Hammond 12 (October 6-11, 1971); *United States Steel v. Air Pollution Appeal Board, Transcript,* pp. 231–324 (testimony of Peter Madinis, Civil Engineer, U.S. Army Corps of Engineers), and pp. 187–88 (testimony of Warren Reeder, a local historian); U.S. Department of Health, Education, and Welfare, *Conference in the Matter of Pollution of the Interstate Waters of the Grand Calumet River, Little Calumet River, Wolf Lake, Lake Michigan and Their Tributaries* (March 2-9, 1965); and *United*

States Steel Corporation v. Indiana Stream Pollution Control Board, Proceedings (April 27, 1971), Case No. 570-1212, pp. 1189–90.

53. Moore, *Calumet Region,* p. 102, and *United States Steel Corporation v. Russell Train et al.,* 556 F2d 822, Court of Appeals, 7th Cir. (May 13, 1977), p. 830, note 6. Generally see Edward G. Fochtman, "Lake Michigan: Can It Survive?" *Frontier* 30, no. 1 (Winter 1970): 5–6; Charles F. Powers and Andrew Robertson, "The Aging Great Lakes," *Scientific American* 215, no. 5 (November 1966): 94–104; N. William Hines, "Controlling Industrial Water Pollution: Color the Problem Green," in *Environment Law Review,* 1970, ed. H. Floyd Sherrod, Jr. (New York: Boardman, 1970), p. 285; and Paul A. Share, "Pollution of the Great Lakes: A Study of International Environmental Control Efforts," *Wayne Law Review* 19, no. 1 (November 1972): 165–79.

54. *United States Steel Corporation v. Russell Train et al.,* p. 830; *New York Times,* January 9, 1974; and Faulkner P. Walling and Louis C. Otis, Jr., *Water Requirements of the Iron and Steel Industry,* Water Supply Paper 1330-H (Washington, D.C.: Government Printing Office, 1967).

55. HEW, *Conference,* Vol. I, pp. 45–50, 103, 112. See also Commoner, *Closing Circle,* pp. 35–36; Council on Economic Priorities, "Environmental Steel," p. 11; interview with Dr. Herschel Bornstein, June 8, 1971; and *United States Steel Corporation v. Russell Train et al.,* p. 831.

56. Brian J. L. Berry et al., *Land Use, Urban Form and Environmental Quality,* Report to EPA Office of Research and Development (Chicago: University of Chicago Department of Geography, 1974), p. 99, table 2.12. Between 1957 and 1971 gross water discharge by all manufacturing firms increased by 40 percent. Council on Economic Priorities, "Environmental Steel," p. 16.

57. U.S. Environmental Protection Agency, *A Progress Report* (Washington, D.C.: Government Printing Office, 1972), p. 11, and Council on Economic Priorities, "Environmental Steel," pp. 17–20.

58. Cannon and Armentrout, *Environmental Steel,* p. 204, and David Zwick and Marcy Benstock, *Water Wasteland* (New York: Grossman Publishers, 1971), p. 223.

59. *Post-Tribune,* November 13, 1971, and November 14, 1971.

60. Council on Economic Priorities, "Environmental Steel," p. 31. In another instance, a second steel company offered an aggressive local public official who was vigorously enforcing environmental statutes a remarkably highly paid consultantship while he was

pursuing remedies against U.S. Steel; there was no mention that he should be less assiduous in his public duties.

The Gary official who wrote the ineffectual air pollution ordinance for Mayor Chacharis had previously worked for a steel company, and his replacement resigned to take a job designing air pollution control equipment with a firm selling to steel companies. *Post-Tribune*, February 12, 1969; January 3, 1970; and January 4, 1970. The Allegheny County air pollution chief resigned his post after five years of enforcing controls on U.S. Steel's Clairton Works "to accept a position with United States Steel as director of environmental control." Jones, *Clean Air*, p. 93. Indiana's water pollution statute was drafted by William D. Ruckelshaus when he was working at the Indiana attorney general's office. He later served as director of EPA and is currently a partner in a Washington, D.C. law firm specializing in representing large industrial polluters. Another partner in this firm had been an assistant to Vice President Nelson Rockefeller and appointed by him to the National Commission on Water Quality, where he served simultaneously the American people and his corporate clients. *New York Times*, August 6, 1972, and December 9, 1975.

61. Indiana Statutes, Chapter 214, Acts of 1943 as amended. The law has been upheld in court. *Manner v. Terre Haute*, 163 N.E. 2nd 577, and *Plymouth v. Stream Pollution Control Board*, 238 Ind. 439, N.E. 2nd 625. See also Davies III, *Politics*, pp. 122–23, and sources cited in note 18 above.

62. HEW, *Conference*, Vol. III, pp. 606–23, and Vol. IV, p. 1253; Davies III, *Politics*, pp. 44, 142–43; State of Indiana, Stream Pollution Control Board, *Regulation SPC8, Grand Calumet River* (June 13, 1967); and *A Progress Report*, pp. 13, 75.

63. *United States Steel Corporation v. Indiana Stream Pollution Control Board*, Proceedings (April 27, 1971), Transcript, p. 63; *In the Matter of the Stream Pollution Control Board of the State of Indiana v. U.S. Steel Corporation, Gary Works*, Case No. B-82; *United States Steel Corporation v. Indiana Stream Pollution Control Board* (Lake County Superior Court, 1971) Case No. 570-1212; *United States Steel Corporation v. Air Pollution Appeal Board of the City of Gary, Indiana* (Lake County Superior Court, 1971), Case No. 571-585.

64. During this period, operating costs of pollution control equipment were only about one-fifth of capital costs. Leonard Lund, *Industry Expenditures for Water Pollution Abatement* (New York: The Conference Board, 1972).

65. Cannon and Armentrout, *Environmental Steel*, pp. 6, 40–41, 170–72.
66. *In the matter of NPDES Permit for U.S. Steel Gary Works*, Case No. NPDES-V-027 (AH), before the Regional Administrator, EPA, Region V, *Initial Decision* (May 11, 1976).
67. *United States Steel Corporation v. Russell Train et al.*, and *Chicago Tribune*, June 16, 1977.
68. *New York Times*, December 8, 1975.
69. Council on Wage and Price Stability, *Prices and Costs in the United States Steel Industry* (Washington, D.C.: Government Printing Office, October 1977), p. xiv.

   For a detailed survey of the state of the steel industry, see Edward Greer, "The Political Economy of U.S. Steel Prices in the Postwar Period," in *Research in Political Economy: An Annual Compilation of Research*, Vol. I, ed. Paul Zarembka (Greenwich, Conn.: JAI Press, 1977), pp. 59–85, and Edward Greer, "Placebos for a Sick Industry," *The Nation* 226, no. 8 (March 4, 1978): 235–39.
70. One is reminded of the chemical companies' claim that the regulation of polyvinyl chloride "would close the industry and bring on national economic disaster. They even offered a study warning that a shutdown would put 2.2 million people out of work and cost the economy \$65 to \$90 billion." After the standards went into effect, however, the price of the product "has been running about 10 percent below the pre-regulation price." *New York Times*, December 28, 1975. See also Cannon and Armentrout, *Environmental Steel*, p. 172, and Council on Wage and Price Stability, *Prices and Costs*, p. 35.
71. This is true not only in Gary: for Allegheny County see the full-page ad in the *Pittsburgh Press*, May 18, 1976, and the article on its impact in the Greensburg *Tribune-Review*, May 19, 1976; and generally, see "Corporate Advertising and the Environment," *Economic Priorities Report* 2, no. 3 (September-October 1971): 28–29, and *Wall Street Journal*, November 19, 1971.
72. Indiana Statutes, Chapter 174, Acts of 1967. This bill was passed while William Ruckelshaus was majority leader of the Indiana House of Representatives. *New York Times*, April 28, 1973. See note 60 above; *Annual Report and Official Opinions of the Attorney General of Indiana: 1969*, Official Opinion No. 39; and "Tax Incentives for Clean Industries," *Environmental Science and Technology* 5, no. 8 (August 1971): 692–93.

Conclusion

1. See Sam Bass Warner, Jr., *The Urban Wilderness: A History of the American City* (New York: Harper and Row, 1972), pp. 154–56.

2. A similar perspective with respect to the Federal Trade Commission is advanced in Alan Stone's brilliant monograph, *Economic Regulation and the Public Interest* (Ithaca, N.Y.: Cornell University Press, 1978).

3. Power in the advanced capitalist nations, Fernando Claudín points out, is not

> the expression exclusively of monopoly capital; rather [political power and the state apparatus] are the expression of a *power bloc* composed of different fractions of monopoly and non-monopoly capital, within which each strives for hegemony. Under monopoly capitalism the State is the institutional condensation of this power bloc (in political, ideological, and organisational terms) and reflects the relationship of forces of its various components.

Eurocommunism and Socialism (London: New Left Books, 1978), p. 105.

4. Ralph Miliband, *Marxism and Politics* (Oxford University Press, 1977), p. 21, and Nicos Poulantzas, *Classes in Contemporary Society* (London: New Left Books, 1978), pp. 9, 193. Classically, of course, leading Marxist thinkers did address this problem. See, for instance, Lenin's astute comments in "State and Revolution," in V. I. Lenin, *Selected Works*, Vol. II (New York: International Publishers, 1967), pp. 288–90, and George Lukacs, *History and Class Consciousness* (Cambridge, Mass.: MIT Press, 1971), p. 307.

5. Cf. Anthony Giddens, *The Class Structure of the Advanced Societies* (New York: Harper and Row, 1975), pp. 177–78, and C. Wright Mills, "The Middle Classes in Middle-Sized Cities," in *Power, Politics and People: The Collected Essays of C. Wright Mills*, ed. I. L. Horowitz (New York: Oxford University Press, 1967), pp. 274–91. Also see the "Debate" following the publication of a draft section of this book on the police over just this question between Gerda Ray and the author in *Crime and Social Justice*, no. 9 (Spring-Summer 1978): 63–71.

6. Antonio Gramsci, *Selections from the Prison Notebooks*, ed. and trans. Quinton Hoare and G. Nowell-Smith (New York: International Publishers, 1971), p. 182. As Nicos Poulantzas recently put it:

> In working for class hegemony, the State acts within an unstable equilibrium between the dominant classes and the dominated. The State therefore continually adopts material measures which are of positive significance for the popular masses, even though these measures represent so many concessions imposed by the struggle of the subordinated classes.

State, Power, Socialism (London: New Left Books, 1978), p. 31.

7. On this point see Don Hamerquist's critique of Louis Althusser for picturing the working class "as the object, or the effect of historical development." "A Tension Between the Theory and the Politics," *Urgent Tasks*, no. 4 (Summer 1978): 49. Also cf. the pungent comments of Jean Chesneaux in *Pasts and Presents* (London: Thames and Hudson, 1978), pp. 136–38.

8. "Can the Bolsheviks Retain State Power?" in Lenin, *Selected Works*, Vol. II, p. 395. As Rosa Luxemburg contemporaneously asserted, "The main feature of the socialist society is to be found in the fact that the great mass of the workers will cease to be a governed mass, but, on the contrary, will itself live the full economic and political life and direct that life in conscious and free self-determination." Quoted in Miliband, *Marxism and Politics*, p. 177.

9. Gramsci, *Selections*, p. 172.

Index

283